BY
BARBARA DEMICK

Logavina Street

Nothing to Envy

Eat the Buddha

EAT THE
BUDDHA

EAT THE BUDDHA

Life and Death in a Tibetan Town

BARBARA DEMICK

RANDOM HOUSE · NEW YORK

Copyright © 2020 by Barbara Demick
Maps copyright © 2020 by Jeffrey L. Ward

Published in the United States by Random House,
an imprint and division of Penguin Random House LLC, New York.

RANDOM HOUSE and the HOUSE colophon are
registered trademarks of Penguin Random House LLC.

LIBRARY OF CONGRESS CATALOGING-IN-PUBLICATION DATA
NAMES: Demick, Barbara, author.
TITLE: Eat the Buddha : life and death in a Tibetan town /
by Barbara Demick.
DESCRIPTION: First edition. | New York, N.Y. : Random House, [2020]
IDENTIFIERS: LCCN 2019044133 (print) | LCCN 2019044134 (ebook) |
ISBN 9780812998757 (hardcover) | ISBN 9780525510697 |
ISBN 9780812998764 (ebook)
SUBJECTS: LCSH: Tibetans—China—Aba Zangzu Qiangzu Zizhizhou—
Social conditions. | Tibetans—China—Aba Zangzu Qiangzu Zizhizhou—
Social life and customs. | Buddhism—Social aspects—China—
Aba Zangzu Qiangzu Zizhizhou. | Refugees, Tibetan. | Aba Zangzu
Qiangzu Zizhizhou (China)—Social conditions. | Aba Zangzu
Qiangzu Zizhizhou (China)—History.
CLASSIFICATION: LCC DS797.77.A63 D46 2020 (print) |
LCC DS797.77.A63 (ebook) | DDC 951/.38—dc23
LC record available at https://lccn.loc.gov/2019044133
LC ebook record available at https://lccn.loc.gov/2019044134

International edition ISBN 9780525510697

Printed in the United States of America on acid-free paper

randomhousebooks.com

2 4 6 8 9 7 5 3 1
First Edition

Book design by Barbara M. Bachman

IN MEMORY OF

LOBSANG CHOKTA TROTSIK

(1981–2015)

CONTENTS

AUTHOR'S NOTE

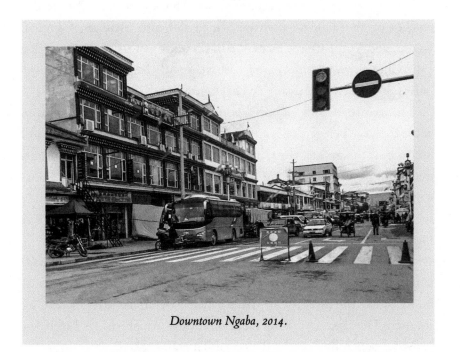

Downtown Ngaba, 2014.

FOR CENTURIES, TIBET WAS KNOWN AS A HERMIT KINGDOM. Its charms were hidden by the natural barrier of the Himalayas and by a reclusive theocratic government ruled by a succession of Dalai Lamas, each believed to be the reincarnation of his predecessor. Nineteenth- and twentieth-century literature about Tibet is replete with accounts of foreigners trying to sneak into the country disguised as monks or hermits.

Nowadays it is not the Tibetans shutting the door, but the Chinese Communist Party. China has ruled Tibet since 1950 and is a most un- welcoming gatekeeper when it comes to foreign visitors. There is a modern airport in Lhasa with a Burger King and ATMs, reducing what was once a holy city into a tourist trap for the pleasure, almost exclusively, of Chinese tourists. Foreigners must obtain a special travel permit in order to visit what China calls the Tibet Autonomous Region. That permit is granted sparingly to academics, diplomats, journalists, and anybody else inclined to ask hard questions. The eastern reaches of the Tibetan plateau, which fall into Sichuan, Qinghai, Gansu, and Yunnan provinces, are in theory open to anybody with a valid Chinese visa, but foreigners are frequently turned away at checkpoints or refused permission to check into hotels.

I moved to Beijing as correspondent for the *Los Angeles Times* in 2007, the year before the Summer Olympics. As part of its successful bid to host the games, the Chinese government made a raft of promises about improving human rights and opening the country to journalists. The reality on the ground was that much of the country remained off-limits to reporters. Among the most impenetrable was Ngaba.

Ngaba is an obscure place. To the extent that it appears on English-language maps, Ngaba is referenced by its Chinese name, Aba (pronounced like the Swedish pop band). The Tibetan name is challenging for non-Tibetans, but comes out sounding roughly like Nabba or Nah-wa, depending on the dialect of Tibetan spoken.

Ngaba has been an irritant to the Communist Party since the 1930s. Every decade or so, Ngaba is the scene of anti-government protests that invariably leave a trail of destruction and death. Tibetans adhere to the teachings of the 14th Dalai Lama, Tenzin Gyatso, who won a Nobel Peace Prize for his embrace of nonviolence, so notably most of the deaths in recent years have occurred on the Tibetan side. During protests in 2008, Chinese troops opened fire on protesters in Ngaba, killing several dozen people. In 2009, a Buddhist monk doused himself in gasoline on the main street, while calling for the return of the Dalai Lama, who lives in exile in India. A wave of self-immolations followed. As of this writing, 156 Tibetans have self-immolated, nearly one-third of them from Ngaba and its environs, the most recent in

November 2019. These deaths deeply embarrassed Beijing, belying as they do the claim that Tibetans are happy under Chinese rule.

After the immolations began, the Chinese authorities redoubled their efforts to keep journalists out of Ngaba. New checkpoints were erected at the entrance to the town, with tank traps, barricades, and paramilitary peering into the cars to make sure no foreigners slipped in. With varying degrees of success, some intrepid journalists folded themselves up in the back seat and held up their cameras like periscopes to shoot out the window.

Journalists are contrarian creatures. If we are told we cannot go somewhere, then predictably we try to go. The subject of my last book was North Korea, which I must admit intrigued me in part because it was so closed to Western visitors. Once I had decided I would profile one Tibetan town, I set my sights on Ngaba. I wanted to know what it was in Ngaba that the Chinese government was so anxious to hide from view. Why were so many of its residents willing to destroy their bodies by one of the most horrific methods imaginable?

Tibet also piqued my curiosity in much the same way it has other Westerners. Although I'm not a Buddhist, and have not sought solace in the religions of the Far East (or of the West for that matter), I appreciated that Tibet was a place infused with a spirituality that had inspired a rich culture, philosophy, and literature that stood out in an increasingly homogeneous world. Since I'd studied Chinese history, I knew the basics of the Chinese invasion and the flight of the Dalai Lama. But I had very little sense of Tibetans themselves other than the caricatures of the hollow-cheeked holy men in caves and the cheerful nomads fingering their prayer beads. What was it like to be a Tibetan in the twenty-first century living at the edge of modern China?

Technology has robbed the world of much of its mystery. Google Earth with a few clicks allows you to peer into the most inaccessible reaches of the world, but can't explain what is happening below. I needed to go to Ngaba.

A geographical note here: Only half of the Tibetan plateau is designated as the Tibet Autonomous Region by the Chinese government, for historical reasons that are explained later in this book. But the majority of Tibetans live in parts of Sichuan, Qinghai, Gansu, and Yunnan provinces, which, although outside the "official Tibet," are just as Tibetan. And in recent decades, these eastern reaches of the plateau have become the heartland of Tibet, producing a disproportionate share of the famous Tibetan musicians, film directors, writers, activists, and lamas, including the current Dalai Lama.

NGABA IS IN SICHUAN PROVINCE, roughly at the point where the Tibetan plateau collides with China, making it a front line of sorts. To get there, you usually go through Chengdu, the capital of Sichuan province and another of China's new megacities.

Leaving behind the gaudy new shopping malls with their Gucci and Louis Vuitton boutiques and the slabs of high-rise apartment towers, you head out on the ring roads and then turn north into the mountains. As the crow flies, Ngaba is only 220 miles away, but the drive takes a full day through the Qionglai Mountains, a temperate rain forest that is the natural habitat of China's beloved pandas. It is a steady climb through narrow mountain switchbacks wet with rivulets of water dripping down the rock. Once you reach the plateau, the trees melt away and the landscape bursts open. The transition is so abrupt it is like stepping through a magical wardrobe and exiting into another dimension.

In every direction, an expanse of nubby green carpet rises and falls with the contours of the mountains. In coffee-table books about Tibet, the sky is always blue, but during my visits, which were mostly in the spring, thick clouds like wadded cotton hung low enough to obscure the mountaintops. The villages along the road consist of clusters of squat earthen houses. Shaggy yaks and sheep ignore the few passing cars. At key points along the road are offerings to the deities that Tibetans believe inhabit every mountain pass and hill. Prayer flags, sun-bleached to pale pastels, flutter from the mountain ridges.

Ngaba is at nearly 11,000 feet elevation, although the altitude is not immediately obvious because the place is rather flat. The downtown is little more than a narrow ribbon of urbanity slicing through the grasslands. The main road, Route 302 on maps, goes straight through town; you can drive from one end to another in about fifteen minutes. The town got its first traffic light in 2013. For this rural area it is not uncommon to see men on horseback, although people nowadays usually ride motorcycles or travel by pedicab. Most older people and some young wear a traditional Tibetan robe called a *chuba,* belted at the waist; but many opt for a compromise between tradition and ready-to-wear practicality with cowboy hats and puffy jackets made of sheepskin or down. The women often wear long skirts.

Rising up like bookends on either side of Ngaba are two Buddhist monasteries, their gold-plated roofs reflecting the sunlight. They are painted in deep tones of vermilion and egg-yolk yellow, colors reserved for monastic buildings that contrast with the drabness of the landscape. Se Monastery (pronounced "say") is near the first checkpoint as you enter Ngaba from the east. At the western end of town is the larger Kirti Monastery, which was at the center of the self-immolations.

In between the monasteries, the streetscape is a clutter of low-rise buildings with tile exteriors, as though they were bathrooms turned inside out. The ground floors are mostly storefronts; when their metal doors are open they reveal an ugly assortment of merchandise: auto parts, buckets, mops, plastic stools, cheap sneakers, agricultural tools.

The imperative of Chinese development has stamped a kind of uniformity on the town. Signs advertise the China Peoples Bank, China Mobile, China Unicom. Ngaba is a county seat (the town's population is about 15,000; that of the larger Ngaba county roughly 73,000) with the usual complement of drab government offices, a hospital, a large middle school, and police and public security bureaus, all conspicuously waving big red flags. The same as any county seat in western China, but with more police cars and military vehicles. An armored personnel carrier is often parked outside the town's only department store. Overhead cameras record the license plates of cars entering and leaving town. Green canvas-covered military trucks frequent the main road, heading back and forth from the army base located on the other side of Kirti Monastery. By one count, some 50,000 security personnel are stationed in Ngaba, about five times the normal deployment for a place this size.

Ngaba is sufficiently remote that it is not yet overrun by Chinese chain stores and fast-food restaurants, but there are plenty of small Chinese establishments advertising hot pot and dumplings. A few years ago, in response to complaints that Ngaba had become too Sinicized, local authorities ordered up Tibetan motifs to be painted on the buildings along the main street. Murals of lotus flowers and conch shells, golden fish and parasols convey a forced cheerfulness. Matching red metal shutters embossed with Buddhist symbols complete the look. Chinese shopkeepers were told to add Tibetan lettering to their signage, though Tibetans told me the words were often misspelled. I could only guess from the peculiar English added to some of the signage.

NGABA BENEVOLENCE AND GARAGE

BRILLIANT DECORATION

Over the seven years I lived in China, I improved my skills at navigating the Tibetan plateau without attracting attention. I didn't want to wear a ridiculous disguise like those nineteenth-century explorers, but I did buy a floppy hat with polka dots and one of those pollution face masks so common in Asia. I wore long, dusty coats and flat lace-up shoes. The fact that it was frequently raining allowed me to add an umbrella to hide behind.

I managed to make three trips of varying lengths into the heart of Ngaba. I also interviewed people from Ngaba in other parts of the plateau that were less restrictive. The Tibetan exile communities in India and Nepal included many people from Ngaba, who gave generously of their time and recollections. I even ran into a Ngaba Association in Kathmandu. For centuries until the coming of the Communist Party, Ngaba was ruled by its own kings and queens, and their survivors provided a wealth of historical information about the area and the dynasty. A Chinese scholar kindly shared with me translations of Chinese-government documents and memoirs about Ngaba. For all of the people featured in the book, I also interviewed relatives, friends, and neighbors in order to corroborate their accounts, in anticipation of critical Chinese claims that the hardships depicted in these pages are exaggerated.

All the people, events, dialogue, and chronology are as reported. There are no composite characters, although I have changed some names to protect from retribution those who spoke honestly.

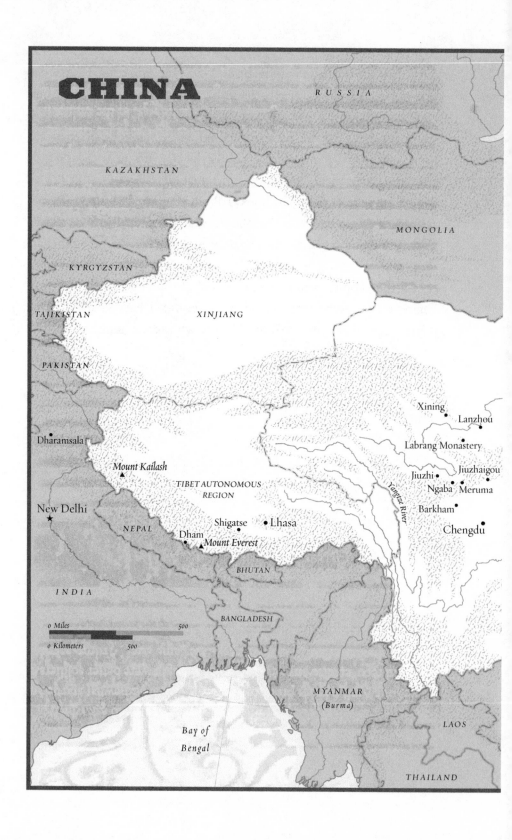

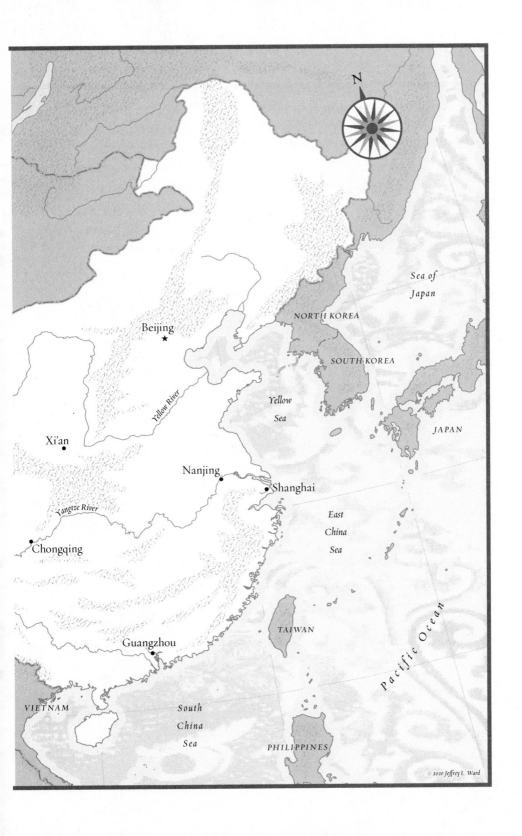

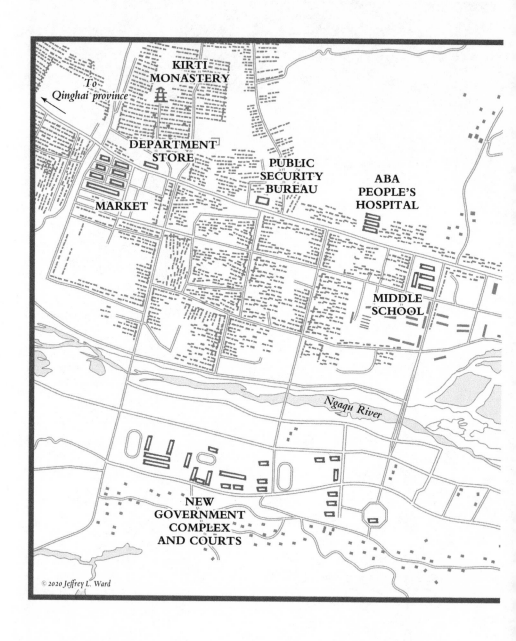

KIRTI
MONASTERY

To
Qinghai province

DEPARTMENT
STORE

PUBLIC
SECURITY
BUREAU

ABA
PEOPLE'S
HOSPITAL

MARKET

MIDDLE
SCHOOL

Ngaqu River

NEW
GOVERNMENT
COMPLEX
AND COURTS

© 2020 Jeffrey L. Ward

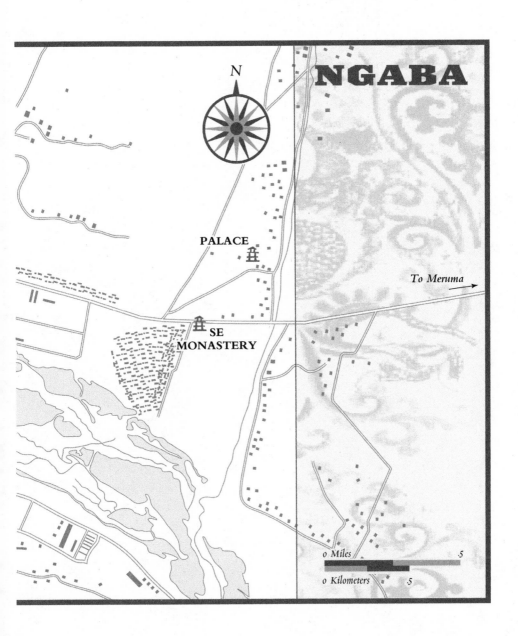

PART ONE

1958 – 1976

CHAPTER

I

...

THE LAST
PRINCESS

*The royal family of Ngaba. Gonpo is center front
with her father, the king, behind her, 1957.*

1958

GONPO COULD SMELL THE SMOKE BEFORE SHE COULD SEE
what was happening. Although she was just seven years old and not
well versed in the politics of the day, it confirmed a nagging feeling
she'd had for weeks that something was amiss. She was on her way

home with her mother, sister, an aunt, and a convoy of servants. They had been away, attending the funeral rituals for her uncle. It had been summer when they set out for her uncle's village, but they'd been away for forty-nine days, the traditional mourning period between death and rebirth for Buddhists. Now it was early autumn, and the evening chill whispered of the snow that would soon creep down from the mountaintops. Gonpo wore a thick sheepskin robe trimmed with fur, but the wind whipped up from underneath her horse and made her shiver. Everybody was on horseback: Gonpo, like most Tibetans, was a seasoned equestrian at a young age. They followed the course of a road that had recently been laid out by Chinese military engineers, though not yet paved, heading due west, into the setting sun. Their route forked off at a stream that led north to Gonpo's home, and as they emerged from behind a thicket of shrubbery, Gonpo could see where the smoke was coming from. From her vantage point atop the horse, she had a clear view of half a dozen bonfires and a corresponding number of tents. As they approached, she could see that these weren't the black yak-hair tents used by Tibetans, but the small white tents of the People's Liberation Army.

This was 1958, nine years after Mao Zedong had proclaimed the People's Republic of China, so it was not unusual to see encampments of the Red Army around the countryside. But this was on the family property, and that was surprising. Gonpo had been fighting off sleep on the last leg of the two-day trek, but now she was jolted awake by curiosity and a touch of fear. She was one of the first to dismount, sliding off her horse without waiting for the servants to help her. She ran up to the gate, wondering why nobody had come out to greet the returning convoy. She banged hard on the gate—a slab of wood twice as high as a grown man with a massive lintel across the top. There was no response, so she shouted at the top of her lungs.

"Hello, hello. Where is everybody?"

Her mother walked up behind her and called out as well.

Eventually, Gonpo's nanny came and unlocked the gate. Instead of a warm welcome, the maid leaned over the child as if she weren't there, bringing her face close enough to Gonpo's mother to whisper directly into her ear. Gonpo couldn't hear the words, but she discerned from her mother's reaction that it couldn't be good. Gonpo had seen her mother crying a lot lately; the uncle who died had been her favorite brother—and Gonpo thought maybe her mother was crying again because she was still sad about his death. At least that's what Gonpo wanted to believe, in spite of all the evidence to the contrary—the smoke, the tents, the stone-faced maid. Her instinct told her that this was the beginning of the end of the world as she knew it.

GONPO WAS RAISED A PRINCESS. Her father, Palgon Rapten Tinley,* a name that roughly translates as "Honorable Enlightenment Steadfast," was the fourteenth in a line of rulers in what was known as the Mei kingdom. Its capital was Ngaba, in what is now Sichuan province. When Gonpo was born, in 1950, Ngaba was a nondescript market town where traders came to sell salt and tea and where herders came to sell their butter, skins, and wool. This entire region was a patchwork of small fiefdoms governed by various chieftains and kings, princes, khans, and warlords. The Chinese used the term *tusi,* often translated as "landlord," to refer to local rulers like Gonpo's father, but the Tibetans called him *gyalpo,* or king. English-language chronicles from the early twentieth century also refer to him as royalty. That was certainly how Gonpo perceived her family's position in society.

As a child, Gonpo was dressed in the floor-length robes called chubas, cinched at the waist. Almost all Tibetans wore similar garments, the quality reflecting their status. Gonpo's robes were trimmed with otter fur. Around her neck she wore ropes of beads, big as grapes—coral, amber, and, most precious of all, *dzi,* a Tibetan striped agate thought to protect against the evil eye. Otherwise she wasn't a very girlish princess. She was cute rather than pretty, with gapped teeth

---

* Many Tibetans do not have surnames in the Westernized sense, but they will often have more than one given name.

and a snub nose that gave her the look of a mischievous little boy. Like many young girls in Ngaba, Gonpo had her hair cropped short—a signal that she was not of marriageable age. Her mother and other adult women in the royal family wore long braids, held in place by tassels and strands of coral, so elaborate that they might take servants two days to braid.

The family lived in an imposing manor house—technically a palace, though it looked more like a fortress, stout and sturdy, built to endure—located on the east end of Ngaba, just outside the downtown area. The house was designed in a traditional Tibetan style out of rammed earth, dun-colored so that it blended into the landscape during the dry season when the plateau was bare of grass. The massive walls—up to nine feet thick at the bottom—tapered inward toward the top to provide stability in case of earthquakes; the narrow slits of windows were similarly trapezoidal, framed by wooden latticework. The walls were unadorned except for two protruding wooden balconies on either side—one on the east, the other on the west. The balconies looked elegant, but in fact they accommodated the toilets. Human waste dropped below, where it was mixed with ash and spread on the fields as fertilizer.

What the house lacked in modern amenities, it made up for in scale. It measured 80,000 square feet with more than 850 rooms ranging from dungeons, stables, and storerooms on the very bottom, to the rooms of increasing elegance and purpose as they rose upward. There were the bedrooms for the children and their mother, then the king's retinue of assistants and his private officers. The rooms on the upper levels were paneled in wood that masked the dirt exterior.

The upper floor was appropriately dedicated to spiritual practice. The rooms came alive with frescos and *thangka*s, Tibetan wall-hangings, all in eye-popping shades of poster colors. Since Buddhist figures are reincarnated over and over again, they appear in countless manifestations, male and female, familiar and fanciful. There was the Buddha, past and future, and many more of the bodhisattvas, enlightened beings who forgo nirvana to be reborn for the benefit of others. The most prized piece was a statue of Avalokitesvara, or Chenrezig, the bodhisattva of compassion, the patron saint of Tibetans, given to the king by the 14th Dalai Lama, the centerpiece of his chapel.

The king was a dedicated bibliophile who had an extensive collection of books and scriptures. Some were printed with gold and silver. The reception room under the scripture hall was large enough to accommodate thousands of monks. On Buddhist holidays, the palace would echo with a cacophony of chanting, cymbals, horns, and conch shells. And the untranslatable mantra uttered by Tibetans to invoke their patron saint, the bodhisattva of compassion,

om mani padme hum

Daily life inside the palace was measured out by the rituals of Buddhism. The king began every morning in front of a shrine, with repeated prostrations. Standing upright with hands clasped in prayer up over his head, he'd then in one movement extend his body in full horizontal position, prone on the floor, and stand again. The ritual kept his physique lean and his mind clear.

It was impossible to distinguish that which was religion from that which was culture or habit. When Gonpo was caught in a lie, she was made to do repeated circumambulations around a nearby monastery, spinning countless prayer wheels, big vertical cylinders of metal, wood, and leather with prayers written on them. Each time you turned them on their spindles it was like reciting the prayer aloud. They were heavy for a child, and the penance forced her to reflect on her wrongdoing.

The children—Gonpo and her sister, who was six years older—lived with their mother in separate quarters on one side of the house. Upon awakening, their mother would take the girls to their father's chambers to wish him good morning. They would repeat the visit at bedtime to wish him good night. The family ate most meals together, and their father strictly enforced their manners. Prayers were said before eating. The children waited while the elders ate first. Their father made it a point to clear his plate down to the last grain of rice, reminding his daughters of how hard farmers toiled to produce their meal. He insisted also that the staff get the same portions of food as he did, although they often ate their food later when it was cold. The king was a fastidious man who didn't want his daughters, despite their royal bloodlines, to be spoiled. Although the house was full of servants, the king made his own bed.

A man ahead of his time, the king was steadfast in the belief that girls should get the same education as boys. He had no son and he anticipated that one of his daughters might become the next monarch. Gonpo had a tutor who came every morning to teach her the Tibetan alphabet, using a traditional method of spreading ash on a slate and giving her a quill to trace the letters. Tibetan is a difficult language to write; its script is adapted from Northern India, with consonants stacked on top of each other. Gonpo spent hours glassy-eyed, staring at the swirling letters.

She was a restless child who chafed at the confines of life within the palace. Her nanny attached a bell around Gonpo's waist when she was a toddler so she would hear if the child tried to go outside. It was not until much later that Gonpo would appreciate how fleeting was this cloistered period of her early childhood. She had no playmates her own age. Her older sister, pale and studious, was not inclined to join Gonpo in her quests to make mischief. Gonpo's happiest moments were when the monks came to visit, since some were just boys her own age. She had a favorite, who as it happens had been identified as a reincarnate lama, a *tulku*. The adults treated the boy with great reverence, but Gonpo would tug at his sleeve, demanding that he kick a ball around the reception hall. Gonpo frequently snuck out of the palace to play with children at a neighboring house. There, she didn't behave like a princess. One of those children would later remember that she insisted on helping with the chores at his home. Uncomfortable with the fact that she had more than other children, she tried to give away items of clothing. Once, she joined the neighborhood kids when they snuck into the private gardens of the palace to pilfer beans. Gonpo didn't realize, of course, that the beans she was stealing were her own.

As she grew older, her father worried that she did not have the comportment of a princess. He tried to prevent her from playing with the neighboring children, the offspring of his subjects. She had to content herself with peering out the windows onto the walled courtyard and beyond to the hills that rolled onward until they disappeared into the snowy mountains to the north. As far as the eye could see, this was her father's realm.

The Mei kingdom extended at least as far as Dzorge (Zoige in Chinese), ninety miles to the northeast. Exactly how much territory the kingdom controlled is unclear because this was a society in which power was measured not by land but by people. Borders were not as important as loyalty, and there were few bonds stronger than the extended family. Tibetan accounts say the Mei king controlled twelve tribes and 1,900 households. Chinese documents say there were 50,000 people directly under his leadership. Wealth was similarly measured by the number of animals a family owned, and so the chronicles recorded very carefully the tallies: the kingdom had 450 horses and 800 head of cattle, including yaks, which were sometimes crossbred with the cows.

Pastures surrounded the palace, but most of the animals were kept near a village fifteen miles to the east called Meruma, which had been established for the kingdom's herd. The king also had a summer palace in Meruma. Yet another, smaller palace was located a few miles to the west on the grounds of Kirti Monastery, which was founded by the king's ancestors. It was used for pilgrimages and on Buddhist holidays.

From Gonpo's perspective, her father was the unchallenged ruler of his lands. He decreed what hours the markets were open, what could be sold, which animals could be hunted. As a devout Buddhist, he banned the hunting of birds, fish, marmots, and other small animals; since each was thought to be a reincarnated soul, it was better to kill a large animal like a yak or a sheep that could feed many mouths. He maintained a strict ban on the sale of opium.

From breakfast on, the king received a stream of visitors who petitioned him to address their grievances and adjudicate disputes. If somebody was quarreling with their neighbor about land or trying to open a business, they would implore the king to pass judgment. So many came to call that there were always people camped out in the meadow in front of the palace waiting for their audience. Not just Tibetans came to seek his wisdom. The region was home to dozens of ethnic groups—Mongols, who had swept onto the plateau in the thirteenth century, and the Qiang, who physically resembled Tibetans although they had their own language and culture. Chinese Muslims, known as the Hui (pronounced *Hway*), were ethnically Chinese but identifiable by the wispy beards and white skullcaps on most men and the headscarves on women.

Increasingly, ordinary Han Chinese were moving in. The Han were the Chinese majority, and most of those Gonpo encountered were somehow attached to the Chinese government. But they too appeared to be deferential to her father, and she'd had no ill feelings toward them. She'd watched with delight as Chinese engineers and construction workers built a new road paralleling the river—the road on which they'd come from the funeral rites. One of Gonpo's earliest memories was of participating in a ceremony for the opening of the road that ran from Ngaba to Chengdu and passed close to their palace. Dressed in their finest Tibetan robes, bedecked in beads, they handed bouquets of flowers to the Chinese officials attending the ribbon cutting. It was the first time the young girls had seen motor vehicles. Their mother joked afterward that the girls had tried to feed the trucks grass because they thought they were horses.

THAT NIGHT IN 1958 when the royal family came home from the funeral, Gonpo didn't know why the Chinese were camped out in front of her home. She pushed her way inside and ran up to the third floor. The servants were as unsmiling as her nanny. They worked silently, packing boxes. Some had tears in their eyes. Gonpo could no longer deny that something was wrong, very wrong. Her father was not to be found—somebody said he had gone to a meeting, but she was not convinced. She ran from room to room looking for him, looking for someone who could explain what was going on. Nobody had answers for her. The servants moved between rooms, their arms stacked with clothing and linens. All of this only made Gonpo more agitated. In the way that very small children can make very loud noises, her feet reverberated on the wooden floors, thump, thump, until her nanny caught up with her and grabbed her by the arm.

She needed to be quiet, the nanny admonished. Couldn't she understand this was serious? No, she did not. She definitely did not understand. But since everybody else was packing, Gonpo figured she should too. She went into her room and pulled out her toys.

"You're not going to need those things. Leave them behind," snapped her nanny, a woman who had taken care of Gonpo since she was a baby and had never before spoken so harshly.

And so she said goodbye to her most precious possession—a plastic apple from India that when opened contained smaller and smaller plastic apples stacked like Russian nesting dolls. Decades later, when she was well past middle age, graying and arthritic, she would search the toy stores of Asia to find a toy apple like the one she left behind.

THE NEXT MORNING, when the light broke, Gonpo saw that the house was being sealed with tape. The soldiers were tacking up posters handwritten with large Chinese characters. They seemed to convey an urgent political message that Gonpo couldn't understand since she didn't read Chinese. Neighbors stood outside the cordon of soldiers with tears streaming down their faces. Some of them were the kids with whom she stole beans.

Gonpo still hadn't accepted the gravity of her situation. What most caught her eye was the motor vehicle waiting to drive them away. Although it was only a Russian-made jeep, nothing fancy even by the standards of 1950s China, Gonpo had never ridden in a private car before, only a bus. She was so excited that she momentarily forgot the unfolding tragedy and ran out after the car, jumping up and down with anticipation.

Her mother got her attention with a sharp slap on the cheek—the only time either of her parents ever struck her. She had violated a key tenet of Tibetan etiquette by not undertaking a respectful departure from the home. She slunk back to stand next to her sister, her two cousins, and her aunt. Together, they raised their hands as though in prayer and prostrated themselves to show gratitude for the home that had sheltered and protected her all those years. Then they climbed into the jeep with their suitcases piled on the roof and were driven away.

EAT THE BUDDHA

The Chinese Red Army on their way to the Tibetan plateau, crossing Jiajinshan Mountain, June 1935.

THE TIBETAN PLATEAU IS LIKE NOTHING ELSE ON THIS planet, a unique geological feature that rises three miles above sea level from the heart of Asia, propelled upward by the same tectonic forces that created the Himalayan Mountains. The roof of the world, as it's often called, for good reason. Chinese like to boast that the Great Wall is visible from space, but in fact it is Tibet that catches the eye when you look at satellite images of China. It appears as a vast landlocked plateau fringed with brushstrokes of white, the glacial peaks of the highest mountains in the world. Threaded through the landscape are the headwaters of the great rivers of Asia, the Yangtze, the Mekong, and the Yellow Rivers among them—called by the Tibetans the Drichu, Dzachu, and Machu, respectively—which provide water to half the world's population.

The plateau extends from Mount Everest all the way to northern Pakistan, then clear across central China to the edge of the Gobi desert. At one million square miles, it is as large as India, or about the equivalent of one quarter of China's landmass, although the punishing terrain, high altitude, and hypoxic atmosphere have made it one of the most sparsely populated areas of the planet, with fewer than six people per square mile.

The origin of the Tibetans is a puzzle to geneticists. Although they share common ancestry with the Chinese, Japanese, Mongol, and Siberian populations, and strongly resemble some Native Americans, the Tibetans have a unique genetic mutation that enables them to thrive at high altitudes.

Tibetans themselves have a fanciful origin myth with nods to both Darwinism and Buddhism. Although there are various permutations to the story, the gist is that the Tibetan people are the descendants of an ape and an ogress who mated on a cliff above a vast inland sea that once covered the Tibetan plateau. (The part about the sea is supported by geological evidence.) The ape was said to be a manifestation of Avalokitesvara, the bodhisattva of compassion, gentle in nature, and the ogress a pitiless warrior.

These qualities would be inherited by their descendants, the Tibetan people, whose destiny would be shaped by competing strains of compassion and cruelty.

Even after the introduction of Buddhism, imported from India in the seventh century, the Tibetans were hardly pacifists. Nor were they particularly insular, contrary to the latter-day reputation of Tibet as a hermit kingdom. In an era when horsemanship was the most essential skill of war, Tibetans ranged across central Asia, sacking cities and subduing other peoples who were incorporated into the Tibetan nation. Under the great emperor Songtsen Gampo, the Tibetans built an empire that rivaled those of the Mongols, Turks, and Arabs. For a brief moment in history, fleeting but hardly forgotten, the Tibetans were even more powerful than the Chinese. In 763 the Tibetans sacked Chang'an, the Tang dynasty capital city now known as Xi'an, home of the terracotta warriors. Their occupation of the city lasted only fifteen days, but it would be long remembered by Tibetans with pride.

The Tibetan empire collapsed in the mid-ninth century and fragmented into minor principalities. It was not until 1642 that a strong, centralized Tibet was reestablished under the leadership of a succession of Dalai Lamas installed and supported by the powerful Mongols. The fifth Dalai Lama had the Potala Palace built on the ruins of the fortress of Songtsen Gampo, giving the impression of an unbroken line of succession with the past. But his Tibet was less than half the size of the former empire, with most of the formerly Tibetan lands to the east split up among various smaller kingdoms and fiefdoms, of which the Mei kingdom of Princess Gonpo's ancestors was one of many.

Gonpo's ancestors came originally from the western reach of the plateau, near Mount Kailash—a region called Ngari, which might account for the name Ngaba. Perhaps to enhance their legitimacy, they claimed to have migrated during the ninth century, the golden age of Tibet, as warriors under the command of the great emperors. When the Tibetan empire collapsed and receded, an official history suggests, they remained behind in the east, establishing their own fiefdom.

Ngaba was the perfect place to go rogue. It was the very embodiment of the old Chinese chestnut "Heaven is high and the emperor is far away." It was more than one thousand miles from Beijing—at least a month's journey by horseback—and nearly as far from Lhasa. By the time the Mei kingdom was firmly established in the eighteenth century, the eastern reaches of the Tibetan plateau had been annexed by the Manchus, who had conquered China and established the Qing dynasty. But the Qing emperors were stretched too thin to bother with the tiresome task of governance. They would send in the cavalry only if fighting between fractious chieftains threatened the empire. The attitude seemed to be "Let the barbarians rule themselves." They even gave imperial seals to many of the local rulers, Gonpo's ancestors included, confirming their authority to rule.

Ngaba also clung to its independence from Lhasa. The people from Ngaba did not consider themselves subjects of the Dalai Lama, even if they revered him as their spiritual leader. They made pilgrimages to Lhasa, studied at Lhasa's great monasteries, and conducted business in Lhasa, where they were renowned as savvy tradesmen. They were bound to other Tibetans by their common ethnicity, beliefs, and lifestyles. They had the same written language—based on a northern Indian alphabet—even if their dialects were mutually unintelligible. They ate the same staple, *tsampa,* the roasted barley that was so essential to survival on the plateau that the term *tsampa eater* was practically synonymous with *Tibetan.* But they were not subjects of the Tibetan central government in Lhasa and didn't follow its laws. Rather than identify themselves as *bodpa,* Tibetan, they usually referred to their tribe or chieftain. Or they acknowledged their common ancestry by calling themselves the people of the "land of snow."

If this region wasn't technically part of Tibet, neither was it a backwater as far as Tibetan culture is concerned. The eastern reaches of the plateau, which Tibetans call Amdo (the northeast) and Kham (the southeast), and which the British sometimes called "inner Tibet," produced a disproportionate share of illustrious lamas, scholars, and artists. From Amdo came Tsongkhapa (1357–1419), a brilliant Buddhist philosopher who established the Gelug school, which would come to dominate Tibetan Buddhism—and the most famous living Tibetan of all, the 14th Dalai Lama, born in 1935 in a village called Taktser, about two hundred miles north of Ngaba. The 10th Panchen Lama, the second-ranking Tibetan lama and one of the pivotal figures in twentieth-century Tibetan history, was also an Amdo man. Kham produced rebels of varying political stripes—among them some of the first Tibetans who joined the Communist Party, and a little later the fiercest of the anti-Communist guerrillas. The legendary warrior king of the *Epic of Gesar* was supposed to be from Kham. The majority of Tibetans today live in the eastern half of the plateau—in parts of Qinghai, Sichuan, Gansu, and Yunnan provinces. This is something that causes much confusion because the Chinese government doesn't consider this to be Tibet, but if you visit these areas, they are undisputably Tibetan in character. If you meet people in New York or London today who tell you they are Tibetan, there is a good chance this is where they are from.

THE MOST VIVID DESCRIPTIONS of life within the Mei kingdom come from *A Brief Chronicle of the Origins of the Mei King for the Ears of Future Generations,* a slim volume with a silk brocade cover, privately published in 1993 by a man named Choephal who was secretary to Gonpo's father. The Mei kings ruled uneasily, constantly watching over their shoulders for assassination plots from rivals. When swords and firearms were not sufficiently powerful, the warring parties hired shamans to cast incantations to undermine their enemies. Disputes were resolved by paying reparations—villages were traded back and forth like pawns. The vanquished were punished by having limbs, ears, or noses amputated. It wasn't all warfare and revenge, though. The Mei prided themselves on being hard-nosed tradesmen and on giving their subjects enough freedom to do the same. The unique environment of the Tibetan plateau produced rare products like the fragrant pods of the musk deer that were in high demand by perfumers in the Arab world and salt collected from Tibet's many evaporated lakes. Ngaba developed a reputation as a business-friendly environment; its traders prospered selling products from China to central Tibet and Nepal, particularly tea, which was loaded onto caravans of yaks that traversed the plateau.

The Mei kingdom wasn't a matriarchy by design; it just happened that the queens tended to outshine their kings. Females were allowed to ascend the throne if there wasn't a suitable male heir, a not uncommon event since members of the royal family struggled with infertility and at least one king was insane. The queens built monasteries, signed treaties, and led armies into battle. One queen went to war to avenge the infidelity of a daughter-in-law on behalf of her cuckolded son. Men couldn't take care of such matters without their mothers.

The eighteenth-century queen Abuza forged an alliance that would become the defining feature of the Mei dynasty. Abuza was an outsider who married into the royal family, but quickly ended up eclipsing her husband in power. Around 1760, she met the head of Kirti Monastery, which was headquartered in Dzorge at the far north-eastern corner of the Mei lands. She invited Kirti Rinpoche (an honorific title for the head of the monastery) to visit Ngaba. The rinpoche endeared himself to the queen by taming a wrathful deity who had troubled the kingdom—in Amdo, every hill, meadow, and stream had its own deity—and by appointing another deity as protector of the ruling house. They developed a relationship based on a template known as *choyon,* priest-patron. The lama imparted spiritual guidance and legitimacy to the ruler; the ruler provided material support in the form of money, herds, or land. Together, they thrived, increasing their power and presence. A century later, Kirti would open a branch of the monastery in Ngaba that would eventually become one of the most influential and politically active, contributing to Ngaba's later reputation for rebelliousness.

The queen also inaugurated a month-long prayer festival in Ngaba each spring. Tibetans would gather to burn juniper branches and incense and release animals intended for slaughter, a Buddhist gesture of compassion. For entertainment, they raced horses and competed at archery. People from around the region would bring clay pottery to sell. The pottery festival, as it came to be known, was a popular event in eastern Tibet until 2009, when Chinese authorities suspended it because of Tibetan unrest.

———

THE MOST GLORIOUS OF the queens was Gonpo's grandmother, Palchen Dhondup. Although no photographs or paintings of her exist today, she was described in the family chronicles as a "very beautiful woman," also as "broad-minded and intelligent." Gonpo was once told by her father that her grandmother "was a real warrior and when she tucked her hair up in a cap to go to battle she looked more splendid than any man." She was born in the late 1890s under tragic circumstances. Her mother died in childbirth. Her father, King Gonpo Sonam, was killed in a freak accident in 1913 while overseeing the construction of a congregation hall at Kirti Monastery. The roof collapsed, crushing the king. That left the orphaned teenaged princess, an only child, to run the kingdom. Although Tibetan tradition could accept a young woman as ruler, a man in the family was still a requirement. The princess was hastily married off to a noble prince from Golok, northwest of Ngaba, who became the nominal king. But again, it was evident that Palchen Dhondup held the reins of power, which she did not relinquish even after her own son—Gonpo's father, Palgon Rapten Tinley—became the Mei king.

The queen, Palchen Dhondup, completed the ill-fated construction project at Kirti Monastery that had killed her father. She donated jewelry from her hair ornaments to fund the carving of wooden blocks that would be used to print the complete works of Tsongkhapa, the founder of the Gelug school.

The queen was respected for her literacy and her tolerance. In 1924, an American missionary, Robert Ekvall, came through Ngaba with his wife and infant son to distribute Tibetan translations of the Bible. Although monks tried to chase him away, he was granted an audience with the queen. He quickly realized that she was the true ruler. "The king was just the prince consort in a way," Ekvall later told an interviewer.

Ekvall presented the queen with gifts—a barometer, a compass, binoculars, and one of the translated Bibles. As the missionary looked on anxiously, the queen flipped through the Bible, commenting on the high quality of the printing. She then read some of the passages aloud. The queen showed no inclination to convert, but she told Ekvall that she liked the opening of John 1:1—"In the beginning there was the word and the word was God"—which was in keeping with Tibetan Buddhist beliefs that speech is integral to the human soul.

"Now this makes sense," she told Ekvall.

The queen impressed Ekvall as articulate, intellectually curious, and, as he told the interviewer, "full of compassion." He recalled that she was particularly struck with the couple's young son, since she, like others in her family, had struggled to procreate and at that time had only one child, Palgon Rapten Tinley, who had survived.

QUEEN PALCHEN DHONDUP MIGHT have had a glorious reign had it not coincided with the tumultuous start of the twentieth century. Britain and Russia had been locked in a rivalry for influence in central Asia so intense that it threatened anybody who stood in the way. In 1903, a British colonel, Francis Younghusband, who was stationed in India, led what he euphemistically called an "expedition" into Tibet. Several thousand Tibetans were killed. Although he had the backing of the viceroy, Lord George Curzon, the British government repudiated the mission and pulled out its troops. But the damage was irreparable in that it yanked the Qing dynasty out of its complacency. The Manchu Chinese rulers had been so preoccupied by European campaigns to pry open treaty ports on the coast that they had neglected their western flank. They certainly did not want Britain peering down on China from the roof of the world or controlling their water supply. Once the British tipped their hand, the Chinese realized the strategic importance of the plateau. To this day, many Tibet scholars blame Britain for the subsequent calamities that befell Tibet.

Enfeebled though they were, the Qing mounted their own invasion of Tibet in 1909 and remained until 1911, when their own empire came crashing to an end. At that point, the Tibetans deported all Chinese representatives. For all intents and purposes, Tibet reestablished itself as an independent country. It issued its own travel documents and its own currency. But it was a de facto independence. Tibet did not apply to become a member of the League of Nations, the precursor to the United Nations, not fully appreciating the value of this fledgling international organization. In fairness to the Tibetans, the very concept of statehood was still a work in progress in the early twentieth century, and the international relations of imperial Asia meshed imperfectly with European definitions. The Tibetans tried to get the British to recognize their independence, but ended up having to settle for a deal that gave China the rights of "suzerainty," which had the advantage of being a term that nobody quite understood. Correspondence in the years following the empire's collapse showed the British and the Tibetans wrestling over translations and definitions of words like *suzerainty, sovereignty, independence,* and *autonomy.* In the end, Tibet's status was left vague at precisely the wrong time.

THE COLLAPSE OF THOUSANDS of years of imperial rule in the early years of the twentieth century had left behind a dangerous vacuum in China. The Republic of China, founded by Sun Yat-sen, had only the most tenuous hold on power, with most of the country run by feuding cliques—the so-called warlord period. The boy emperor Puyi, evicted from the Forbidden City, was by the 1930s a dissolute young man living in a puppet state called Manchukuo that had been set up by the Japanese in northeastern China. What was left of China was led by the hard-headed generalissimo, Chiang Kai-shek, who had succeeded Sun as head of the Kuomintang, or Nationalist Party. He clung desperately to power with the Japanese advancing into the country and a fast-growing new rival, the Communist Party of China—soon to be led by Mao Zedong—nipping at his heels.

The Tibetans in Ngaba knew little of Chinese politics. They were concerned with their own clashes with rival Tibetan chieftains and paid little attention to this distant war. After all, Chinese fighting Chinese was an internal affair that seemed to have nothing to do with the Tibetans.

The Communists were ensconced 1,200 miles away at the borders of Jiangxi and Fujian provinces, where they had formed a mini–Soviet state. When Chiang's forces launched an attack to dislodge them in 1934, the Communists broke into three armies and escaped in a retreat that would become known as the Long March. For the Chinese Communist Party, this is an epic event, enshrined in revolutionary ballads and operas—roughly the equivalent of the exodus out of Egypt, except it was not Moses but Mao leading the Red Army to safety.

With Chiang's army in hot pursuit, the Communists fled farther and farther west into China before turning north in Sichuan province. For Tibetans, it marked their first encounter with the Chinese Communist Party. It did not go well.

The Red Army of the 1930s was not yet the formidable fighting machine that it would later become. The Chinese soldiers were short of equipment, food, and local knowledge. The last overlords of the plateau, the Qing, were Manchus, not Han; the envoys they sent to the plateau were usually Manchus or Mongols. Many of the maps and documents were in Manchurian. The Red Army soldiers were mostly Han from the lowlands of eastern and southern China.

Idyllic though Tibet looks in those coffee table books, the habitat is brutal to the uninitiated, the weather perilously unpredictable. You can be soaked through the skin one minute, charmed the next by a magnificent double rainbow, then shriveled by ultraviolet rays of the high-altitude sun. Hailstones big as chicken eggs can kill an adult yak and occasionally humans. The oxygen-starved atmosphere leaves newcomers faint and headachy. Even Tibetans get lost in swirling blizzards and die of exposure. The Tibetan plateau was terra incognita for the Chinese.

"Where are we? Have we left China?" one bewildered young soldier asked his commanding officer as they trekked through grasslands to the east of Ngaba, this according to a book by Sun Shuyun, *The*

Long March: The True History of China's Founding Myth. The commanding officer admitted that he didn't know himself. He suggested they wait until they encountered somebody who spoke Chinese. They didn't.

The most pressing concern for the Red Army was a lack of food. The Chinese soldiers started by picking crops from Tibetan fields—some of them unripe—and stealing stockpiles of grain. They captured sheep and yaks for slaughter. Many young Communists were still idealistic about helping the poor, and the memoirs reflect that they sometimes left IOUs after they looted Tibetan larders. It didn't do much good because there was a limit to how much food could be raised. The plateau couldn't support a large population, certainly not the thousands of newly arrived soldiers. For the first time in living memory, Tibetans experienced famine conditions.

At some point, the Chinese discovered that the Buddhist monasteries contained not only the treasures of Tibetan civilization, but potential comestibles. Drums were made of animal hides that could be eaten if boiled long enough—a technique the soldiers knew because they'd already consumed their own belts, rifle straps, leather bags, and the reins of horses. They even ate figurines that had been sculpted out of barley flour and butter, according to a memoir discovered by scholars Jianglin Li and Matthew Akester, who have extensively researched this period. One revealing anecdote they uncovered comes from the memoirs of Wu Faxian, a former political commissar in Mao's first army. He wrote:

> One of our quartermasters visited a Lamaist temple. He walked around, and somehow he touched those tiny statues, then licked one. To his surprise he found it tasted sweet. He licked again, and it was indeed sweet. It turned out that all those dust-covered little Buddha (statues), big or small, were sweet. It was wonderful, like Columbus discovering the New World! He brought some of the small Buddha (statues) back,

washed them clean, then added water to boil. They were all made of flour, and tasted really good. . . .

From then on, whenever we arrived at a place, the quartermaster went everywhere searching for Lamaist temples, and brought back flour Buddhas to eat.

Tibetans who survived this period say that what the Chinese ate were actually *tormas*, votive offerings that are not exactly Buddha statues. But as far as the Chinese were concerned, they were literally eating the Buddha. They knew it was sacrilegious, but they didn't care.

THE TIBETANS PUT UP fierce resistance. The queen ordered women and children to evacuate to the mountains while she enlisted the able-bodied men to fight. Although strict Buddhists abhor killing animals and will often pray over a fly that's drowned after falling into a bowl of soup, they can be merciless warriors when under attack. But raising an army has always been a problem for Tibetans because, in their traditional society, some 20 percent of the males are monks, pledged to the compassionate side of the Tibetan character. The queen decreed it would be pointless to allow an exception. "If we fight it is for the defense of religion, not just the country," the queen instructed her subjects, one elderly Tibetan later told oral historians.

Armed with spears, flintlocks, and muskets, wearing charm boxes for protection against bullets, they fought hard on their home turf and scored some initial successes, blocking the advance of the Red Army near Tsenyi Monastery. The monastery is on the road from Chengdu, about ten miles southeast of Meruma, where the Mei army was headquartered. Nearly half of the Chinese regiment of 1,300 soldiers perished, according to Wu Faxian's memoir. But reinforcements from the rear guard arrived within days, forcing the Tibetans to retreat.

Everyone was ordered to flee to the mountains, into the high-elevation passes where the enfeebled Red Army soldiers were too weak and hungry to follow. They took whatever animals they could herd into the mountains and the food they could carry, hiding the rest. The Red Army quickly scoured the grounds of abandoned properties, digging for hidden caches of valuables and grain, picking bare the fields. They took over the vacated premises, the monasteries usually being the most choice accommodations. Mao himself did not come through Ngaba, but Red Army commander Zhu De picked for himself the assembly hall of Kirti Monastery, the largest in the region. The Red Army soldiers tore up the floorboards and rafters for firewood, stripped the walls of the *thangka*s so that the canvas could be used for seating. Copper bowls and silver statues were melted down for munitions.

Queen Palchen realized that the Red Army would likely take over her palace. She went into the chapel to pray for guidance. Her subjects would later suggest she consulted an oracle, who told her she could not allow the enemy to use her home to advance their causes. The chapel flickered with row after row of butter lamps, the ceremonial candles that are the most distinctive feature of Tibetan monasteries and temples, burning clarified yak butter. She took one of the lamps, small but with a long enough flame to lick the curtains and tapestries. And although the exterior of the palace was mud, the wooden interior, the furnishings, paintings, and textiles, were highly flammable and the palace was quickly consumed. The queen and her family fled with the rest of the Tibetans into the mountains.

The family stayed away for about four months, waiting for the Red Army to leave, then returned to Ngaba, settling into a palace behind Kirti Monastery. These were lean years. The army had decimated the fields. In 1936, the Red Army came back through and the people fled again into the mountains. By that time, Queen Palchen Dhondup was delighted to learn that she was pregnant again. In her late thirties, nearly two decades after the birth of her first child, Gonpo's father, she had a baby girl, Dhondup Tso. Tragically, like her own mother, she would die in childbirth.

RETURN OF
THE DRAGON

*From left to right, the young Panchen Lama, the Mei king,
the Dalai Lama, and other officials on a 1954 tour of China.*

PALGON RAPTEN TINLEY WAS TWENTY YEARS OLD AT THE
time of his mother's death, and he would simultaneously inherit responsibility for a baby sister and a kingdom.

The future Mei king was so soft-spoken and contemplative that people assumed he was destined for the monastery. He was even identified as a reincarnation of a famous lama. But Queen Palchen put a stop to that; Tibetan monks are celibate and her son as heir to the kingdom would be obliged to provide an heir. She had handpicked a bride for him the year before she died. Tashi Dolma was the daughter of a minor neighboring chieftain, a plump girl with thick black braids. She was pious, well-mannered, and, like her husband, literate. The queen's ministers had wanted a more strategic match that could help patch up a feud with a rival, but the queen insisted that Tashi Dolma was the right personality for her son.

Although she was only fifteen when they married, Tashi Dolma quickly stepped up to share the burdens of ruling. Photographs of the couple are a study in the physiognomy of contrast. In later life, she would grow stout with an enormous shelf of bosom, while her husband remained rail thin, upright in carriage and bearing, with protruding cheekbones that gave him a foreboding look. The arranged marriage evolved into a love match as well as an efficient partnership. Together, they raised his baby sister, Dhondup, along with their own two daughters, Gonpo and her older sister, Dolma. They rebuilt the palace burned down by the queen in 1935 and set about repairing the damage done to the monasteries during the Red Army's occupation.

By the end of 1936, the last stragglers of the Red Army had vacated the Tibetan plateau, many of them moving on to Yan'an, where Mao had consolidated his grip on the Communist Party. The Chinese Civil War flickered on and off, at times overshadowed by the Japanese rampage through eastern China and the massacre of hundreds of thousands in Nanjing. With World War II raging and the world in crisis, the Tibetans hoped that the larger powers would for once be too busy elsewhere to bother with them.

The young Mei king proved himself to be a natural ruler. An official Chinese history of the Mei kingdom, published by the local government, praised him as "scrupulous, shrewd, capable, and experienced." The American missionaries who visited Ngaba—otherwise dismissive of Tibetan chieftains as backward and superstitious—pointed to Ngaba as a rare example of good governance on the plateau. Ekvall, the missionary, remarked that literacy was much higher in Ngaba than in other parts of the Tibetan plateau and that it was not confined to the clerics and aristocracy. Robert Dean Carlson, another missionary who followed Ekvall's footsteps in the 1940s, later told interviewers that Ngaba was thankfully free of the bandits who terrorized other Tibetan areas. "The king just didn't tolerate that sort of stuff," he said.

Communist propaganda would later portray life in pre-Communist Tibetan society as a feudal hell with the serfs subjected to grotesque tortures by their cruel masters—it was one of the pretexts for their conquest of Tibet. But Carlson describes a society quite to the contrary. "In Ngawa [Ngaba], there were the ordinary people, and then there was the ruling family, and there were good relations with the ruling family there. But I don't think you could say that in that part of Tibet there were clear cut class distinctions, scholars and ordinary people, or upper-class and lower-class. The feeling was that there was pretty much equality," he told an interviewer years later.

The kingdom had what might today be referred to as progressive taxation. The people were divided into five categories depending on their wealth. A very wealthy family would have to supply the king's military with three horses, two guns, and 300 rounds of ammunition. A poor family had to supply one horse and one spear. If the family was too poor to afford the tax, one family member would be commissioned to serve as a *keigyak,* or caller, who would travel to the next village to inform people of royal edicts and dictates. Families also sent young women to serve at the palace for one year. They had their hair cut short—to indicate they were not of sexual maturity and shouldn't be taken as mistresses or wives—and they brought their own supply of tsampa. People north of the Ngaqu River, which runs through Ngaba, paid more in taxes because their side got more sunlight with the mountains facing the afternoon sun. The "shade side" was the poorer side of town. Families also paid taxes in the form of barley, yak dung, and juniper branches, which were used for smoke offerings in religious ceremonies. In the king's own home, servants were fed the same food as the aristocrats.

Under Palgon Rapten Tinley, the Mei kingdom's connections to

Kirti grew even stronger, since his wife's family had long been involved with the management of the monastery. In the interest of effective governance, the king also had to maintain good relations with the often-bickering monasteries in his realm. Ngaba was home to at least eighteen Buddhist monasteries as well as a well-known monastery called Nangshik, following the Bon tradition, which claimed to be Tibet's indigenous pre-Buddhist religion. During Losar, the Tibetan New Year, the king would host monks from all the monasteries in the palace's huge reception room.

The Mei king opened a market catering to Hui Muslim traders in Ngaba and created a system of standardized measures for grains and cereals to ensure that the market was a success. The Hui were integral to the success of the economy; since Buddhists weren't supposed to slaughter animals, the Hui served as butchers and ran many of the restaurants. They were keen traders as well. The main market was conveniently located near Kirti Monastery; when nomads and farmers traveled to town, they could make it both a pilgrimage and a shopping excursion. The market sold all the products of the region, salt, meat, cheese, butter, tea, barley, and wool, in addition to manufactured goods such as shoes, bowls, utensils, and tents. Another market in the town sold livestock, horses, sheep, and yaks.

Most exceptional was an alliance that the king maintained with Ma Bufang, a powerful Muslim warlord (many Chinese Hui use the surname Ma, which is short for Muhammad) who controlled neighboring Qinghai province. Throughout the 1920s and 1930s, Ma terrorized Tibetans in Golok, home of the king's paternal relations, and was implicated in a ghastly massacre where thousands of Tibetans were beheaded at Labrang Monastery in Gansu province. Even as the Mei kingdom welcomed refugees fleeing Ma's atrocities, the king never severed relations.

That was the nature of the king's personality. He was business-minded and pragmatic. He tried to accommodate and compromise with whomever he needed in order to survive. There was only one group with whom he could not get along.

———

ON OCTOBER 1, 1949, Mao Zedong proclaimed the People's Republic of China with a ceremony in Beijing's Tiananmen Square. He vowed to restore China to its past glory after a century of humiliation that had begun with the first Opium War in 1839. The many affronts against Chinese sovereignty included the British invasion of Tibet in 1903–1904. Mao vowed to protect the western flank of his nation by establishing firm Chinese control over Tibet.

He wasted little time. On October 7, 1950, some 40,000 People's Liberation Army troops crossed the upper reaches of the Yangtze River, which roughly delineated the border with the territory controlled by the Tibetan government. Within two weeks, the Chinese had captured the border town of Chamdo and forced the Tibetan Army to surrender. China radio enthusiastically declared the "peaceful liberation" of Tibet to be complete.

The Chinese invasion couldn't have come at a more vulnerable time for Tibet. The major powers that might have leaped to Tibet's defense a few years earlier now stood paralyzed. Britain had lowered the Union Jack over India in 1947 and wasn't looking for a new entanglement in the region. Newly independent India wasn't willing to antagonize Beijing. Tibet's situation is often contrasted to that of Mongolia, which gained its independence after the collapse of the Qing dynasty, thanks to the support of Russia and later the Soviet Union. Tibet had no such patron. The United States wanted to curb the expansion of Communist China, but was too preoccupied with Korea. In a strange confluence of events, the People's Liberation Army entered Tibet on the very same day that an American-led U.N. coalition crossed the 38th parallel to fight North Korean forces that had invaded South Korea earlier that year.

To make matters worse, Tibet was ruled by a teenager, albeit a very intelligent and respected teenager: Tenzin Gyatso, the 14th Dalai Lama, who was just fifteen years old at the time.

Of the many defects in Tibet's theocratic system of government, the most glaring is the appointment of a head of state through reincarnation. In this construct, the new leader can't be born until the old one dies, necessitating a long transition before the little boy—it has always been a boy—is identified and then raised to adulthood. In the interim, you have a power vacuum that makes your country vulnerable to external threats and infighting between regents.

The 14th Dalai Lama was born in 1935. His home village, Takster, is about 220 miles north of Ngaba, in Amdo. He was a toddler when a search party, seeking a successor for the 13th Dalai Lama, who had died in 1932, stumbled into his village, following various omens, including ripples in the water of a lake that appeared to spell out the beginning of the word *Amdo*. The story is so often retold that nobody would dare to question its accuracy, but as it goes: The precocious boy, then named Lhamo Dhondup, was able to identify the head of the search party as a senior lama although he had disguised himself as a servant. He proceeded to ace a series of tests, in which he was required to select from an assortment of objects that had belonged to the 13th Dalai Lama—eyeglasses, a drum, beads, and a walking stick. He reportedly was able to speak the Lhasa dialect of Tibetan, almost incomprehensible to those from Amdo.

And so Lhamo Dhondup was recognized as the next incarnation in a venerable lineage. (The title had been bestowed in 1577 by a Mongol ruler, Altan Khan, who was so awed by a visiting Tibetan lama that he decreed him to be the "Dalai lama"—*dalai* being Mongolian for "ocean"—and adopted the Buddhist religion.) After two years of negotiations and payment of a large ransom of silver to Ma Bufang, whose forces surrounded the village, the little boy was transported to Lhasa in a palanquin and installed in a private suite in Potala Palace, a sprawling edifice twice the size of Buckingham Palace, perched high on a hill over Lhasa. He was tutored intensively in the Tibetan language, calligraphy, philosophy, and the metaphysics that Buddhist monks employ in a dialectical debate. He memorized scripture. What little he learned of the outside world was gleaned from ancient maps he found in his library and geography lessons given by the Austrian mountaineer Heinrich Harrer, author of the memoir *Seven Years in Tibet*.

As the Dalai Lama would later write in his autobiography, *My Land and My People,* "I grew up with hardly any knowledge of worldly affairs, and it was in that state . . . that I was called upon to lead my country against the invasion of Communist China."

The king watched the happenings in Lhasa with foreboding. He was better acquainted with the Red Army than most Tibetans. His experiences as a teenager during the Long March left him with a profound distrust of the Communist Party. He was inclined anyway to the Nationalist Party since it had the support of his ally Ma Bufang and the other Muslim warlords, who saw the Communist Party as hostile to Islam.

The king fretted that the Tibetans were too consumed with their own internecine feuds, accusing rivals of launching raids on caravans, stealing territory or animals. The Mei were in a virtual state of war with a rival clan known as the Chukama and had exposed an assassination plot against the king himself.

"We have to put aside these small issues," the king told fellow Tibetan chieftains whenever he had the chance. "The real enemy of the land of snow is coming."

But the king was also a pragmatist. After the defeat of the Japanese in World War II, the Communists won battle after battle; and once it became obvious that they would prevail in the civil war, he deftly switched his allegiance. He sent a gift of musk and deer antlers to Peng Dehuai, Mao's senior general in Sichuan, along with a pledge of support. He helped the Communists round up the remnants of the Nationalist Party still fighting in Sichuan, including some with whom he'd been friendly. When the People's Liberation Army established bases in Ngaba and Dzorge, he loaded up caravans to bring food for the Chinese soldiers.

In return, the Chinese piled on titles and honors. In the convoluted

Communist bureaucracy, the Mei king was simultaneously named Vice Governor of Ngaba, Deputy Director of People's Committee of Sichuan province, and Vice Chairman of Sichuan province's Chinese People's Political Consultative Congress, and as a representative of the first, second, and third National People's Congress. He was named to the Preparatory Committee for the Autonomous Region of Tibet, which was supposed to be setting up a new administration for Tibet along Communist lines.

IN 1951, A TIBETAN delegation was summoned to Beijing and strong-armed into signing away its independence in the form of the Seventeen-Point Agreement. "The Tibetan people shall return to the family of the Motherland the People's Republic of China," declared the first point of the agreement. The Tibetans would give up their military and their right to conduct foreign relations. In return, the agreement promised the Tibetans no immediate changes in their society. "The religious beliefs, customs, and habits of the Tibetan people shall be respected."

Mao launched a charm offensive. Contrary to popular impressions, the first few years of Communist rule in Lhasa were relatively benign. Chinese troops in Lhasa followed a strict code of conduct. They were to pay for any goods they took with silver coins rather than paper money—which Tibetans didn't like. They were supposed to give alms to monks and to show respect for the Buddhist religion. Mao invited the Dalai Lama to Beijing, where he assumed the role of the avuncular older ruler advising the impressionable teenager. "His appearance gave no sign of intellectual power," the Dalai Lama later wrote of Mao, noting his frayed cuffs and slovenly dress, and his constant wheezing. "Yet his manner of speech certainly captured the minds and imaginations of his listeners, and gave the impression of kindness and sincerity." Mao made no secret of his antipathy toward religion. At one point, he sidled up close enough to the Dalai Lama to whisper in his ear, "I understand you very well. But of course, religion is poison." And yet the Dalai Lama believed Mao's promise that he would not interfere with the Tibetans' faith. "I was also convinced that he himself would never use force to convert Tibet into a Communist state," the Dalai Lama wrote.

The Dalai Lama was taken on a tour of the wonders of modern China—factories, shipyards, roads, and schools. He later told Mao "truthfully that I had been greatly impressed and interested by all the development projects I had seen." What he found most intriguing, however, were Mao's messages about social equality.

Along with many Tibetan intellectuals, the Dalai Lama found himself nodding in agreement when the Communists criticized the wealth of the monasteries and aristocrats in contrast to the abject poverty of their subjects. In later life, the Dalai Lama would tell interviewers—myself included—that he considered himself a socialist at heart. The Marxist message of equality was a comfortable fit with the Buddhist emphasis on compassion. The shortcoming in his own education convinced him that Tibet needed more schools. The Dalai Lama's chief complaint about Mao was that he smoked too much.

It was obvious to the Dalai Lama as well that Tibet needed reforms, development, and modernization. The ease with which the Chinese had conquered Tibet drove home the inadequacy of Tibet's institutions and military in the twentieth century. The Communist vision appealed to many educated Tibetans. These included the Panchen Lama, who had initially embraced the Party.

Like other influential Tibetans, the Mei king was invited to Beijing as a delegate to the first National Party Congress along with other top Tibetan leaders whose loyalty the Communists hoped to cultivate. He was given the grand tour of the marvels of modern China. "They made every effort to show us only the best and prettiest of China in order to impress us. We ate the best food and stayed in the nicest rooms," said Jamyang Sonam, an octogenarian from Kirti Monastery who was on one of the trips. "They told us to report what we saw to our people back home and tell them how developed China was and how good life was under Communism."

The Mei king was less easily persuaded. An official photograph taken in 1954 of his visit to Beijing, with the Dalai Lama and Panchen Lama also in attendance, captured the moment. The lamas—the Dalai Lama, then eighteen, a bespectacled, gawky teenager; and the moon-faced Panchen Lama, already plump at sixteen—are smiling, if hesitantly. Two decades older and more skeptical, the Mei king stands behind them, scowling, his brows knit together as though he is contemplating the disaster about to befall his kingdom.

In 1956, Chinese authorities permitted the Mei king to visit Lhasa for the inaugural session of the Preparatory Committee for the Autonomous Region of Tibet, which was supposed to be setting up a new administration along Communist lines. He dutifully attended the meetings. He followed the usual pilgrim circuit—visiting the great monasteries of Lhasa, Ganden, Sera, and Drepung, and the Tashilhunpo Monastery in Shigatse. He had an audience with the Dalai Lama, who presented him with seven golden statues and a prayer book.

He brought along the entire family; Gonpo would remember it as her first family vacation, a trip marred mostly by her older sister getting sick with what would turn out to be a chronic stomach ailment. They traipsed up endless sets of stairs to the monasteries high in the mountains, draping white silk scarves called *khata*s and prostrating themselves in front of endless statues of Buddha and his bodhisattvas. Gonpo was unaware that these conspicuous displays of piety were in part a cover for the secret meetings her father was holding with monastery officials.

The king was preparing for the future by divesting himself of the family's wealth, making large donations to the monasteries of central Tibet. He was arranging for his land to be transferred to Kirti Monastery. The king also used the visit to warn the Dalai Lama about the troubles the Chinese were causing Tibetans to the east.

In the Seventeen-Point Agreement signed in 1951, the Party had promised not to impose Communism by force on the Tibetans. But they insisted the deal covered only the former territories of the Lhasa government, excluding the eastern half of the plateau, where the majority of Tibetans live. Already by 1956, the Communists were starting to confiscate land in parts of Sichuan province.

When the king returned to Ngaba, it was clear that his fears were justified. The Chinese were demanding that the Tibetans surrender all firearms. Some of the hotheads in Meruma, among them his former generals, were resistant; they wanted to fight. The king was insistent. He was painfully aware of the superior firepower of the People's Liberation Army. Even back in the 1930s, when they were a ragtag army in retreat and on the edge of starvation, the Chinese had easily defeated the Tibetans in Ngaba. Now they were battle-hardened soldiers who fought in mechanized columns with tanks and aircraft. The king advised his generals that they should follow Chinese orders to turn in their firearms. When they balked, he sent emissaries out himself and collected five thousand guns and pistols.

The king was compliant until the very end, dutifully carrying out the dictates of the Communist Party. He served on their committees and assemblies. He showed up at meetings. In the summer of 1958, when Gonpo, her mother, and her sister were mourning the death of her uncle, the king was summoned to Barkham, the capital of the prefecture, for what he was told was an urgent meeting. This was a common ruse employed by the Party for deposing those who stood in their way. While the king was out of town, supposedly attending this meeting, the army seized his palace and escorted his family away from Ngaba. Now the rulers were out of the way and the Communist Party could do what it liked with their former subjects, who in the end would be treated with even more brutality.

THE YEAR THAT
TIME COLLAPSED

Amdo Delek as an adult.

—

1958

—

DELEK WAS BORN ON AUGUST 15, 1949, SIX WEEKS BEFORE the founding of Mao's China, in Meruma village. Of all the villages of Ngaba, Meruma is the one most closely associated with the Mei kingdom—the very name loosely translates as "the place of the Mei tribes." Most of the working men of Meruma were in some way employed by the ruling family, serving in the court or the military or maintaining the king's herds of yaks and sheep. Delek's father, Ratsang Wangchen, was an illustrious general. In 1935, he commanded the intrepid troops who tried to head off the Red Army at the pass near Tsenyi Monastery. It was one of the few times Tibetans won a battle against the Chinese, and that made Delek's father a war hero, even though the Tibetans were ultimately defeated by Red Army reinforcements. The general, already in his late fifties, died suddenly of a heart attack when Delek was still an infant. The family carried his body by yak to the hill behind Tsenyi Monastery where he'd fought so bravely and there they conducted the traditional sky burial—the body hacked up and fed to vultures. (Barbaric as the custom may appear to outsiders, it is one of the most ecologically sound funeral practices: returning a body to nature without digging the land, polluting the water, or chopping down trees for cremation.)

Afterward, Delek's grief-stricken mother gathered the remaining bones to be blessed in Lhasa. As was the habit of the many devout pilgrims, she walked the entire way, stopping periodically to prostrate herself. Since the journey took more than two years, it left Delek a virtual orphan. He went to live with his maternal grandparents, shared a bed with his grandmother, and at night would snuggle close and suckle on her shriveled breast.

Delek was an unprepossessing slip of a boy, small of stature, tiny in every which way, except for his protruding ears and a nose that by middle age would grow big as a gardening spade. That nose was perpetually dripping and his face was always dirty from wiping the snot with the sleeve of his lambskin robe.

Nevertheless, Delek grew up with a sense of superiority because of his family's association with the king. A maternal uncle had also served as a general, and another cousin was a minister. After his father's death, Delek was brought by an uncle for an audience with the Mei king. When they were ushered into the palace, they found the king not in a formal reception room or office, but in the kitchen surrounded by his advisors. He was wearing a black chuba and a white shirt and had a long braided tuft of hair on the back of his head. What Delek would remember most clearly was that the king's complexion had an unearthly pallor, so unlike that of the Tibetans who worked outdoors. The king put his hands on Delek's head in affection and gave him a horseshoe-shaped candy made of molasses.

MERUMA IS ABOUT FIFTEEN MILES east of Ngaba, along the main road, Route 302, leading in from Chengdu. The village was divided between herders and farmers. The farming families lived off the main road where the terrain was flat enough and the altitude, at 12,000 feet, just low enough to support the growth of barley, the grain best suited for high altitudes. The herders, or *drokpa,* are frequently referred to as nomads, but they had a fixed home in the long winter, from September until June. Then they would head to summer pasturelands, pitching their black felt tents in the mountains and moving every few weeks to provide fresh grass for their herds. The two communities, farmers and nomads, were essential to support each other: the nomadic families would supply the farmers with butter, cheese, and meat, while the farmers would supply grain.

Delek's family lived in a neighborhood called Serda, or "gold hill," where the terrain begins a gradual climb up from the administrative center. The houses were constructed of rammed earth and surrounded by courtyard walls—smaller versions of the king's palace.

Over the course of 1958, Delek noticed that the working-age men had begun to disappear. Then the women too. In time he learned that many, including his older brother and an uncle, had been arrested— for what crime he never knew. Others had run away. In time only old people and children were living in the neighborhood.

What Delek didn't understand until later was that the Communist Party was about to launch what would be the first of the many wildly ambitious and ill-conceived schemes to transform Tibetan society. Preemptively, officials had rounded up people they thought likely to resist. The process began in the mid-1950s in other parts of Sichuan province, and it hadn't gone well. The forced collectivization had led to revolts among the Khampas—a term for the natives of Kham, who were so fierce that the name is practically synonymous with warrior. Determined not to make the same mistake in Ngaba, the Party started by offering an amnesty for households who turned in their weapons voluntarily. When too few were turned in, they insisted that the king implement the policy.

Of all the king's edicts, this was the most unpopular. Tibetans had an ambivalent relationship with guns. Although they disapproved on religious grounds, most households kept at least one firearm—maybe an antique, a musket or flintlock dating back to the nineteenth century, but still something that could kill. After decades of civil war and feuds with warlords, the plateau was awash with guns of various vintages. This was the Wild West, and there were bandits and even whole tribes that made it their business to rob caravans of travelers; if you didn't encounter bandits on the road, you might run into wolves or bears. At times Tibetans would hunt to supplement their diet, sometimes going after small game like marmots.

Even the king's military advisors were grumbling about the edict to turn in weapons. One of them, Meigang Jinpa, a respected and outspoken man who was married to Delek's aunt, was walking through the small alleys toward Kirti Monastery to visit his brother, a monk, when from around the corner gunshots rang out. He was hit. He stumbled toward the monastery, trying to contain his entrails with the sash of his chuba, before collapsing into the arms of one of his relatives. Although Meigang Jinpa never saw his assassin, he suspected he had been targeted by the Communist Party to prevent him from organizing the resistance.

"They are up to no good. They will destroy everything we have if we don't prepare," he told the relative just before he died.

Slowly but surely, the now-ruling Communist Party was making its presence felt. There were military barracks all around Ngaba and in Dzorge—the very same barracks that the king had supplied with food when he was still trying to ingratiate himself with the government.

Now the town was full of Han Chinese—engineers, surveyors, teachers, and bureaucrats. Delek watched with fascination as the Chinese engineers etched into the grasslands a web of roads that connected Ngaba with Chengdu. Some of the roads cut right through his village. Meruma was no longer the remote place it once was. Some of the Tibetans said that it would make their life more convenient, while others warned that the real purpose of the roads was so the military could roll in.

ON A COLD AFTERNOON in late autumn 1958, Delek was playing in the courtyard outside his grandparents' house when the dogs started the furious barking that heralded the arrival of unwelcome visitors. He peered out the gate and saw men on horseback—a mixed group of Tibetans and Chinese—heading up the hill. They were riding nice horses and wearing expensive clothes—new sheepskin cloaks and brocaded coats, so elegant that Delek suspected they must have been confiscated from richer Tibetans. They carried guns, another sure sign that they had official permission since ordinary Tibetan households had already given up their weapons.

As the men tied their horses to pegs outside the house, Delek ducked into the basket that his grandmother used for carrying laundry. At nine, he was still small enough to hide in that tight space and be completely out of sight.

Delek smelled smoke, so he knew there was a fire somewhere close by. He heard his grandmother come out of the house to tie up the dogs. Hunched over with age, she was nevertheless moving quickly. A few weeks earlier, government visitors had shot a neighbor's dog, and she wanted hers to escape that fate. The dogs kept up their barking, but the men on horseback shouted above the din.

"Give us your gold. Give us your silver. We know you have it hidden in the floor," one of the men shouted at his grandparents in Tibetan, translating for the Chinese who were clearly in charge.

Delek could hear the thumping—whack, whack, whack—over

and over, and his grandparents' screams. They were being beaten. His first instinct was to rush out of the basket to protect them, but he was so small and so scared. He dared not cry out for fear of being discovered. He shoved his hand into his mouth to keep quiet, even though tears were streaming down his face.

When at last he heard the horses heading back down the hill, Delek jumped out of the basket and dashed into the house into his grandmother's arms, so happy to see her that at first he failed to notice that she was bleeding from her head. She wore her hair Tibetan-style in skinny, tightly woven braids—three on each side of her head, held in place by an amber hairpiece. The men had yanked the braids out, leaving her scalp red and bloodied.

"Grandma, your hair! Where is your hair?" he cried.

"Never mind my hair. Help me with your grandfather!"

Delek looked up. The men had tied his grandfather's hands behind his back and then run the rope over the horizontal wooden beams, creating a makeshift pulley. He was suspended from the ceiling, tangled in ropes. His grandmother wasn't able to pull him down, but Delek was nimble. He ran to get a stool and a knife, then shinnied up to the beams to cut the ropes. He and his grandmother eased the old man down. His grandfather crumpled onto the floor, barely conscious, his brittle skin bleeding from the ropes. Delek's grandmother took his head in her lap and spoon-fed him tsampa porridge, while Delek rubbed his feet.

The house was filled with smoke. Still smoldering was everything that the men had tossed into the fire. Delek's grandparents were literate and had a fine collection of Buddhist manuscripts, handwritten in gold and silver, works of art as well as holy books. Also burning in the fire were precious pills, herbs, and minerals wrapped in silk pouches and blessed by a lama, and hairpieces for the braids his grandmother no longer had.

This was the beginning of what the Chinese called "Democratic Reforms"—a redistribution of the land from the nobility and the monasteries to benefit the poor. Socialist theory called for a gradual process in which the people first organized themselves into "mutual-aid teams" so that they learned to work together. These teams would eventually form collectives and then larger communes. But hard-liners in the Party were in a hurry, and Mao himself was impatient. In a speech in 1955, he complained that "some of our comrades are tottering along like a woman with bound feet."

The Communist Party had identified feudalism and imperialism as the greatest evils of society. Their dilemma was how to destroy feudalism without becoming imperialists themselves; they couldn't simply force "reforms" on the Tibetans. In order to live up to their own lofty propaganda, they needed the Tibetans to carry out reforms voluntarily, joyfully. To convince them, they dispatched young Chinese recruits, some of them still in high school, to spread the word. These young Chinese cadres lectured about the corruption of the aristocracy and the monasteries, which also had large holdings of land. Delek remembers their speeches.

"You will be your own master," the Chinese promised poorer Tibetans. "We will topple the feudal landlords."

"Nobody will be able to exploit you anymore."

"Religion is superstition. You are worshipping demons."

The mass uprising never materialized. But the pitch did appeal to those Tibetans who hoped the redistribution of wealth would improve their lot in life. Tibetans who joined forces with the Communist Party were known as *jiji fenzi,* which loosely translates from Chinese as "activists." The Tibetan term was *hurtsonchen*—the lowest level of enforcers, the collaborators who squealed on and beat up neighbors who resisted Communist rule. As a reward, *hurtsonchen* were allowed to loot clothing, shoes, and household goods from their wealthier countrymen. But anything of real value went to the Party-controlled communes, which turned out to be far greedier than the worst of the feudal landlords.

Tibetans of this generation refer to this period simply as *ngabgay*—'58. Like 9/11, it is shorthand for a catastrophe so overwhelming that words cannot express it, only the number. But there are some evocative figures of speech. Some will call it *dhulok,* a word that roughly translates as the "collapse of time," or, hauntingly, "when the sky and earth changed places."

The "Democratic Reforms" in eastern Tibet roughly coincided with the Great Leap Forward, Mao's misguided experiment in jump-starting the Chinese economy. Like so many catastrophes, it was the result of ambition run amok. Mao was a utopian who hoped to create not just a new society, but new, improved human beings. He believed that people could transcend their individual desires for the greater good and through collective enterprise boost their living standards and the country's output. This was to be accomplished by herding 700 million people into cooperative farms.

Even to a child as young as Delek, it was obvious that Mao's reforms were doomed to failure. The Chinese cadres in charge of the Tibetans had no experience with herding and even less with farming at high altitudes. Most of the Chinese troops came from lower-lying regions; they didn't realize that barley was the only grain that thrived in the plateau and that the higher altitudes couldn't support crops at all and were better used for grazing. Giddy from Mao's exhortations, they denied the expertise of the people who had lived off the land for generations, insisting that the Tibetans were backward. "As the Han are the bulwark of the revolution . . . any thinking against learning from the Han nationality and welcoming the help given by the Han nationality is completely wrong," expounded one propagandist at the time. The nomads were made to hand over animals to the collectives that didn't know how to keep them alive, and to farm land that would never produce crops.

The result was years of failed harvests and dead animals. Grasslands where the crops failed were now stripped bare of vegetation, exposed to the winds that swirled through the plateau spewing dust into the air. The Communist cadres didn't understand that the Tibetan way of sustenance required both nomads and farmers; in order to obtain enough nutrition, people needed to swap their animal products for grains, and that required markets. Now the markets were closed. Buying or selling grain was forbidden. Internal travel restrictions were imposed so people could no longer barter goods with other villages. When Delek's mother returned from Lhasa, she would saddle up a horse in the dead of night to visit a cousin in another village with whom she could trade some butter for barley to prevent her family from starving. She only dared make the trip a few times a year.

Unlike Han Chinese, Tibetans had little experience with famine—the exception being the Long March interlude of 1935 and 1936 when the Red Army decimated their food supply. In the past, Tibetans were poor, often poorly nourished because of the scarcity of fresh fruit and vegetables, but they rarely went hungry.

Few Tibetans were vegetarians at the time; eating meat was essential in a habitat that didn't support many vegetables. They slaughtered yaks, but sparingly, saying a prayer to apologize for taking the life of a sentient being, possibly the reincarnation of somebody they'd known. A single yak could feed a family for months.

Yaks were the sustenance of village life. Yaks were often crossbred with cows to produce a *dzomo,* an amazing dairy machine that could produce seven liters of milk per day. Every part of the animal was consumed, not just the choice cuts of meat. Tibetans churned the milk into butter that was spooned into salty tea or clarified to fuel the butter lamps that provided spiritual illumination. They made lumps of hard cheese that were a convenient protein source for a peripatetic people, perfect for a nomad to tuck into the pockets of his robe along with the dried meat. The intestines were used to make sausage, stuffed with the blood or the meat of the less desirable organs. Stomachs became bags for storing other food. The skins were made into shoes and rugs, and even coracles, small boats used to navigate rivers. The bones became combs, buttons, and ornaments. The long coarse hair on the flanks of the yak was woven to make blankets and tents. Yak dung was collected and shaped into bricks and hockey-puck-like patties to be used for construction or burned as fuel. Without the animals, the Tibetans lost their food supply, their clothing, their shelter, their light.

All of Delek's family's animals—300 head of sheep and 200 head of cattle, including yaks—were transferred to a commune. There, Chinese Muslims slaughtered the yak with industrial efficiency. The skins and the meat were immediately taken away; to where Delek didn't know at the time, although it turned out much of the lamb was exported to the Soviet Union since Han Chinese don't care for mutton. If the butchers were kind, they would allow Delek and other children to stand around with their enamel mugs to catch the blood oozing out from the slit throats of the animals. That was all they got of the animals they had once owned. They received no wages, only work points they could swap for food at the communal kitchen.

It was forbidden to cook at home. Utensils and dishware had been confiscated from private homes to discourage violations. At mealtimes, Delek would walk down the hill to the administrative center of Meruma. A communal kitchen had been set up inside a house that had been confiscated from a wealthy family. A chef ladled out a gruel that was something between a soup and a porridge, filling Delek's enamel rations mug just halfway. Delek would quickly swallow his food, then, still hungry, he would rush out with other children to look for more food. The children would forage in the mountains. They searched for edible plants, like *rambu,* an alpine flowering weed with red seeds, and *droma,* the root of the silverweed, which tastes a little like sweet potatoes. They picked out undigested seeds in the horse manure.

Delek was a quick-witted boy so he went hungry less often than others. His specialty was in finding bones, which could be smashed to expose the marrow and then boiled into a nutritious broth. He wasn't particular about what kind of bones—sheep, yak, dog, or even human. Although he doesn't remember any incidents of deliberate cannibalism, he says nobody looked too closely at what was thrown into the soup pot. Tibetans who found something edible in the mountains would wait to cook until after the neighbors were sleeping, for fear somebody would report the smoke.

The elderly, who had very limited rations, were the first to perish. Delek's grandfather never recovered his health after being brutalized by the invaders and died about a year later. The family performed a sky burial on the same hill where they had seen off Delek's father. This time, though, they were unable to call monks to say the prayers so they did it discreetly on their own. Afterward, they dug a hole in the ground and secretly burned a butter lamp. Spies were everywhere. The pro-Communist Tibetans were encouraged to squeal on their neighbors who showed any religious inclination, even those who quietly recited prayers at home.

"You're trying to resurrect ghosts and talk to spirits. It's all superstition," offenders would be scolded.

Harsh punishments were meted out at public struggle sessions known as *thamzing*. They took place in a tent that had been erected near Delek's home. People were summoned with cymbals, horns, and drums that had been confiscated from monasteries. Since the cadres didn't know how to play them, the instruments made what Delek would remember as a terrifying cacophonous noise. He was about nine years old when he attended his first session. The accused was a wealthy young man named Rachung Kayee who was charged with hiding gold and silver and lighting butter lamps. With his hands tied behind his back, he was dragged onto a makeshift stage, slapped and kicked and whipped with sharp branches of the sea buckthorn that punctured his skin. Delek and other children had been arranged in rows in front of the stage. They were instructed to raise their fists and shout their approval. Chinese officials observed from their chairs, smoking cigarettes. The spectacle started at nine A.M. and dragged on until sunset. Delek had nightmares for weeks after.

Although elsewhere in China the Communist Party's assault on religion began in earnest with the start of the Cultural Revolution in 1966, it happened much earlier in the eastern reaches of the Tibetan plateau. By 1960, the monasteries around Ngaba had been largely demolished or appropriated. The largest, sturdiest buildings at Kirti Monastery were requisitioned for administrative offices. Lesser structures became barns and warehouses. The monks' dormitories, made of adobe, were crushed to be mixed in with the soil and their foundations plowed for planting barley and wheat. At Se Monastery, across from the king's palace, the monks' quarters were preserved, but given to poor families who had been told to vacate their homes so that the land could be requisitioned for government use. The monks, many of whom had lived in the monastery since they were seven years old, were evicted and sent back to their villages. They remained stigmatized; even without their robes, they were banned from visiting the towns.

Delek remembers that you could tell who had been a monk because they looked so uncomfortable in lay clothing. "They couldn't walk in the heavy lambskin robes and pants. They were so clumsy," he said.

Seeing the monks humiliated, statues smashed, and paintings burned shook Tibetans to the core. Buddhism provided the rituals through which the seasons were measured, births celebrated, and deaths grieved. The monasteries were Tibetans' museums, libraries, and schools. Whether or not you were a true believer in the faith, there was no denying that Tibetan Buddhism had inspired an artistry that some compared to the splendors of medieval Christendom. The attacks on religion alienated Tibetans who might otherwise have supported the Communist Party's efforts to stamp out feudalism and create social equality.

Tibetans were not alone in their suffering. Between 1958 and 1962, during the Great Leap Forward, an estimated 36 million Chinese are believed to have perished, a death toll that rivals the greatest calamities of a brutal century.

As bad as it was for the Han Chinese, the Tibetans got it worse. The abuses started earlier and lasted longer. The Chinese deaths during the Great Leap Forward were primarily due to famine. Although many Han Chinese were killed during the struggle sessions, the preemptive arrests didn't approach the same level. In some Tibetan areas, as much as 20 percent of the population was arrested, and among those as many as half perished, according to Tibetan accounts. Some of the prisons consisted of little more than pits in the ground crammed with hundreds of people.

"When people were taken to prison, they did not come back," Delek said.

How many Tibetans were killed as a direct result of Chinese policy depends of course on who is counting. Chinese government statistics do not classify excess deaths by ethnicity, but one can extrapolate by the geographic data. In 1960, for example, the mortality rates in Sichuan, Gansu, and Qinghai provinces—all with large Tibetan populations—were nearly double the national average of 25 deaths per thousand people.

The Panchen Lama, whom the Communists initially hoped to enlist to their cause, visited his birthplace in 1962, and was so appalled by what he saw that he remarked afterward that in feudal times at least the beggars had a bowl in which to put their alms. He penned a lengthy complaint, which would become known as the 70,000-Character Petition, which would earn him nine years in prison and another four under house arrest. Although the petition opened obsequiously with the obligatory encomium to the "great, correct, and wise Chairman Mao," it went on to warn that the Tibetan nationality is "sinking into a state close to death." He noted the "evident and severe reduction" of the Tibetan population. "The anguish of such severe hunger had never been experienced in Tibetan history and was such that people couldn't imagine it even in their dreams."

Treatment of Tibetans in Meruma was somewhat more lenient because of the Mei king's initial compliance with the Communists. By insisting that his subjects turn in their weapons, the king might have prevented the massacres that took place in less cooperative villages. In one village, Marang, south of the river, the men who resisted were summarily executed along with their families, according to a compilation of testimonies published in exile. According to one:

> My father surrendered to the Chinese by raising his arms in the air. But the Chinese shot him. They killed him, his body rolling down. The soldiers ran towards us and fired on us. I didn't die but I lost consciousness.

When I regained consciousness, I found that bullets had hit my arms and legs. As a result, I couldn't move them at all. My three-year-old sister was dead, while my nine-year-old brother was severely injured; his entrails had come out.

The testimonies are too similar and too numerous to dismiss. A Tibetan monk in his seventies who lives on a mountain west of Ngaba told me a harrowing story about how people from his village, starving because of the rations, tried to escape into the mountains, hoping to fend for themselves as nomads. The PLA pursued them. They were chased to a rocky escarpment where they couldn't run any farther and were shot at close range.

"They were shooting at us like we were wolves. They had us surrounded," said the monk, who was fifteen at the time. He and his twelve-year-old brother escaped, but two young friends were shot and killed. Out of his village of two thousand people, he believes only about five hundred survived the 1950s.

It is impossible to fathom current Tibetan attitudes toward the Chinese government without grasping the enormity of what befell them in the 1950s and early 1960s. Tibetans often speak about "when the Chinese invaded"—only to be chastised by Chinese who point out that this eastern part of the plateau had been part of the Qing dynasty's China since the early eighteenth century. But the Qing emperors were Manchus, a northern people who were nominally Tibetan Buddhists. The Han Chinese were virtually strangers. And what difference does it make? When somebody who speaks a different language comes to your town, confiscates your home, your clothing, your shoes, and your food, destroys that which is most sacred to you, imprisons the young men in your family, and shoots those who resist, it feels like an invasion whether that person is a fellow citizen or not. Tibetans aren't talking about the fine points of international law or the definition of sovereignty: they are speaking honestly about what they experienced.

As context, the estimated death toll of 300,000 Tibetans during this period is greater than the massacre in Nanjing by Japanese occupying troops, for which the Chinese government insisted on repeated apologies. Except for one instance in 1980 by China's most liberal leader, Hu Yaobang, the Chinese government has never apologized— instead it keeps up a barrage of propaganda about how lucky Tibetans are to live under the beneficent rule of the Communist Party.

The resistance in Meruma was fairly modest, involving some thirty men who fled into the mountains with weapons to stage guerrilla attacks on the Chinese. Although they were badly outnumbered, they managed to inflict some casualties. Delek remembers coming home from a Chinese-run school around 1959 and seeing trucks carrying dead Chinese soldiers. "There were many dead in the back of the truck and they had clearly been killed recently because the truck was dripping blood," he said.

Elsewhere, the resistance was better organized and better funded. A guerrilla movement called Chushi Gangdruk, literally "four rivers, six ranges," a traditional epithet for Kham, started up during the late 1950s. The guerrillas received some logistical and training support from the Central Intelligence Agency—just enough to infuriate the Chinese, but not enough to change the balance of power.

Recently uncovered Chinese archives suggest that the fighting during this period was deadlier and more widespread than the Chinese government initially acknowledged. The closest anybody has come to piecing together the whole story is the Chinese-born scholar Jianglin Li, who scrutinized county and provincial records. In her book *When the Iron Bird Flies: The Secret War on the Tibetan Plateau, 1956–1962,* Li concluded that the Chinese Air Force flew almost 3,000 bombing sorties in Qinghai province. A publication called *The Sichuan Military Gazetteer* described "over 10,000 big and small battles." Columns of tanks fired mortar shells into recalcitrant enclaves. Entire villages were obliterated. On her blog, *War on Tibet,* Li estimated that at least 300,000 people died in eastern Tibet during the years after the reforms were implemented. She did not find records for Ngaba, but in one nearby prefecture, Yushu, the Tibetan population dropped 41.4 percent from 1957 to 1963.

In one of the most famous incidents in 1956, thousands of Tibetans took refuge in Changtreng Sampheling Monastery, one of the largest in the region with three thousand monks. The Chinese Air Force sent in a Russian-made Ilyushin bomber that reduced the monastery and the refugees within to ruins. Another historic monastery in Lithang was similarly destroyed. To terrified Tibetans, most of whom had never seen an airplane, the death from the air evoked a famous prophecy by an eighth-century lama who predicted that "when the iron bird flies and horses run on wheels, the Tibetan people will be scattered like ants across the world."

DURING THE 1950S, Mao still hoped he could enlist the support of the Dalai Lama, whose popularity he thought would convince other Tibetans to voluntarily embrace Communism. Though the Party more or less abided by the Seventeen-Point Agreement, postponing any provocative changes in central Tibet, the veneer of civility was wearing thin. Some hard-line leftists within the Party believed Mao was moving too slowly and that he should dump the Dalai Lama in favor of the Panchen Lama, who'd been more enthusiastic about Communism at the outset. The tensions were exacerbated by guerrillas from Sichuan province. The Chinese government demanded that the Dalai Lama dispatch Tibetan troops to fight the guerrillas—to which he responded that his troops would likely defect and join forces with the guerrillas.

By early 1959, some 50,000 refugees from eastern Tibet had poured into central Tibet, setting up tent cities around Lhasa. They told of starvation and persecution and the desecration of Buddhist sites. The refugees and their supporters pressed the Dalai Lama to end any cooperation with the Chinese Communist Party.

The fragile détente fractured in March 1959. The Chinese military invited the Dalai Lama to a theatrical performance, requesting that he leave behind his usual security retinue. The Tibetans suspected it might be a ruse to arrest him or worse. Tens of thousands of Tibetans surrounded Norbulingka palace, vowing to protect him. The crowds grew rowdier, demanding the expulsion of the Chinese from Tibet. Chinese troops reinforced their military camps with sandbags and moved heavy artillery into place. Shots were fired. Mortar shells exploded nearby. Shortly before midnight on March 17, 1959, the Dalai Lama, dressed in layman's clothing and high leather boots, and without the eyeglasses that made him easily recognizable, left the palace via a back exit, and with a small retinue of family members and aides made his way on horseback out of Lhasa and into exile in India.

A THOROUGHLY
CHINESE GIRL

*The last photo of Gonpo's family, taken in Chengdu in 1966, months
before the start of the Cultural Revolution. Only she (top left)
and her aunt (top center) would survive.*

THE NIGHT THEY WERE EVICTED FROM THE PALACE, GONPO,
her mother, and her sister were driven in a Russian jeep piled high
with their suitcases to Chengdu, the capital of Sichuan province. The
journey took three days as the jeep bounced its way through the
switchbacks of the mountain roads. It was downhill almost the entire
way. Chengdu was hot and sticky, overgrown with subtropical fo-
liage. Gonpo felt like she was in a foreign country.

Gonpo and her family were housed in a suite in the Nationalities Reception Center, a government-run hotel that had been built on orders of Sichuan's Communist Party secretary for the express purpose of assimilating minorities into the motherland. With its passion for categorization, the Communist Party had used a Stalinist model for classifying the population by ethnicity. The Chinese government eventually identified fifty-six nationalities. (The people from eastern Tibet, who had considered themselves somewhat apart, were lumped in with the Tibetans from central Tibet—which some scholars believe contributed to the greater sense of Tibetan nationalism.) Other prominent ethnicities were the Uighurs, a Turkic people from the northwest, and the Mongols.

"All nationalities of our nation have already united into a great family," boasted a propaganda poster of the day with smiling, rosy-cheeked young men and women in their ethnic costumes.

The Nationalities Reception Center was like a cross between a dormitory and a hotel. The accommodations were comfortable enough. They had adequate, if rationed, meals that were served in a downstairs canteen. But the atmosphere was at times unfriendly. Although the other residents were also ethnic minorities, many of them Tibetan, they kept their distance from Gonpo and her family. It took Gonpo some weeks to comprehend the status her family had and what they had lost.

Gonpo's mother didn't like to eat in the cafeteria with the others, so she often asked Gonpo to go and bring up a tray of food. One day when Gonpo ventured into the cafeteria, she was recognized by Communist hard-liners.

"This is the child of a landlord," somebody yelled while the others got up and kicked the empty metal tray out of her hands. She picked it up and ran from the building. She hid behind a tree, sobbing. It was not so much that she was offended or hurt, but she feared the incident would upset her mother. She waited until she was able to collect herself, then picked up the tray from the floor and headed back upstairs.

"Oh, I tripped and dropped the tray," Gonpo told her mother, who had noticed that the tray was dented. She braced herself for a scolding, but her mother just nodded. The next day they scraped together some coins and went out to buy bread.

The family's greatest hardship by far was that the king did not rejoin them for more than a year, and for much of the time they were unsure of his whereabouts. Gonpo's mother fell into a deep depression. She rarely went out; she stayed alone in her room, reading Buddhist scriptures. Once a large matronly woman, she shrank in her grief.

When the king finally rejoined the family, he was withdrawn and taciturn and barely spoke to his family. Gonpo's mother improved, relieved to have her husband back, but now her father was the one who refused to leave his room. He'd close the windows and draw the curtains so that the warm, humid air of Chengdu couldn't penetrate. He kept his hands tightly folded into the sleeves of his chuba as though cocooning into himself. He recited the same mantras over and over. A doctor was called in to examine him, but did not come up with any diagnosis. Later Gonpo learned that her father had been abused in struggle sessions and kept for nearly a year in solitary confinement in a dark room.

Gonpo was the youngest member of the family and the most adaptable. While her parents battled their demons, she thrived. She absorbed Mandarin so quickly it began to push aside her mother tongue; she even lost the guttural accent that identified her as a Tibetan.

Although her eyes were rounder and more deeply set than those of most Han Chinese, her hair curlier and her complexion a shade darker, she was barely distinguishable from Chinese schoolgirls when dressed in her school uniform with its crisp white blouse and red tie. Instead of the tiny braids worn by Tibetans, she tied her hair back in one thick plait like the Chinese girls. She carried in her schoolbag the little red book of quotations of Chairman Mao, which had become the national bible. Some of Mao's most famous quotes strangely reminded her of her father's admonitions ("We should be modest and prudent, guard against arrogance and rashness") and she thoroughly approved. It was how they had tried to live and protect themselves all those years. Nobody would have suspected she was a Tibetan princess. She could pass.

Her father slowly came out of his shell. He recovered his ability to speak and socialize. He continued to attend meetings of rubber-stamp assemblies. He would frequently travel to Beijing. He got extra rations of food—six meal coupons instead of the usual four—which he shared with his family and servants. But Palgon Rapten Tinley was no longer a king; it wasn't just that he no longer wielded power, it was that he no longer had the disposition of a king. He was more of a doting father than an authority figure. He insisted on inspecting Gonpo's homework, which mostly consisted of worksheets of Chinese calligraphy. He couldn't read the actual characters, but he would make her recopy an entire sheet if he spotted a tiny inkblot on the page. He was clueless about the math.

Gonpo thrived academically and socially. She earned high enough marks to win a place at a prestigious high school in Beijing that was affiliated with the Nationalities University, designed to groom future cadres in the minority populations. Mindful of her aristocratic past, Gonpo had learned how to make herself inconspicuous when needed in order to avoid situations that might provoke jealousy or conflict, but she also knew how to use her intellect and talents when she needed to stand out. She had a clear, confident soprano voice and was chosen to head the school's cultural club. She had somehow survived the various Communist Party campaigns—Speak Bitterness, the High Tide, the Anti-Rightist Campaign, the Democratic Reforms, the Great Leap Forward—each of which rolled in succession over the Tibetan plateau like destructive summer storms. But in China, there was always another storm brewing in the distance. If one didn't knock you down, the next would.

THE SUMMER OF 1966 Gonpo would remember as the happiest of her life. She came back from Beijing to vacation with her family. Her sister, Dolma, who was in training to be a medic at a PLA military school, returned as well for a reunion. Their father gushed over how well his daughters were growing up. Thoroughly indoctrinated by now by the Communist Party, or at least pretending to be, the king told Gonpo with approval, "Mao's Red Book has had a good influence on you."

They went on picnics. They went to a photo studio to have a family portrait taken. The girls wore flowered dresses with high collars cut in the classic Chinese style of the cheongsam. Her parents wore crisp white shirts. In the photograph, her father looks less gaunt than before, with more flesh in his cheeks. He was insistent that they all smile for the photo, and so they did.

The third week of August, Gonpo received a telegram that instructed her to return to Beijing immediately to resume her studies. The family went to see her off at the train station. Her father was in a generous mood and rushed between kiosks buying her gifts for the journey. Later, as she was leaving, her father pressed in her hands a large bag of *mihuatang,* a sweet cake made of puffed rice that is a ubiquitous snack food in China.

"Share it with people you meet on the train. Even if you have only one piece of candy, you must share," he advised.

As the train pulled out of Chengdu station, Gonpo settled contentedly into her seat. She had never seen her father so loving with his children. Only later did it occur to her that he must have known what was about to happen. The Cultural Revolution had begun.

After the disaster of the Great Leap Forward, Mao worried that his grip on leadership had slipped. So many people had died of starvation during the Great Leap Forward that not even the most talented propagandist could spin it into anything but an abject failure. Relations with the Soviet Union had been souring since the late 1950s. Then leader Nikita Khrushchev had denounced the excesses of Mao's former ally, Joseph Stalin, an implicit criticism of Mao too. In a preemptive strike against real and imagined enemies within the Party, Mao deputized his wife, the former actress Jiang Qing, who also saw her power eroding due to Mao's affection for young women, to begin a purge.

While Gonpo was enjoying her summer idyll in Chengdu, Mao was preparing to do battle within his own party. Beijing's mayor, the chief of staff of the People's Liberation Army, and the director of the propaganda department were all swept out of the way. Mao made a conspicuous display of his own fitness with a swim across the Yangtze River. On the night of August 8, the Party's central committee made it official with the "Decision Concerning the Great Proletarian Cultural Revolution," a sixteen-point statement that was read on the radio and published in the newspapers the following day.

> Our objective is to struggle against and overthrow those persons in authority who are taking the capitalist road, to criticize and repudiate the reactionary bourgeois academic "authorities" and the ideology of the bourgeoisie and all other exploiting classes and to transform education, literature and art and all other parts of the superstructure not in correspondence with the socialist economic base.

In mid-August a series of rallies took place in Tiananmen Square that were attended by a million students. They were exhorted to destroy what were named the "four olds"—old thoughts, old cultures, old customs, and old habits.

Gonpo could feel the excitement from the moment her train pulled into Beijing. The station was pulsing with students, all dressed alike with caps and baggy military uniforms cinched tightly around their skinny waists. The kids were about her age, fifteen, or even younger, and they had been arriving en masse in Beijing following Mao's order. It was her first glimpse of the Red Guards, the youthful vigilantes who would soon tear China apart.

They had set up makeshift checkpoints throughout the station where they were inspecting passengers' documents in an effort to discern their class background. She saw they had stopped some women and were crudely cutting their hair with shears. Class enemies, she

suspected. Despite the steamy August temperatures, Gonpo was fortunately wearing a jacket; she tucked her thick braid inside and scur-
ried out through a side door.

Loudspeakers blared propaganda. Posters written with ever-larger
characters were plastered on the walls, omens of the violence that
would soon engulf the country.

BOMBARD THE HEADQUARTERS

WAGE WAR AGAINST THE OLD SOCIETY

*BEAT TO A PULP ANY AND ALL PERSONS WHO
GO AGAINST MAO ZEDONG THOUGHT*

When Gonpo returned to her school, she could see that her status
had changed and not for the better. Most of the students came from
prominent families, but few as illustrious as hers. Up until that time,
her family had retained some of its privilege; the Communist Party's
strategy was to co-opt the former nobility with creature comforts to
prevent them from making trouble. Now her world was once again
turned upside down, her aristocratic roots her greatest liability. One
People's Daily editorial at the start of the Cultural Revolution encouraged the Red Guards to "sweep away the monsters and demons,"
Gonpo among them. She was forced to resign as head of the cultural
club. She had a habit of singing much of the day, whether she was
walking or bathing or cooking, but that was forbidden. Laughing and
smiling too were prohibited. She was supposed to behave as though
she were in mourning.

Her activities became increasingly constricted. Afternoons, when
classmates played basketball in the big courtyard, Gonpo was not allowed to join in. Her class background precluded her from joining the
Red Guards, the ambition of all of the school's students. The fashion
among teenagers at that time was to wear the oversized army uniforms
of the Red Guards, but that too was forbidden. Once Gonpo had bor-

rowed a uniform, but other students threw red paint on it. She was no longer allowed to wear the round red badges with Mao's profile. That really stung because Gonpo had worshipped Mao as much as any of her classmates.

In January 1967, Gonpo heard that a delegation of fifteen students from Ngaba was coming to visit the school. The Red Guards were traveling through China, encouraged by Mao to spread the word of the Cultural Revolution and ferret out suspected enemies. Gonpo was so happy she could barely contain her excitement. She was lonely and hoped there might be somebody she knew among the group or possibly a new friend from her hometown. She had no welcoming gifts for them, but the night of their arrival, she prepared a fire in the dormitory stove so that they could warm themselves in the dead of winter.

Gonpo was waiting in line to use the toilets when a Mongolian classmate called her aside. The girl was a member of the Red Guards, proudly wearing her Mao badge on the army uniform, and one of the popular students. But she had always been kind to Gonpo. As other girls turned against Gonpo, she remained protective. Now, as they stood talking in a cold corridor outside the girls' toilet, the girl took off her Mao badge and handed it to Gonpo.

"You can have this but pin it inside your clothing so nobody sees," the girl told her.

Gonpo did as instructed, pinning the badge underneath her thick coat. Before Gonpo had time to wonder about this unexpected generosity, she noticed the pity in the eyes of the Mongolian classmate. The girl spoke to her softly, confiding a secret. She wasn't supposed to divulge what she had overheard, but she thought Gonpo should know.

"Your parents are no more," the girl told her, before advising, "Don't cry. They were counterrevolutionaries, so you shouldn't grieve for them."

NEWS TRAVELED SLOWLY IN 1960s China. It had happened three months earlier. Gonpo's mother, Tashi Dolma, had attempted to travel back to Ngaba. The king had been asked to sign documents ceding the title to additional property to the government, and his wife volunteered to make the trip. The king and queen often worked together as partners in what remained of the royal enterprise. She was stopped by Chinese authorities along the way and told she would not be permitted to advance farther. She had no choice but to spend the night in Lixian, a mountain retreat on the road between Chengdu and Ngaba, perched at the edge of the fast-moving Zagunao River. She told her manservant that she would send a telegram to her husband, asking for his guidance. The next morning, the servant found the door to her hotel room ajar and no sign of the queen, only the sash to her robe lying on the bathroom floor.

The king flew into a panic at the news that his wife was missing. He rushed up from Chengdu to find his wife. Although theirs had been an arranged marriage, the king considered his wife his best friend, partner, and only true ally.

After a day of fruitless searching, he found no trace of the missing queen. Somehow the king knew that it would be useless to continue the search. He was sure she was dead. Fearing it was too dangerous to stay in Lixian, he started back toward Chengdu, getting as far as Wenchuan. (The city would become famous in 2008 as the epicenter of one of the biggest earthquakes in recent history.) That night the king jumped from a bridge, leaving behind only his *gyasha,* a brocaded Tibetan hat. Family members later told Gonpo that the king had been deeply depressed even before his wife's disappearance. He was under pressure to denounce the Dalai Lama and to take a job in Beijing, which would turn him into a puppet for the Communist Party.

"I'm useless. There is nothing more I can do for my people," he had told his sister a few days before. The family presumed that he committed suicide, although some Tibetans whispered that he had been pushed into the river.

As for Gonpo's mother, neither she nor her body was ever found.

———

THE MORNING AFTER SHE learned that her parents were dead, Gonpo was called to a public struggle session in the school. The students were assembled in the courtyard, the uniformed Red Guards standing in front, shouting revolutionary slogans.

"Be honest and the government will be lenient," they yelled in unison. Gonpo tried to follow the advice of her Mongolian friend: Do not cry. Pretend you don't know anything. Just go with the flow. Gonpo joined the crowd, shouting the slogans as loudly as she could to drown out the heartbreak, until she realized what was going on: she was the target of the struggle session.

The delegation from Ngaba, the very same students Gonpo had been so eager to befriend, had a long list of accusations against her.

"Your father had a telegraph set in his house. He was in contact with the Dalai clique." By this time, the Dalai Lama had set up his headquarters in India where the nascent Tibetan exile government was taking shape.

"Your father killed many people. He ate his meals out of their skulls!" shouted another accuser.

Gonpo knew she was supposed to confess, but she could honestly say she had no idea what they were talking about.

"I'm so young. I have never seen a telegraph set. I don't know," she stammered her response. To the other accusation, she was adamant in her denial. "My father would never, never eat out of somebody's skull. I swear in the name of Mao Zedong."

The delegation from Ngaba had been instructed to bring Gonpo back to be struggled against. She was lucky, however, that a headmaster insisted that she did not have permission to leave the school. She believed he might have intervened to save her life. But staying in Beijing was barely endurable. Until that time, the abuse was tolerable— just above a level of playground bullying; now it was serious. Gonpo's accusers spit at her. They slapped her in the face and kicked her in the shins. She was made to stand with her head bowed, her hands raised behind her back. She had to crawl back to the dormitory on her hands and knees. Everybody now knew who she was—the daughter of a king—which made her a prime target. She had "black bones," as they said—meaning she was rotten to the core. Even the people who ran the small shop across from the campus refused to sell to her. There was no escape.

The struggle sessions continued for the next year. At times, Gonpo was the target; other times she was a spectator and, if not wittingly, a participant, forced to cheer on the tormentors. The iconic image of the Cultural Revolution was the accused wearing a dunce cap and a placard around their necks, but it was much worse. Gonpo remembered one accused counterrevolutionary who was the wife of a lecturer at the teacher training college. The woman could barely walk and had to be carried into the struggle session. In the crowds, standing close enough to Gonpo that she could overhear their conversation, were the woman's sons. One was about twelve years old and the other nine. They held hands as they watched.

"Brother, I'm so scared," she heard the younger boy whisper to his brother.

The teacher's wife was accused of being a supporter of Chiang Kai-shek. They claimed she had been heard saying it would have been better if the Nationalists won and not the Communists.

"Be truthful and you will be spared," the students chanted.

Unable to stand, the accused woman collapsed in a heap on the pavement. Her accusers kicked her in the back and head. When she could no longer move, they threw a bucket of cold water on her. Still, she didn't move. The chant switched to a new theme, menacing the onlookers.

"Tell the truth or you will end up like this woman."

Gonpo presumed she was dead.

When Gonpo found out that she was going to be exiled to the northwest, to the farthest, coldest, most remote reaches of China, to do hard labor, it came as a relief. She would be far from Beijing and that suited her just fine.

RED CITY

A bonfire of Buddhist scriptures, Lhasa, 1966.

OF ALL THE PEOPLE TO EMBRACE THE RED GUARDS, DELEK would seem to be the most unlikely, given the terror the marauding bands had inflicted on his family. But the Cultural Revolution was to evolve in ways that made it unexpectedly appealing to Tibetans.

Delek was seventeen years old at the start of the Cultural Revolution. He'd grown into a sinewy teenager with protruding ears and a prominent nose. Although still short, he was stronger than most of his peers, the result of working in the mountains where he could forage for food. He had managed to get in a few years of education at a new primary school in Meruma. Instruction was entirely in Chinese. He had learned to read and write with enough proficiency that he was awarded an armband with red stripes for his academic achievements. He too prized his copy of Mao's Little Red Book. His family had a large portrait of Mao at home; his school displayed portraits of Stalin and Lenin as well.

Delek closely followed the news during this tumultuous period. By 1968, the second year of the Cultural Revolution, Chinese cities were in a virtual state of war. The Red Guards, after rooting out real and imagined class enemies, turned on one another, each claiming that they alone were the true upholders of Mao's will and that their rivals the counterrevolutionaries. They'd looted enough weapons from the military to do serious damage. Rival Party leaders stoked the divisions, enlisting Red Guard factions for their own protection.

One of the Red Guard factions that started up in Chengdu was called the Hongcheng, "Red City" in Chinese. It had the backing of Zhang Guohua, a former general who had been ousted as Party secretary of the Tibet Autonomous Region earlier and moved to Sichuan province. Many of its young leaders were sons of PLA officers. A Tibetan in his early twenties from Ngaba who would later be known as Hongcheng Tashi (Tibetans often take on an extra name to identify them by their work or hometown) had been introduced to some of the Red Guards in Chengdu and vowed to start a branch in Ngaba. The fact that so many prominent military-connected Han Chinese had enlisted with Red City made Tibetans believe it was politically correct to join in themselves.

In March 1968, thousands of Tibetans convened in Ngaba from the villages and surrounding towns to pledge their support to Red City. They came from a cross-section of Tibetan society—commune employees, nomads, farmers, and even former monks who had time on their hands since the monasteries were closed. They elected four leaders who fanned out around the region to recruit.

This was a time to question authority. It felt like anything was possible in the chaos that engulfed China. There were no rules. Nobody was untouchable. The hierarchy of power had been turned upside down; sacred figures in Communist lore, like Zhu De, the general who had occupied Kirti Monastery during the Long March, and Peng Dehuai, the commander of the victorious troops in Sichuan province against the Kuomintang, had been purged. Other Red Guard factions had ousted lower-level Party officials in Ngaba. One had hung himself in a bathroom.

It might be coincidental that 1968 was the same year that students were rioting from Paris to Berkeley and that Soviet tanks rolled into Czechoslovakia to crush the Prague Spring. Rebellion was in the air.

One of the idiosyncrasies of Chinese public opinion is that people tend not to blame the emperor. There is a tendency to assume the emperor to be a benevolent being above reproach whose underlings must be the ones at fault. And so it was with attitudes toward Mao. Tibetans couldn't believe that Mao—their god, their father, around whom the whole edifice of the new China was constructed—was responsible for their suffering. They just couldn't make the psychological leap that would require them to admit to themselves that everything they were taught the past decade was a lie.

They took Mao at his word when he said the Cultural Revolution was a movement to root out corruption within the Communist Party. With more than a touch of wishful thinking, Tibetans interpreted that to mean the Party was admitting that everything it had done since the 1950s was a mistake. All the abuses, the killings and repression, the arbitrary arrests, the forced starvation, and the destruction of the monasteries had gone against Mao's original intent.

"This is not Chairman Mao's doing, but the Party leaders beneath him. We will struggle against them and march forward on the correct path shown by Chairman Mao," the Red City leaders told Tibetans.

"This was done by corrupt Leftists in the Party. There was no approval from the Tibetan side, no approval to set up the cooperatives and confiscate everyone's property."

They evoked the Seventeen-Point Agreement of 1951 in which the Communist Party promised to respect Tibetan tradition and religion.

"From now on, you can practice religion without any restriction. That has always been Mao Zedong's position."

The pitch was irresistible. One cadre, Yangling Dorjee, who was the highest-ranking Tibetan in the regional Communist Party, later told an interviewer that virtually every Tibetan family in the region supported the Red City movement.

Tibetans in Ngaba were fed up with the collectivist economy. It had been nearly a decade since they'd been herded into communes, with little sign of loosening. They still worked like slaves for the communes, which took the meat, milk, butter, cheese, and animal skins, handing out only the dregs to the workers.

In June of 1968, representatives from each village in Ngaba were appointed to meet with Communist Party leaders in downtown Ngaba. The representatives were mostly older people and they politely presented their demands. They wanted the dismantling of the communes, the distribution of livestock to the people, and the right to reopen the monasteries. When, as was expected, the Party leaders refused their demands, they went home and started organizing their own militia.

Most of the monasteries around Ngaba had been demolished or repurposed in 1958. In 1966 and 1967, Han Chinese factions of Red Guards trashed what few remained and went after the small shrines that Tibetans kept at home. Now the Red City faction in Ngaba, dominated by Tibetans, engineered a 180-degree reversal. Former monks started returning to what was left of the monasteries, reciting prayers in the rubble. They brought out the crimson robes that had been hidden away for years.

Tibetans on horseback galloped to a prison on the outskirts of town to release political prisoners. They forced some of the Chinese-run agricultural communes to shut down and distributed the animals to nomadic families who had lost them a decade earlier. According to a report by one Party cadre, 26,945 animals from five livestock farms were taken.

"Ngaba was in chaos. They were looting public properties and were swollen with arrogance," complained a Communist Party cadre based in Jiuzhi, northwest of Ngaba in Qinghai.

Emboldened by their success, the Tibetan Red Guards fanned out across the plateau. They were not able to capture downtown Ngaba, which was by then controlled by the rival Red Guard faction Bingtuan, or "Brigade," which was primarily Han Chinese and backed by the military. But the rebellion spread through the marshy grasslands to the east and to the west in the region known as Golok, where many of Ngaba's Tibetans had relatives.

Before long, the Communist Party officials declared that the Red City rebels were not true revolutionaries, and sent in the People's Liberation Army to quash the uprising. The Red City rebels fled the center of Ngaba and shifted their operations to Meruma. Over the summer of 1968, they moved again into the mountains, following the nomads who were heading out anyway to bring their yaks and sheep out to graze for the season. Meruma had its own designated summer pasturelands, in the middle of which was an open pasture that they called the Mandala plain. It became the new headquarters for Red City. They erected a large tent as a makeshift monastery. Monks openly wore their crimson robes and led prayers. They burned juniper branches and made smoke offerings to the protectors, something they hadn't dared do for years. Volunteer fighters came from all six of the townships that made up Ngaba and from surrounding counties. By the end of the summer, the rebels had formed an army of a thousand men and were drawing up plans for an ambush on Chinese government offices.

That summer, Delek was tending horses during the day, volunteering his service for the rebels after hours. He and another groom had responsibility for 120 horses, which they agreed to turn over to the rebels. Battle would be waged on horseback using the same tactics their fathers and grandfathers had employed when they fought on behalf of the Mei king.

As for weapons, some Tibetans had primitive muskets they had been given to protect the herds from wolves that preyed by night. Delek didn't have access to a gun, but he was friendly with the blacksmith that shod the horses, so he gathered together some farm implements that the blacksmith forged into spikes. Delek carved a wooden stave into a handle, making himself a spear. He was proud of his weapon—the other teenagers had only swords.

The rebels' next step was to dig up the roads used by motor vehicles and cut the power lines. Meruma had been electrified in the early 1960s, but the lines ran mostly to offices and administrative buildings used by the Chinese and the Tibetans who worked with them. With the electricity cut and the roads blocked, the Chinese administrators would not be able to call for backup.

"We, the nomads, don't need electricity. Only the Chinese do," Delek remembers the leaders instructing the troops.

The plan of attack called for the troops to be divided into three divisions. Two divisions were to take over the township offices in Meruma. The third was assigned the most dangerous mission: they were to capture a concrete bunker above Serda Hill, where Delek had lived with his grandparents.

The bunker was constructed by the PLA in 1958 at the start of the forcible collectivization. (It is still there, and years later, children in Meruma would use it to play hide-and-seek and war games.)

On a crisp, clear autumn day, the men galloped down from their command post in the summer pasture. Delek would later question why they hadn't waited until after dark. The fighters had hoped for an element of surprise, thinking they could storm the offices. But they found the premises long vacated and booby-trapped with grenades.

They deftly avoided the trap, but when they approached the granary—another target on their list—the ground started exploding.

The Chinese had concealed trip wires through the grass so that the grenades would go off like land mines. Horses vanished into clouds of earth, shrapnel, and blood, while those behind them stumbled and reared in fright, ditching their riders. In the midst of it all, bullets started raining down from the hill above.

The division assigned to capture the bunker had failed, and Chinese snipers moved in. From the bunker, they had clear sights of the Tibetans below. Pop, pop, pop. One after the other, they were hit and tumbled off their horses.

One Tibetan by the name of Tsering Dhonkho, who would become legendary for his bravery, made it up to the bunker and grabbed for the barrel of a Chinese sniper's gun while reaching inside with his sword to kill him. It was a heroic yet ultimately futile gesture; he burned his hand on the smoking gun barrel and would later die of an infection.

As one of the teenaged grooms, Delek was stationed near the granary with orders to wait for the fighters to descend the hill and to care for their horses. He stood there waiting, clutching his homemade spear, wondering if he would have the courage to use it against the Chinese. He never had a chance. From a vantage point of relative safety, he watched the unfolding massacre in horror. The Tibetans on horseback galloped up and down the street in a haphazard manner, yelling battle cries while the bullets rained down on them. The hill was strewn with the bodies of the fallen men and horses.

"It was like a shooting range," Delek said later. "This group of nomads didn't stand a chance with the Chinese."

The shooting went on for more than three hours. A succession of Delek's friends and relatives were hit—a work colleague shot in the leg, a cousin toppled over backward from his horse. His uncle, Konchok, took a bullet in the shoulder. Delek helped to hoist him onto a horse semiconscious so that he could be returned to safety.

It was a swirl of confusion. Some of the fighters wanted to storm the bunker, but that would mean riding into a hail of bullets—certain suicide. There was nobody to ask for guidance. The commander of Delek's unit lay on the ground, his face covered with so much blood he was unrecognizable, one leg blown off at the thigh. A woman tied a rope around his remaining leg and started to drag him away for funeral services, when he suddenly shouted out, "I'm alive. Get me some water." The woman picked up a plastic shoe and scooped water from the river into his mouth.

When night fell, they made a stretcher out of sack cloth and carried the commander first to his mother's house and then to the summer pasture where they were retreating. One of the senior leaders of Red City, Alak Jigme Samten, known as a spiritual man, recited prayers for the man's rebirth. Knowing that they both loved tobacco, he lit a pipe and exhaled the smoke as a blessing into the dying man's mouth. The commander expired shortly afterward.

Altogether, fifty-four men were killed in battle, along with a hundred horses, who are often included in the death tolls reported by Tibetans.

LATER IN LIFE DELEK would become the unofficial historian of Ngaba. He reflected on how the Cultural Revolution evolved into a Tibetan uprising. "There wasn't a sense of this being part of a broader nationalist struggle since many of the people were illiterate, but they saw it as an opportunity to fight for basic rights that had been denied the Tibetans," he said. "Looking back, it was recklessness that cost us the battle. We were high on enthusiasm but low on battle readiness. It was the natural reaction of an overzealous mob."

Further insight into the rebellion comes from a man named Louri, the younger brother of Hongcheng Tashi, the leader of the movement. Louri was the same age as Delek and one of the more hotheaded of the teenaged fighters. He remembers charging up the hill under gunfire. He sustained seven gunshot wounds when his horse was hit by gunfire, but he managed to grab another horse that had lost its rider, jump on, and escape to the mountains. A large man with bulbous features, powerfully built even in his early seventies when we met in Chengdu, Louri too would struggle to explain why he was willing to ride into a fusillade of bullets.

"I didn't have a weapon, not even a knife," he said with a self-deprecatory laugh.

Unlike Delek, Louri came from a family of illiterate, landless farmers—exactly the Tibetans who were supposed to be beneficiaries of the Communists' redistribution of wealth. They had in fact been moved out of a dilapidated shack in the center of Ngaba and relocated into a sturdy house in Se Monastery after the monks were banished. But their initial satisfaction with their new housing was outweighed by the desecration of the monasteries.

"We were very angry. As Buddhists, everything we worshipped had been destroyed. The monasteries had been burned and the Buddha statues smashed. That is why ordinary people joined the rebellion," he said. His brother, he said, convinced him and other young men that their participation in the Hongcheng was sanctioned by Mao as part of the mandate of the Cultural Revolution to overthrow the establishment.

"People believed this was all very official. We thought it was organized. We were confused," Louri said.

Nonetheless, the surviving leaders of Red City were dealt with harshly. Of the four main leaders of the movement, one died and two were executed, Alak Jigme Samten and Gabe Yonten Gyatso. Louri's brother, Hongcheng Tashi, was spared the death penalty because of his connections to powerful people in Chengdu, but he received a fourteen-year prison sentence. Some 30,000 people were arrested. Delek was held and interrogated for three months in the township offices. Almost every Tibetan family within a hundred-mile radius of Ngaba had a man in prison. It was one of the largest uprisings of Tibetans during the Cultural Revolution and established Ngaba's reputation for rebelliousness.

Although this uprising was ultimately a failure, for six months the Tibetans had raised their own livestock, worshipped freely in the monasteries, chanted prayers, and conducted rituals. The monks had worn their robes. It had given Tibetans a taste of freedom, the memory of which could not so easily be extinguished.

EXILE

Gonpo and Xiao Tu.

GONPO ARRIVED IN XINJIANG, FOR CENTURIES CHINA'S equivalent of Siberia, in 1969. On the first leg of the train ride to Urumqi, the main city of Xinjiang, a group of students figured out who she was and threatened to throw her off the moving train. Gonpo spent three days darting up and down the train, hiding between cars, trying to avoid her tormenters. When she at last arrived, she was horrified by her surroundings. When she'd learned she would be exiled,

Gonpo had asked to be sent to a nomadic area, thinking it would be like Ngaba.

Now she despaired of what she had gotten herself into. The landscape was open and uncluttered as she'd hoped, but it was nothing like home. The sky had none of the crystalline sharpness of Tibet. As far as her eye could see, there was only sand, emptiness, and desolation. Her farm was located near the border with the Soviet Union, in a place called Qinghe county. Its only claim to fame was that a meteor had fallen there in 1898. It was the middle of nowhere.

Together with Tibet, Xinjiang (the name means "new frontier") fills in the entire western half of the map of China. At the edge of central Asia, Xinjiang is home to Kazakhs, Mongols, and Uighurs, a Turkic minority who called the place East Turkestan. Although just to the north, Xinjiang is set apart from Tibet by mountains and desert; Gonpo would not encounter a single Tibetan during her time there.

Gonpo was sent to work at a vast military-run complex that had a farm, a dairy, and a cattle ranch. It was a town in itself with a population of about three thousand people. Almost everyone was Han Chinese. Besides political outcasts like herself, the farm was home to hundreds of "sent down" youth who had been ordered to the countryside by Mao, ostensibly to learn the lessons of hard labor but also to ease increasingly violent street fighting between the Red Guards. Of higher status were decommissioned PLA soldiers who made up much of the leadership. But all of them were in effect pioneers, sent west by the Party to develop the frontier.

Because of her class background, Gonpo was assigned the most difficult jobs. She had to dig trenches, plant fields, and milk cows. When the rest of the farmhands finished work at the end of the day, she was sent to clean the stables. Her dormitory was seven miles away from the workstation where she had to report each morning. She had to walk the first three miles through marshlands, a perilous trek to make alone since there were brown bears and wolves in the region. She usually set out before the sun came up. If she was lucky, when she reached the main road she might see a passing horse cart and hitch a ride. The temperatures overnight reached minus 22 Fahrenheit (minus 30 Celsius). One early morning during an especially cold winter, her feet got badly frostbitten, the treatment for which was submerging them in cold water. It could have been worse. Another girl used her hands to cover her ears and suffered such serious frostbite that one hand had to be amputated.

The Chinese government was determined to transform unproductive marshes into agricultural land no matter what the human or environmental cost. Xinjiang was full of evaporated lakes that had turned into salt marshes, too saline for corn, the primary crop. The Chinese had devised a technique of digging trenches in the fields so that the melting snow would flush away the salt. It was exhausting heavy labor. Gonpo dislocated her shoulder digging. Her supervisors refused her medical attention, insisting that her bad class background precluded her from seeing a doctor. Her feet and her shoulder would trouble her for the rest of her life.

The cooperative also operated a dairy with herds of black-and-white cows crossbred from Holsteins and Chinese yellow cattle. When she wasn't working in the fields, Gonpo milked the cows, twice a day. She was also assigned to raise money by selling the milk. If she didn't fulfill her quota, she was penalized with a deduction from her salary. She was paid for her labor—18 Chinese yuan a month, roughly four dollars—but she needed to pay for her own food. If her salary was docked, she was in danger of starvation. Fortunately, she had made a friend, a young man who would buy her leftover milk and insist that his friends do the same. He'd also give her extra coupons to buy food.

Xiao Tu, or Little Rabbit, was his nickname, since he was born in the year of the rabbit. It suited his personality. Xiao Tu was a lively, preternaturally cheerful young man who seemed to view exile in Xinjiang as a grand adventure. He was a year younger than Gonpo, but he seemed like her senior. Having been sent to the farm in his early teens, he was an old hand who knew how to navigate the system. Like Gonpo, he was a political exile with a bad class background. He came from Nanjing, the city in eastern China where Chiang Kai-shek's capital was located. His grandfather had been a supporter of the Nationalists. Most of the family fled to Taiwan after the Nationalists lost the civil war, but his father, alone of the siblings, remained to take care of an elderly mother who was too ill to relocate. When Gonpo heard that story, she figured that Xiao Tu had inherited his innate sense of compassion from his father, and that endeared him to her.

Xiao Tu had a choice job at the farm. He worked in the broadcasting unit, running the movie projector. The farm had only a handful of scratchy old prints that he frequently spliced. The most popular was a revolutionary opera, *Shachiapang,* about the proprietress of a tea shop who secretly aids the Communist resistance against the Japanese. Another, *The Flower Girl,* was from North Korea, about an impoverished flower seller and the landlord who brutalizes her family. No matter that they were overt propaganda pieces, no matter that they were shown over and over again, the films drew a good crowd because the farm offered little in the way of entertainment.

To keep themselves occupied, the young people at the farm organized themselves into singing groups. Gonpo wasn't invited to join—she was still a pariah—but the farm also had a propaganda troupe under the auspices of the Party and they were less picky, since there were few qualified sopranos who could reach the high notes. Xiao Tu was also assigned to the propaganda troupe. He couldn't carry a tune, but he danced while Gonpo sang. The songs were all paeans to Mao; regardless of whether you agreed with the politics, they had catchy tunes that were hard to resist.

In her clear soprano, Gonpo sang enthusiastically about the Long March—of course without mentioning that her grandmother had burned down their palace to prevent the Red Army from using it. Another song extolled the Communist Party's liberation of Tibet.

> *From that golden mountain in Beijing*
> *The sun's rays shoot out to illuminate the four directions.*
> *And Chairman Mao is that Golden Sun,*
> *How warm, how beatific,*

Bringing light to the heart of the liberated serfs of Tibet.
We are now walking on the great socialist highway
Of good fortune!

BY THE 1970S, the Cultural Revolution was collapsing under the weight of its own contradictions. Party leaders knew you couldn't run a country without educated citizens, so they quietly allowed the reopening of some of the universities that had been closed since 1966. New students were admitted with recommendations from their work units at factories, farms, villages, and the military. Among the schools reopening was the Nationalities University, Minzu Daxue, which was affiliated with Gonpo's former high school in Beijing.

Gonpo planned to take the exam for admission. She saw it as her only way out of Xinjiang. Xiao Tu asked his parents to send her the study materials from Nanjing. Gonpo was nervous about studying in the dormitory, where roommates might report her. But her job at the time was relatively easy—she guarded the tomato crops, shooing away the birds that tried to eat them. Xiao Tu had an idea. He took one of his old shirts (a big deal because clothing was hard to come by) and stuffed it with straw. He added a hat and mounted it on a stick, so that it would wave in the wind. The scarecrow did the trick. Gonpo could sit in the middle of the tomato fields with her nose in her books, while the birds were duly deterred.

She took the exam at the county seat and passed with high marks, but when authorities found out that she was the daughter of a king, her application was rejected. She persisted, discovering other examinations she could take and studying every minute she could get away from work. In 1973, she passed the admissions test for the Shanghai Medical College. Again she was rejected. She was an excellent student with flawless Mandarin, so in 1975 she applied to Beijing University. She aced the test, but once more was rejected.

"I might as well throw away these books," she told Xiao Tu.

Xiao Tu listened patiently to her complaints, gently tugging her out of her despair. Gonpo was thrilled to have a friend at last. Not only was she still grieving the loss of her parents, but a year into her stay in Xinjiang she learned that her sister, who was working at a military hospital, had died of the stomach ailment that had plagued her since childhood. Now Gonpo was truly alone in the world. She assumed that Xiao Tu's kindness was motivated mostly by pity.

Nobody was more surprised than Gonpo to learn that Xiao Tu had developed romantic feelings toward her. She didn't consider herself much of a beauty. Her dimpled cheeks and the slight gap between her front teeth gave her a girlishly cute, jolly appearance that masked her abject loneliness. Her eyebrows curved upward in perpetual question marks. Working in the fields had darkened a complexion that was already a shade too dark by Chinese standards of beauty. She didn't feel particularly feminine either, dressed in a baggy, padded military-style uniform with two pockets across the chest and two pockets below the waist.

Xiao Tu was one of the most popular bachelors on the farm. He had a long, straight nose like a Manchu princeling and a clear complexion. Not only was he a good dancer, always the most coveted partner, he was invariably onstage doing comedy routines. He came from a family of teachers; despite the Communists' attempt to eradicate the privileges of class, when it came to dating, education and background still mattered.

"You can have anybody you want. Why this one?" his friends asked him. "Why a Tibetan?"

Among the recognized ethnic minorities, some were so assimilated as to be virtually indistinguishable from Han Chinese, who made up 90 percent of the population. That was not the case with Tibetans. For all the Communist propaganda about harmonious relations, prejudices ran deep. Han Chinese often disparaged Tibetans as savages. *Luohou,* or backward, they called them, and often still do. Tibet in Chinese is called Zang, 藏, a character that literally means "storehouse" or "treasure," but Chinese would sometimes use the homophone *zang,* 脏,

meaning "dirty." This was a more conservative era when intermarriage was frowned upon. In Xinjiang, which was largely Muslim, intermarriage between local Uighur women and Han men was illegal until 1979.

It wasn't hard for Xiao Tu to answer the question of why. Gonpo stood out among the other young women who eyed him on the dance floor. She was without pretense or affect. She didn't flirt with him; she didn't tease him. She was utterly straightforward, and, he felt, honest in a way that others were not. She said exactly what she thought without calibrating her words to elicit some reaction from him. He trusted her completely, and she trusted him. With little of the melodrama that often accompanies young romance, the two became inseparable.

His family raised no objection. Xiao Tu's grandmother had been a devout Buddhist before the revolution; she approved of her favorite grandson marrying a woman with core beliefs. They liked that Gonpo was a studious type. They had been quietly supporting Gonpo's studies by sending books. As for Gonpo, she had no surviving family to object one way or another. Xiao Tu's qualities were beyond what she had ever imagined in a partner. But before she could commit to him, there was something important she needed to do.

IN THE SUMMER OF 1975, Gonpo and Xiao Tu got permission to leave Xinjiang for their first vacation away from the farm. They took a bus to Urumqi and then a train to Chengdu. There they caught a bus heading north to the Tibetan plateau. As the bus zigzagged up the mountain road, lurching and bouncing, climbing ever higher, Xiao Tu fell sick from the high altitude and could barely stand. A nurse administered an intravenous drip at the side of the road. They had a stopover in Barkham, the capital of Ngaba prefecture, to get him checked out at the hospital. The interruption was unwelcome since Gonpo wanted to avoid undue attention. They were heading to Ngaba, the home she hadn't seen since she was seven years old.

When they finally got back on the road, Gonpo became increasingly nervous. She began a pitched travelogue, trying to explain to Xiao Tu what she was seeing. They entered from the east, driving past Meruma village, where her ancestors had kept their herds. The road was better than she remembered from her childhood, when they traveled in convoys of horses, but otherwise it looked familiar, as though even the contours of the mountains and the yaks grazing on the hillsides were her old friends. Although the main street had been relocated farther from the river, the houses were the same squat mud-brick structures she remembered.

"We're getting close," she told Xiao Tu, pointing through the bus windows. "This should be the crossroad of town. Then there will be Kirti Monastery."

As the main intersection of Ngaba approached, she lost her orientation. The landscape rearranged itself before her eyes. The market she remembered from childhood was gone. She craned her neck looking for the elegant eaves of the monastery, which she knew should be right there, peeking over the roofs of the surrounding houses. The gate was supposed to be just there, on the right side past the intersection. Behind the gate, there should be a large manor house, the place her family stayed during pilgrimages to the monastery. Right there, she was telling her fiancé, even as the realization was rising like bile in her throat that what she was seeking no longer existed.

The images from her childhood were scrambled to the point that she couldn't get her bearings. Was her memory playing tricks on her? There was only rubble, half-demolished walls, as though an earthquake had scrambled the landscape. Swirls of dust obscured her view.

Gonpo got off the bus and tried to get her bearings. She was sure that she was in the right spot, home; she could feel it even if she couldn't see it. Although she had vowed not to, she began to cry. She leaned against a wall, or rather half of a wall since the upper half was gone. She thought she was about to faint, so she grabbed the frame of a missing door for support. Just then, an old woman walked by. The old woman paused, turned back to take another look at Gonpo, and kept walking.

Suddenly grief was replaced by fear. Gonpo felt her back stiffen again. Had she been recognized? She remembered the students from Ngaba who'd come to Beijing to finger her as a member of the aristocracy, subjecting her to months of struggle sessions. The political situation was better now, but how much better? She wondered if she and Xiao Tu had walked into a trap by returning to Ngaba.

Gonpo decided to check in at one of the government offices before there was trouble. She had heard that a relative of her father was working at the county headquarters, and she decided to ask for her by name. At the office, she was told that the woman was not there, but a Tibetan man working behind the counter was curious. Not many strangers came to Ngaba.

"Who are you?" he asked. "What are you doing here?"

Gonpo tried to explain—using Chinese because she couldn't properly form the words in Tibetan—that she was just touring with her friend. The man was friendly, but persistent. He kept asking questions and finally Gonpo just blurted it out.

"I am the daughter of the last Mei king."

The man gasped. Then he started shouting for everyone to hear. Outside, Gonpo saw that there were people rushing to greet her. An elderly man wobbled on his bicycle toward the office, so excited that he nearly fell off. Others came running into the offices, crying, laughing, smiling, and practically tripping over each other to embrace her. Gonpo realized that yes, she was finally home and that it was safe to be there.

The couple stayed for a month. They'd tried to check into a hotel, but one of the Tibetan officials invited them to stay in his home. There was a steady parade of visitors who came to see her. She didn't remember most of them but they knew her. Her old nannies, guards, butlers, gardeners. People tried to give Gonpo gifts of butter and barley. Gonpo and Xiao Tu had arrived in their Chinese work clothing, but soon they were transformed by their hosts, who brought them gifts of Tibetan robes. They were almost equally confused about putting on the garments. Gonpo struggled with the elaborate sash around the waist, and Xiao Tu with the man's cloak that was draped so that only one shoulder was covered.

An old Muslim beggar came bearing a *khata,* a ceremonial scarf, and a small bag in which he'd collected a few coins. They were all he had, but he wanted to give them to the princess. Another man came who told Gonpo how her father had helped him get land and a house when he was penniless. He brought all his children to see her.

"This family wouldn't exist if it weren't for your father," he told Gonpo.

Xiao Tu was stunned by the reverence shown toward Gonpo. Like others educated in Chinese schools, he'd grown up hearing about how the feudal aristocrats had treated the common people as slaves.

After a few weeks, they were exhausted by the attention. And they needed to return to Xinjiang, to their humble lives as farmhands. They donated their gifts—the butter, the barley, and the coins—to the monastery.

IF THE TRIP TO NGABA was a test for their relationship, Xiao Tu passed with flying colors. But their marriage was not a done deal without multiple layers of permission. They needed approval first from their *danwei,* or work unit, and then from each level of supervisors above them at the farm. The couple were prohibited from having any kind of banquet—lavish weddings were prohibited by the Communists—so they settled for a simple meal in the canteen with their coworkers and supervisors. Gonpo had no immediate family, but Xiao Tu's younger brother made the long trip by train and bus from Nanjing. They toasted their marriage by downing glasses of *baijiu,* a strong Chinese liquor. Xiao Tu wore a Mao suit—a tunic buttoned to a high collar. Gonpo's soon-to-be in-laws sent her a green silk jacket to wear over her own trousers to add a touch of elegance. They also sent an entire bed frame and mattress by train so that the couple could settle into their own home.

Four months after the wedding came another turning point.

On the afternoon of September 9, 1976, Radio Peking interrupted its regular programming with an announcement to the "whole Party, the whole army and people of all nationalities throughout the country." Mao Zedong had died that morning at the age of eighty-two.

Mao's death shouldn't have been a shock to anybody who was paying attention. He hadn't been seen in public for years, and those who'd met him came away with reports of his failing health. China's leader had been a chain smoker who suffered from heart and lung ailments; he was rumored to be afflicted with Parkinson's disease and Lou Gehrig's disease. Nonetheless, Mao's death marked a tremendous rite of passage. While still alive, although infirm, his mere presence effectively paralyzed the emerging leadership from throwing off the shackles of the Cultural Revolution.

"All victories of the Chinese people were achieved under the leadership of Chairman Mao," the Party leadership proclaimed in their statement. Despite urging the country to "continue to carry out Chairman Mao's revolutionary line," the Party was preparing to roll back much of what he had done. The shackles were off.

But first the rituals of mourning had to be observed with the appropriate decorum. An eight-day mourning period was declared throughout China. Mao's body was laid in state on a wooden bier in the Great Hall of the People at Tiananmen Square. Black armbands were distributed throughout the country.

The atmosphere at the cooperative farm in Xinjiang was unusually tense. Not only were they preparing for the funeral on September 18, they worried that this unstable transition period might invite an incursion across the Soviet border.

Gonpo's anxiety was compounded by her husband's job. He had been assigned to set up the loudspeakers that were to broadcast the funeral proceedings from Beijing throughout the farm. The loudspeakers were old, the wires frayed, and the electrical supply unreliable. Gonpo was convinced Xiao Tu could go to prison if the broadcast failed. During the funeral, Gonpo stood at attention with the others, listening to the guns, sirens, whistles, and horns that sounded in observance of the leader, followed by a band playing "The Internationale." She was so nervous about the broadcasting equipment that she almost forgot to be sad that Mao was dead.

PART TWO

INTERREGNUM

1976–1989

the ground underfoot. The government had decided to impose its own sense of order on the town by slicing a straight line through the center for a new road—which would eventually become Route 302—but hadn't gotten around to laying down asphalt. Dust and mud choked the streets. Gutters on either side served as open sewers and toilets.

With the monasteries demolished, there was little to alleviate the drabness or delight the eye. The market nurtured by the king that had made Ngaba worth a detour for traders was long gone. There were no private shops or street vendors, the Communist Party having decreed that any business activity violated the precepts of socialism. The only commercial enterprise that had remained open throughout the Cultural Revolution was a shop that made agricultural tools. Bare shelves collected dust in the government-run supermarket.

It was illegal to buy or sell privately—a big impediment in a rural economy in which herders and farmers needed to barter animal products for grain in order to survive. Even street vendors were banned since Mao had deemed them "tails of capitalism."

One advantage of the Tibetan dress was that the robes were voluminous enough to conceal merchandise within. If you wanted to buy something, you looked for a Tibetan with a bulging chuba, the sign of a merchant. One of those black marketeers was a young man who'd started doing this work at the age of twelve and who would eventually emerge from this economic desert as one of Ngaba's leading entrepreneurs.

Born in 1952, Norbu was an ox of a boy with a bulbous nose and fleshy ears. His father was a former monk who had renounced his vows of celibacy after falling in love with a woman who would become Norbu's mother. The couple married and had three children in rapid succession: Norbu, a girl, and then another boy. One morning when Norbu's brother was still an infant his mother woke up in the morning with a fever. She was dead by evening. It was 1958, that most horrible year when the Communist Party launched their so-called Democratic Reforms. Norbu's family was classified by the Party as

CHAPTER

8

. . .

THE BLACK CAT
AND THE
GOLDEN WORM

A Tibetan woman with caterpillar fungus.

B Y THE TIME OF MAO'S DEATH IN 1976, NGABA WAS A GHOST town, sullen and silent. A quarter century of Communist rule had destroyed far more than it had created. What remained consisted mostly of squat mud hovels in dun tones barely distinguishable from "capitalist," perhaps because Norbu's father occasionally sold herbs and wool for extra money. Norbu could never understand it since they owned nothing more than a crumbling one-room house and the clothes on their backs.

This classification made Norbu's family a target for abuse. Communist activists—the Tibetan collaborators—had carte blanche to seize whatever they liked from the family's house. One of Norbu's earliest memories was seeing another boy who had been given his sheepskin robe. The boy was twirling with happiness in the sunlight outside the doorway, while Norbu peered out from inside and cried. Then they took his shoes. During the long winter, Norbu's feet bled from walking on the ice. Soon, the family had nothing but the wooden bed where the children would nestle together for warmth with their father. Eventually the bed was taken too. After that, the family slept on the floor. At night, sometimes people would come in and start kicking Norbu's father for no particular reason except that they were frustrated by the lack of anything more to steal.

As the oldest and sturdiest child, Norbu was sent out to beg for food. There were no restaurants then, only the canteens of the people's communes, so he would wait outside holding out a tin lunch tray. The kind-hearted would drop in whatever slop was left over— soup, porridge, tsampa, and, if Norbu was very lucky, scraps of gristle and bone—and he would bring this unpalatable mix home to feed himself and the younger children. Once he stole sausages, but the police caught him and pushed his head into a garbage can full of Sichuan peppers, making his eyes tear for days.

Despite poor nutrition, Norbu grew tall and strong, by his early teens towering over many adults. Like a beast of burden, he could pull a plow for hours or carry an improbably large satchel of barley on his back. But children were paid with even fewer work points than adults, so he often had to borrow money for food and living expenses and would end the year owing money. As a teen, he tried to enlist in the People's Liberation Army, but he was rejected because of his class background.

Therein lay the dilemma. Norbu had to feed the family. His father was incapable of earning money; he wasn't strong enough for manual labor and was too honest, Norbu would later say, to succeed in business. Since there was no legal way to make money, Norbu naturally gravitated toward the black market.

Communist Party officials and government employees used to receive coupons known as *liang piao* that they could trade for products ranging from soap to rice. The coupons had a cash value, but the officials couldn't be seen selling them, so they would wave this kid over and ask him to do it for them. Norbu was almost equally illiterate in both Tibetan and Chinese, but he had a way with numbers. He quickly deciphered the logic of the coupons, figuring out what they could buy and how to convert these pieces of paper into cash.

These kinds of transactions could get you labeled anti-Party and anti-socialist, crimes that were punishable with a prison sentence or worse. Norbu was also at risk for shirking his obligation to work in the commune's fields. He didn't care—he was already labeled a capitalist—so he figured he might as well make money.

At twenty-two, fearing arrest, Norbu left for Chengdu, riding the overloaded bus through the mountains. It was the first time he'd descended from the Tibetan plateau. While many Chinese gasped for oxygen at the high altitudes, Norbu felt like he was being smothered in the hot, heavy air of the city. He stared at the young Chinese men strolling past the palm and banyan trees in short-sleeved button-down shirts. He stared at the women, getting an eyeful of more bare leg than he'd ever seen in Ngaba. In turn, the Chinese stared back at this sweaty bear-sized young man in his lambskin robes.

Norbu slept at night under the bridges, using his shoes as a pillow so that nobody would steal them. He befriended other Tibetan boys who had wandered into the city and were also camped out under the bridges, trying to figure out a way to make money. They fed themselves on cheap bowls of noodles.

He fell into the same business of buying and selling coupons, but it was more profitable in the big city. Soon he had enough money to move away from the bridge. He rented a room in an inexpensive hotel. He bought himself a smart white button-down shirt so he wouldn't look out of place, although he kept his hair longer than most Chinese men, letting it curl rebelliously over the collar. He started bathing daily—a habit most Tibetans shunned, believing it bad for the health. He took up the Chinese habit of smoking cigarettes. He patronized a shop near his hotel where the clerks were friendly. He came in one day to buy *baijiu,* the harsh Chinese liquor. When he couldn't produce a coupon, one of the assistants smiled and gave him the bottle for free. He asked her to join him for a meal, which turned into a long walk in the park that evening.

Hua didn't think Norbu was handsome—his nose and ears looked too big for his head—but she liked the way he swaggered when he walked. She was a tiny woman, not even five feet tall, with a heart-shaped face, and she felt protected when accompanied by a man who was a head taller than any of her Chinese suitors. And she was just subversive enough to enjoy the shocked looks of her friends and co-workers when this strapping young Tibetan poked his head into the shop to pick her up for a date.

"What's the problem? You think you're not good enough to find a Chinese guy?" one of her friends snorted. She laughed the friend off. Hua's father was harder to dismiss. He was furious that she was dating a Tibetan and deployed every weapon in the parental arsenal.

"These minorities are rough people. They're crazy," her father yelled. "I won't be able to close my eyes at night if you marry this guy."

It wasn't just that Norbu was Tibetan. Mixed marriages were becoming less unusual—indeed, Communist Party propaganda touted the commonality of all Chinese ethnicities. (Gonpo and Xiao Tu had married the year before Norbu and Hua met.) Another big issue was the difference in their class backgrounds. Hua came from what the Communist Party defined as a good family. Her parents were workers, with nary a taint of capitalist or landlord in their blood. She had been a Red Guard. During the latter part of the Cultural Revolution, when urban youth were sent to the countryside, she had been assigned to Yan'an, in Shaanxi province, Mao's former headquarters, widely revered as the birthplace of the revolution. That gave her impeccable Communist bona fides. In those days, being a shop clerk for a state-owned enterprise carried some prestige. She had her "iron rice bowl"—as the Chinese call a secure job. She even owned a Shanghai Watch, the most prestigious brand of mechanical watch in China at the time and a major status symbol.

Norbu had to admit that he brought much less to the match. He was two years younger. He had almost no formal education. Not only was he poor with a bad class background, police in Ngaba were looking to arrest him.

"I know I have nothing to offer you," he admitted to Hua. "But slowly, I will make money and we can be together and have a good life."

HISTORY WOULD SMILE ON the young couple. Mao's body wasn't yet embalmed before China started reinventing itself. Not even a month had passed before the arrest of the so-called Gang of Four, including Mao's wife, Jiang Qing, for the lunacy of the Cultural Revolution. They were charged with causing the deaths of 34,375 people and of unfairly persecuting 750,000. During her trial in 1981, Jiang protested that she was only following Mao's orders. ("I was Chairman Mao's dog. I bit whomever he asked me to bite," she famously said.)

During the third plenum in 1978, the Party's Central Committee declared that China must put "modernization" ahead of class struggle. The following year, the Party approved the creation of special economic zones as an experiment with the market economy. Soon enough, southern China began replacing Taiwan as the source of inexpensive consumer items.

The Chinese Communist Party couldn't quite toss Mao aside. He was the founding father, the inspiration and the symbol that held it all together. His embalmed body would be put on display in a mausoleum at Tiananmen Square, where it remains to this day, sacrosanct as the standard-bearer of the Party. But Mao's successors, led by Hua Guofeng, chairman of the Communist Party from 1976 to 1980, discarded many of Mao's economic and social policies, while offering the face-saving explanation that there could be no true socialism without the country passing through a capitalist phase. China had entered a new era, one in which getting rich was glorious and class background was irrelevant. As Deng Xiaoping, the architect of China's opening in the 1980s, said, "It doesn't matter if the cat was black or white, as long as it caught the mouse."

Norbu was perfectly positioned to be the black cat. He'd gotten a head start in his childhood. Without being able to articulate the reasoning, he intuited that the coupons he'd traded would soon become obsolete as China transitioned away from a strictly socialist economy and that there'd be plenty of opportunities for a clever young man like himself.

From the time Norbu arrived in Chengdu, he was in awe of the variety of consumer products available. At first they'd been brought in from Hong Kong, but manufacturing was starting to spread to Guangdong province on the mainland. Shoes and clothing, in unfamiliar shapes, colors, and textures. There were products he'd never heard of and could hardly have imagined: carbonated soft drinks, popcorn, tracksuits, electric calculators, audiocassette players. Norbu knew that he could get higher prices for this merchandise in Ngaba. The agricultural communes were being disbanded (a process that would be completed in 1982) and their assets distributed to farmers and nomads. In Meruma, for example, each person received ten yaks, eight head of sheep, and two horses. Tibetans had a little bit of disposable income at last and enormous pent-up demand. They had to replace the household goods that had been confiscated for the communes and the tools that had been melted down in backyard furnaces as part of a half-baked scheme by Mao to increase China's steel output.

Norbu bought a large suitcase, filled it up with merchandise, and rode the bus back to Ngaba. He started making frequent trips, carrying whatever it was that Tibetans wanted to buy. Porcelain cups and bowls were his most popular items.

Hua made her first visit to Ngaba in 1979. Norbu was spending more time there doing business; she missed him and wanted to see where he came from. So she bought a ticket for the bus through the mountains—the same one on which Norbu had first arrived. The trip now took only a day or two instead of three because the Chinese had started blasting tunnels through the mountains to straighten out the road.

Like other Chinese newcomers, Hua did not adjust easily to the plateau. She was dizzy from the high altitude. Her skin became scorched and puckered from the ultraviolet rays, her lips chapped with blisters. She couldn't digest the tsampa. The butter and cheese that are staples of the Tibetan diet disagreed with her stomach.

Not that Chengdu was such a refined city in the 1970s, but Hua was shocked by Ngaba. The open sewers. People defecating in the streets. She was terrified of the mangy yellow dogs that ran yapping through the streets. As Buddhists, Tibetans objected to dogs being culled, so the Chinese dared not shoot them. If you went out at night alone, you had to carry a rock lest the dogs attack you. The men were scary too. The lambskin chubas they wore made them appear larger than ordinary mortals; they strutted with an air of belligerence that made her certain there were knives concealed in the folds of their cloaks.

Even her own beloved fiancé, who'd acquired urban manners in Chengdu, was rougher around the edges back home. Shortly after Hua's arrival, Norbu had been arrested. He'd gone out drinking with some friends and got into a fight. After a few days in the police station, he pleaded that they release him because his fiancée was coming to visit. Norbu had by now been transformed from fugitive to up-and-coming leader of commerce. He had friends among the police who were sympathetic. They even loaned him one of their office chairs so that Hua would have a place to sit when she arrived. Norbu's family had not yet replaced the furniture that had been stolen from them in the 1960s.

A more fainthearted person would have fled back to the city. But Hua was not that kind of girl. She wasn't easily intimidated—that was what attracted Norbu to her in the first place. She was in love with Norbu, and Ngaba was part of the package. And for all the inconveniences, she saw something else in Ngaba—opportunity.

Norbu and Hua started doing business together. One of their first ventures was to sell *mihuatang,* the sweetened puffed rice cakes that were hawked at every Chinese train station, the same snack that Gonpo's father had bought her when she left for Beijing. Tibetans turned out to be crazy about the rice cakes. Norbu and Hua filled up their suitcases and carried the cakes up from Chengdu on subsequent trips. They would eventually open a tea shop and a supermarket. It would be one of the first Chinese-Tibetan partnerships. Together, they prospered, and Hua's family's objections to the romance faded in inverse proportion to their swelling bank account.

One day, when Norbu was back in Chengdu, sitting in a tea shop, he was surprised to see Hua's father walk in, looking for him.

"I hope you've picked out a restaurant," her father told him. Norbu was confused.

"For the wedding, of course. We've already invited the family. You are getting married tomorrow," Hua's father told him.

NGABA'S OTHER TIBETAN ENTREPRENEURS tended to come from the same misfit mold. Some were monks. They had the advantage of being more literate than most Tibetans; and they were also out of work while the monasteries were closed. Perhaps the most successful was a monk-turned-businessman named Kunga from Se Monastery.

"We weren't allowed to be monks and so we had to earn our living as laymen," Kunga recalled.

After the Communist Party closed his monastery and evicted all the monks in 1958, Kunga was left homeless and jobless. It was difficult for him to even remain in Ngaba. His father, who had been an official in the Mei king's palace, had been arrested (he would later die in prison), and Kunga's family was so ostracized that they weren't allowed to eat in the communal kitchen or speak with neighbors. So Kunga hit the road, hitching rides on buses and trucks as far as Shenzhen, the city just across the border from Hong Kong. There he'd buy bootleg cameras, cassette players, wristwatches, coats, and clothing that had been smuggled in from Hong Kong and bring them to the Tibetan plateau to sell. Whether in Ngaba or in Lhasa, he found Tibetan buyers for whatever wares he'd display on a blanket on the ground. Tibetans were especially keen on cotton and silk undergarments to wear beneath their heavy chubas.

After the Cultural Revolution, Kunga became a monk again. He'd made enough money that he was able to fund much of the rebuilding of Se Monastery.

THE MONASTERIES STARTED REOPENING in Ngaba in 1980, but it happened gradually, as former monks drifted back to the wreckage and started to hold ceremonies.

Kirti was one of the first monasteries to get permission to reopen in late 1980, but with restrictions. The monks were only allowed to hold prayers during Losar, the month-long Tibetan New Year. They used as their prayer hall a storeroom that was the only structure that had survived intact. Out of the roughly 1,700 monks there'd been before 1958, only about 300 were still alive. Some were recently released from prison, scared and traumatized. Others had married and were living as laypeople. In 1982, the Panchen Lama, the highest-ranking Tibetan lama tolerated by the Chinese Communist Party and recently rehabilitated himself, was permitted to visit Ngaba. He convinced the local government to return the confiscated property to the monastery so they could rebuild.

Most of the construction was done by local volunteer labor. Money came from newly rich Tibetan traders and merchants, including a businessman named Karchen who admitted that he had been among the Communist youth activists who participated in its destruction back in the 1950s.

"I destroyed Kirti, so I have to rebuild it," he boasted to his neighbors.

BY THE MID-1980S, Ngaba looked like a frontier town on steroids. The main road laid out decades earlier by the People's Liberation Army was at long last paved. Both sides of the street were lined with new buildings of sufficient pomp to mark Ngaba as a proper county seat. The Chinese government was trying to impose modernity, and as gaudily as possible. The Public Security Bureau got an imposing new headquarters, befitting the power of the police. A middle school accommodating a thousand students opened across the street. The Ngaba People's Hospital had a four-story atrium and blue glass façade, the height of mid-eighties Chinese modernism. Norbu gave his brother money to build a new house for their father; now they really did live like capitalists.

Everything was growing upward. Along the main road, the low-slung earthen houses were either razed or expanded, transformed into three- and four-story mid-rises. Ground-floor storefronts flung open their doors like garages to display wares that spilled out onto the sidewalks. Tibetans opened tea shops where they would drink endless cups, often salted with a dollop of yak butter. Tea shops were the most popular venues for men to hang out and haggle over business, but one of Norbu's friends broke with tradition and opened a coffee shop, introducing a beverage that had been almost entirely unknown in Ngaba. The shop had a back room with a pool table, which proved so popular that other pool parlors soon opened nearby.

Pedicabs—rickshaw-like vehicles driven by a man on a bicycle—carried passengers and their parcels after a decades-long ban by the Communists, who'd thought them suggestive of class oppression. Cars were still a novelty, but Tibetans rushed to buy motorcycles. Motorcycles were much better than cars anyway for riding off-road through the hills. Nostalgic for their horses, Tibetans would kit out the motorcycles with lamb's-wool saddles.

Tibetans also discovered a niche that was almost uniquely their own: collecting medicinal herbs. Herbs were commonly used in both Chinese and Tibetan medicine, and many of the more valuable were found on the Tibetan plateau. *Beimu,* an alpine lily used to treat coughs, grew at altitudes of more than 10,000 feet, and Tibetan nomads were perfectly situated to collect it.

Most lucrative was *Cordyceps sinensis,* a prized ingredient in traditional medicine, believed to boost immunity, stamina, and lung and kidney function. Tibetans call it *yartsa gunbu,* meaning "summer grass, winter worm," or simply *bu,* "worm," for short. The worm is actually a fungus that feeds on the larvae of caterpillars. In the past, the worm was commonplace enough that Tibetans would feed it to a sluggish horse or yak, but the Chinese developed a hankering for it that sent prices soaring. Chinese coaches with gold-medal ambitions would feed it to athletes; aging businessmen would eat it to enhance their sexual potency. At one point, the best-quality caterpillar fungus was worth nearly the price of gold, as much as $900 an ounce.

Tibetans had a natural monopoly on the caterpillar fungus. Non-Tibetans didn't have the local knowledge or the lung capacity to compete. The best worm was in Golok, northwest of Ngaba. Nomadic families would bring their children with them, sometimes taking them out of school because their sharp eyesight and short stature allowed them to more easily scan the ground for the worm amid the grasses and weeds. The season ran for approximately forty days of early spring, the time when the melting snow turned the still-brown hills into a spongy carpet. The families would camp out for weeks in the mountains. In a good season, a Tibetan family could make more in this period than a Chinese factory worker could earn in a year.

The Communist Party would later brag about how their policies had boosted the Tibetan economy, but the truth was that nothing contributed as much as the caterpillar fungus, which according to one scholar accounted for as much as 40 percent of Tibetans' cash earnings. Unlike earnings from mining and forestry, industries that came to be dominated by Chinese companies, this was cash that went directly into the pockets of Tibetans. The nomads acquired the spending power to support the new shops and cafés. The golden worm was part of a cycle of rising prosperity.

Until the 1980s, trade between the Tibetan plateau and southern China had gone only in one direction. Tibetans were eager customers for the newfangled electronics and ready-to-wear clothing stamped out by China's new factories, but Han Chinese didn't have much taste for Tibetan products like dairy and lamb. The medicinal herbs gave the itinerant traders something to put in their suitcases when they went on shopping trips to Shenzhen and other southern Chinese cities.

In time, the traders from Ngaba ranged farther west. They mastered the trade routes from southern China's Guangdong province, where the factories were concentrated, all the way to the western border with Nepal. Near Mount Everest, the last town in Tibet, Dham (or Zhangmu in Chinese), was practically taken over by Ngaba businessmen who were sending manufactured goods across the so-called Friendship Bridge to Nepal. They formed an informal support network, advancing each other money, transporting each other's merchandise.

The Ngaba traders also became mainstays of the economy in Lhasa, opening restaurants, bars, and karaoke clubs, some of them named Ngaba, in homage to their hometown. "There were a group of sixty traders from Ngaba in Lhasa, and they would meet regularly to drink tea and guide each other in business. They trusted each other and helped each other. That's why they succeeded," according to the once and future monk Kunga.

As it had been during the time of the Mei king's market, Ngaba would once again become known for its entrepreneurship.

WITH SUCH RICHES TO be reaped, it wasn't long before ambitious Chinese looked to the Tibetan plateau as a place to make money. It was like a Chinese version of "Go west, young man." The new migrants would arrive by bus from Chengdu or Xining with a few thousand yuan in savings. They'd open food stalls at the market, selling fresh produce or cooking up dumplings and hot pot, Sichuan specialties.

Like Norbu and his wife, Tibetans and Chinese often collaborated in business. The Tibetans spoke the language and understood local preferences; the Chinese had the connections with the wholesalers and manufacturers in the east. A retired Tibetan prostitute from a nearby monastery town and a Chinese businessman from Chengdu opened a brothel near the military base. It was a thriving business that employed both Chinese and Tibetan prostitutes, a perfect example of inter-ethnic cooperation.

In the past, few Chinese lived in Ngaba on a permanent basis. There was the occasional oddball like the former Red Army recruit who came during the Long March in 1935 and stayed, a carpenter who married a Tibetan woman and lived in Meruma village, and a community of Hui, the ethnically Chinese Muslims who had their own mosque and cemetery. But the Han Chinese had been mostly Party cadres, bureaucrats and engineers and teachers, who would stay a few years before rotating to a new assignment. Now, however, there were more Han Chinese around town. The construction workers were almost all Chinese. So were the men hired by the forestry companies harvesting lumber to the southeast of Ngaba. Older Tibetans complained they couldn't shop without speaking Chinese.

Tibetans harbored prejudices against the Chinese. Most of the latter were poor—even poorer than the Tibetans by the prevailing standard of measuring wealth by head of yak, sheep, and horses. A persistent rumor claimed that the Chinese restaurants served dog meat, anathema to the Tibetans.

What the Tibetans most resented were government programs enacted to lure Chinese to Tibetan areas. Some localities started offering Han Chinese benefits that had been intended for Tibetans and other minorities. For example, university applicants would get extra points on the all-important *gaokao,* the admissions exam—a perk that had been established to compensate Tibetans for the fact that their mother tongue was not Chinese. Chinese moving to some Tibetan towns could also enjoy an exemption—originally given to ethnic minorities only—from the laws that limited most Chinese families to one child.

By the 1990s, the Chinese government launched successive campaigns with slogans like "Develop the West." The stated intention was to narrow the income gaps between China's undeveloped western provinces and the boomtown cities like Shanghai, Shenzhen, and Guangzhou on the east coast. But Tibetans saw it as a land grab that also had the benefit of transferring the population out of overcrowded eastern China. By the mid-1990s, the Han Chinese outnumbered Tibetans on the plateau, and in Amdo (the region that includes Ngaba), there were an estimated 2.5 million Chinese to only 750,000 Tibetans, according to an analysis of Chinese statistics published by the Tibetan government in exile.

During this period, the government started confiscating land for a new housing development across the river from downtown. It wasn't the choicest land in town (the "shade side" of the river, as Tibetans called it), but the project was worrisome just the same. Although the details were kept secret, word on the street was that the housing was designed for up to 60,000 Han Chinese workers, who would be accompanied by their spouses—which would add 100,000 Chinese to the population.

"It would have completely changed the demographics of Ngaba," Kunga later recalled.

It wasn't just a matter of Tibetan pride. Tibetan businessmen watched the arrival of Chinese competitors with trepidation. Since land in China is not privately owned, development often started with auctions to lease government land, but Tibetans were excluded from the bidding process. They weren't informed when bids would be taken or were sometimes banned from participating. Contracts invariably went to Chinese companies, whether for construction or logging. "There was always discrimination against us. They conducted bidding in a way that the Tibetans couldn't participate," said Kunga.

At the border with Nepal, the military leased space for shops and wholesale warehouses to Chinese firms, squeezing out the Ngaba traders who had once dominated the scene.

Norbu found that Chinese competitors were undercutting his prices because they were able to contract directly with manufacturers in south China. He also accused them of dumping substandard and defective merchandise on the Tibetans, taking them as less savvy.

"We can't compete with the Chinese," Norbu grumbled. "They don't have to do things ethically because they don't have any religion. They don't care about anything but money."

Nonetheless, Norbu often found himself in the position of mediating between Chinese and Tibetans. With his language skills and his Chinese wife, he was often called in if there was a difficult negotiation or a dispute. When a Chinese driver accidentally struck a Tibetan, Norbu made sure the driver paid the medical bills and offered compensation to prevent the family from taking the law into their own hands. He was an affable fellow, he felt, one who could get along with anyone.

The one exception was a Chinese businessman who'd first come to Ngaba as a young soldier in the PLA and later opened a shop.

His name was Peng Yongfan, but the Tibetans referred to him as *Shua Tou*, meaning "Brushhead," because of his military-style buzz cut. Peng was originally from Hunan, Mao's home province, so he spoke with a similar accent. In the military Peng had developed a fondness for the climate of the plateau and its wide-open spaces. ("It's quiet there and cool in the summer. To me Aba felt like a piece of heaven," he told me.) His shop expanded over the years and eventually developed into the Yonganli Department Store, enjoying a prime location at the main intersection near the market and Kirti Monastery. Yongli sold appliances, pots and pans, men's clothing and belts. It was by far the nicest store in town, with uniformed clerks, all Chinese.

Upstairs he opened the Jinli Hotel. Peng's shop also offered something that was a rarity in Ngaba: a pay telephone.

Few Tibetans had telephones at the time and they would line up to make calls. Almost immediately squabbles broke out. Tibetans would complain that the phone wasn't working properly and that they shouldn't have to pay if they couldn't hear the person on the other end. Peng put an end to the complaining by calling in his old buddies from the military.

Norbu remembers a Tibetan man coming into his tea shop with a bad limp, a black eye, and a cut lip.

"It happened at Brushhead's shop," the battered Tibetan told him.

"Why didn't you fight back?" Norbu demanded.

"I couldn't. There were ten guys and some were soldiers," he replied.

Norbu was furious. He knew that if Peng had the support of the military, nobody could touch him. It was a small incident, but the anger festered for a long time.

A TIBETAN
EDUCATION

*Tsegyam,
2016.*

THE TIBETAN MIDDLE SCHOOL OPENED ITS DOORS IN 1983 in the spirit of the intellectual awakening that was accompanying the economic reforms. It offered, for the first time in Ngaba, quality secular education in the Tibetan language.

China had sunk into the academic equivalent of the Dark Ages during the Cultural Revolution, when schools and universities were closed throughout the country. And even after schools reopened, some were more like unstaffed daycare centers than educational institutions. Often teachers didn't show up, leaving kids in the courtyard to fight with each other. Parents complained that their kids finished elementary school unable to write their own names. The closure of the monasteries in the 1960s and 1970s had left a generation of Tibetans illiterate in their own language and barely functional in Chinese.

The Middle School was a commanding edifice. Apart from the monasteries, it was the largest building in Ngaba, dominating the east end of the main road, alongside the banks of a stream. The architecture itself was a tribute to Tibetan aesthetics, with tapered windows rimmed in black and a vast courtyard that one entered through a red gate decorated with Buddhist symbols.

It was more like a college than a high school. Many students were in their twenties, having had no earlier opportunity to be educated. Since many were from rural families and lived too far away to commute, they lived on campus. The school dormitories housed about a thousand students.

One of the founders of the Middle School was an aspiring poet by the name of Tsegyam, who would ultimately transform the intellectual life of Ngaba.

Tsegyam was born in 1964 to a family of barley farmers. He grew into an owlish boy, skinny, with glasses and a long forehead that would become more prominent as his hairline receded in later life. Although his parents were barely educated, they recognized that this second son of theirs was a prodigy. Since the monastery schools were still closed, they arranged to have him privately tutored in Tibetan by one of the many unemployed monks from Kirti. Tsegyam later enrolled in the government-run #2 primary school, where he was assigned to a desk under a portrait of a young Mao with an umbrella tucked under his arm. He quickly became fluent in Chinese. He would spend much of his childhood scouring Ngaba for whatever reading material he could find in either language.

Tsegyam's insatiable curiosity led him to ponder the Tibetan situation. Lacking materials to read on this sensitive subject, he was a keen observer of events transpiring around him. One of his most vivid memories dated back to a snowy day in March 1971 when he was seven years old. Tibetans from the region were summoned to watch a public execution on a field that, as it happens, would later be the site of the Tibetan Middle School. The two men being executed had been leaders of the 1968 Red City uprising. Tsegyam recognized one, a rather famous figure from Ngaba, Alak Jigme Samten. He had been a commander of the ill-fated battle in Meruma in 1969 and was considered a *siddha,* a lay spiritual master. Thousands of people were in attendance, and began to wail and shout at the crack of gunshots from the firing squad.

Tsegyam stood at the edge of the field where the bodies were being loaded onto the back of a truck. He saw Alak Jigme Samten's brother dart out from the crowd to try to slip a small Buddhist amulet into the pocket of the dead man. A Chinese soldier intercepted him, grabbed the amulet, and tossed it into the snow. Discarding the amulet struck Tsegyam as more cruel than the execution itself. He would never forget it.

Five years later, when Tsegyam was twelve, he committed his first political offense. It was the week after Mao's death, when the nation was deep in mourning. The pupils from his school were instructed to wear black armbands and were taken to a stadium for the memorial service. Although many Tibetans quietly rejoiced at Mao's death, they dared not show it publicly. Everybody knew they were supposed to make a histrionic show of grief. Tsegyam and his friends refused to play along. They laughed and joked throughout the solemn ceremony, infuriating their teachers. Threatened with expulsion, they were lucky to get off with writing confessions and apologies.

This small blot on his record did not hurt Tsegyam's career. He was admitted to a school for teacher training in Barkham, the capital of Ngaba prefecture, where a literary society was being formed. He became one of its early members. In his teens, Tsegyam started writing poetry and essays for the local Chinese newspaper, the *Aba Ribao.* He also contributed to two new literary magazines in the region publishing Tibetan writers, one called *Drizzle* and the other *New Grasslands*. When he went home to Ngaba, people would recognize him. In this backwater of yak herders and barley farmers, he was the rarest of creatures—a genuine intellectual.

It was as good a time as any to be an intellectual in China. Shut off from the outside world for decades, the Chinese were practically inhaling new ideas, books, music, and film, getting their first taste of modern Western culture, from the Beatles to Jackson Pollock. Tsegyam was allowed to attend a six-month seminar at the Southwest Nationalities University in Chengdu, where visiting professors from Beijing offered lectures on Western philosophy and democracy. Subjects that would have been taboo a few years earlier were openly discussed. Chinese artists and writers themselves were allowed for the first time to give voice to the sufferings they had experienced in the preceding decades, giving rise to a new genre of what was known as "scar literature."

Hu Yaobang had become head of the Communist Party in 1980, abolishing the title of chairman in order to distance himself from the stain of Mao's dictatorship, assuming instead the title of general secretary. One of the few Communist Party leaders to emerge from a genuinely poor family, Hu had run away from his peasant parents at the age of fourteen to join the Communist Party, becoming one of the youngest leaders of the Long March. Purged twice during the Cultural Revolution, he emerged later as Deng Xiaoping's protégé and as the leading voice of liberalism in China. Asked which of Mao's theories were applicable to life in modern China, Hu famously replied, "None, I think."

Under Hu, the Communist Party came as close as it ever would to apologizing for its treatment of Tibetans. While not exactly acknowledging the staggering loss of life, he stated in a remarkable speech in Lhasa in 1980 that "there has been no great improvement in the lives of the people of Tibet." He promised to promote Tibetan culture and autonomy. "You Tibetans like to eat butter and tsampa; as a southerner, I like to eat rice. If you abolish his right to eat tsampa, and you abolish my right to eat rice, then we couldn't be united." He called for the Communist Party "to energetically and fully develop Tibetan science, culture and education." He criticized Party cadres working in Tibet who couldn't say anything more than *tashi delek,* the traditional Tibetan greeting, and urged that they study the language. "Saying that you should warmly love the minority nationalities is not just empty talk; you should respect their customs and habits, their language, their history, and their culture."

THIS WAS THE GUIDING spirit behind the Tibetan Middle School. But it was still a government institution with mandatory courses in Marxism, Leninism, and Mao Zedong thought. Tsegyam had been educated in the Chinese system and he was well qualified to teach these subjects. He was quickly hired as a teacher, even though he was only nineteen years old, younger than many of the students, and soon was promoted to vice principal.

What was most exciting to Tsegyam about this plum job was the opportunity to teach Tibetan reading and writing. The subject matter was sufficiently new in the government school system that there was no fixed curriculum, which gave the instructor great leeway. Chinese educational authorities wouldn't be able to monitor exactly what Tsegyam was imparting to his students; despite Hu Yaobang's urging, few had bothered to learn Tibetan.

Nevertheless, Tsegyam approached the curriculum with caution. He liked this job and wanted to keep it. When he compiled reading material for his students, he carefully added in a few tracts about Buddhist philosophy and Tibetan astrology, the basis of the Tibetan calendar. He had been specifically instructed not to teach Tibetan history, a most sensitive subject, but he found ways to sneak it in. In language class, the students learned about the invention of the Tibetan alphabet and about the hundreds of thousands of books on every conceivable subject from poetry to medicine and physics that had been published in Tibetan. He wanted to counter what students had been taught in Chinese schools—that Chinese was the language of literacy and that Tibetan was merely a folk language used by old people and monks.

For music class, the students staged an opera about the reign of Trisong Detsen, the greatest of the Tibetan kings. In the course of the performance, the students were thrilled to learn about his invasion of China and the fifteen glorious days back in 763 C.E. when the Tibetans had occupied the Chinese capital of Chang'an, forcing the Chinese emperor to abdicate. The students sang their parts with gusto.

"We wanted Tibetan students to realize the strength of their own race," Tsegyam later explained.

Tsegyam lived on the Middle School campus in a room that he'd turned into a makeshift library with books stacked in every corner. He read fluently in both Tibetan and Chinese, making it somewhat easier to find reading material. His friends who traveled out of town obliged him by picking up new books whenever they were near a bookstore.

One close friend was a businessman and monk who made frequent trips to India. With a large Tibetan exile population, India was the best place to buy Tibetan-language books. Returning from one of these trips, the ex-monk gave Tsegyam a very special gift: a memoir by the Dalai Lama.

My Land and My People was published in 1962, three years after the Dalai Lama fled to India, but few Tibetans inside Tibet had gotten an opportunity to read it. The book came as a revelation to Tsegyam. First, he had seldom read an autobiography and this was a classic of the genre: The Dalai Lama presented himself as a real person, modest and even self-deprecating. He confessed his ignorance of worldly affairs at the time he was called upon to lead Tibet and admitted to his mistakes in governance. Although the book was more memoir than manifesto, the Dalai Lama wrote of Tibet's proud past as an independent kingdom. "Tibet is a distinct and ancient nation, which for many centuries enjoyed a relationship of mutual respect with China."

Tsegyam loaned his copy of the book to a trusted colleague, but the colleague was not as discreet as he should have been. The book was confiscated and the colleague admitted it was Tsegyam who had given him the book. Tsegyam was called in for questioning. He told them he had read it for literary, not political, reasons. When they asked where he'd gotten the book, he lied and named another friend who, conveniently, had died the year before and thus could not be punished. Tsegyam was a prominent figure in Ngaba, and someone authorities hoped would eventually join the Communist Party. And so he was let off without any punishment. That made Tsegyam a little braver, and so he asked his monk friend to bring him another copy.

The book made the rounds. The Dalai Lama's message was compelling to these young educated Tibetans. They categorically rejected the Maoist brand of Communism that had been forcibly imposed in previous decades. On the other hand, they had absorbed some of the Communist Party's teachings about the inequities of Tibet's feudal society. The Dalai Lama's words resounded with these Tibetans struggling to articulate a position that would meld socialist ideas about the equitable distribution of wealth along with new ideas about democracy and human rights.

Up until then, Tibetans in Ngaba knew very little about the current activities of the Dalai Lama. He was revered as a spiritual leader, but he was almost mythical—"like Santa Claus" is how one Tibetan later explained it to me. Now they were learning that not only was he a real person, but the head of an entire Tibet government in exile.

AFTER FLEEING TIBET IN 1959, the Dalai Lama had settled in India, eventually finding a home in a mountaintop village called McLeod Ganj in Dharamsala in the northern part of the country. The Tibetans formed a government in exile, complete with a parliament, civil service and other trappings of bureaucracy, and their own flag depicting a pair of snow lions in front of a sun and a red-and-blue-striped sky. They produced buttons and bumper stickers and human rights literature, some of which began to trickle back into Tibet. Tsegyam's friend, the monk, and other itinerant businessmen often carried these banned items in their luggage when they returned to Ngaba.

It was around this time that the Tibetan plight was gaining traction around the world. The International Campaign for Tibet, Free Tibet, and the Tibet Information Network were founded in the late 1980s. A few years later, actor Richard Gere used the Academy Award stage to denounce human rights abuses directed against Tibetans. The Dalai Lama was emerging as a "lama to the globe," as *Newsweek* would call him.

How could the Tibetans not be emboldened? From afar, they saw their revered spiritual leader lauded on the world stage, embraced by parliamentarians and movie stars. Unfamiliar with the subtleties of the Western democratic process, they didn't appreciate the distinction between interest groups, NGOs, congressional committees, and the policies of national governments. On the eve of Richard Nixon's historic visit to China in 1972, the United States had pulled its support for the CIA-funded Tibetan resistance, but the Dalai Lama's popularity among influential Americans misled many Tibetans into believing that the full weight of the U.S. government was committed to the Tibetan cause. It goaded them to resist beyond a point of prudence and gave them a confidence unwarranted by the political realities.

In September 1987, the Dalai Lama made his first major appearance in Washington, unveiling a five-point proposal before the congressional Human Rights Caucus to turn Tibet into a "zone of peace." By then, he had already abandoned the demand for absolute independence in favor of genuine autonomy within the boundaries of China—what would come to be known as his "middle way."

Beijing reacted with indignation to the Dalai Lama's remarks, reviling him as a "splittist" who intended to destroy China. Nothing inflamed Tibetans more than denunciations of the Dalai Lama. To make matters worse, Chinese authorities flexed their muscles by calling a large crowd to Lhasa's sports stadium to witness the sentencing of Tibetan prisoners, including two who were to be executed. Monks held a march in support of the Dalai Lama and were promptly arrested. Protests grew larger and police fired into the crowd, which led to more protests. The cycle would continue over the next two years, when martial law was imposed.

In Ngaba, Tibetans quietly cheered the protesters in Lhasa. They dared not go into the streets themselves because more troops had been deployed around town in anticipation of unrest, but they too wanted to show their support.

They started by writing messages on the *lungta,* square prayer flags no bigger than handkerchiefs, usually pastel pinks, which are tossed like confetti and dispersed into the wind. Sometimes it was just one word, *Rangzen,* "independence" in Tibetan, or simply "Long Live the Dalai Lama." It was an easy, relatively fail-safe way to express the spirit of rebellion.

Tsegyam wanted to take it a step further. His apartment was located on the third floor of the Middle School overlooking Ngaba's main street. Late one Saturday night, he closed the curtains and took out some letter-size paper he had pilfered from the office's copy machine. He felt guilty for stealing the paper—but not about what he was going to do with it. He took out some ink and a traditional calligraphy brush. Then with a trembling hand, he wrote out his messages in Tibetan as well as in Chinese characters.

FREE TIBET.

CHINESE OUT OF TIBET.

BRING BACK HIS HOLINESS
THE DALAI LAMA.

Tsegyam's letters were not as large as in the famous big character posters plastered around during the Cultural Revolution, but his writing was clear and bold. He was known for the quality of his calligraphy, so he slipped in a few errors and smudges so that the police wouldn't immediately identify him as the author.

By the time Tsegyam finished it was two in the morning. The streets of Ngaba were deserted. Most students were asleep, except for two of them whom Tsegyam had enlisted to put up the posters. Moving as stealthily as one could on a bicycle, they pedaled up to his entranceway and tucked the posters along with bottles of glue into large messenger bags. In the dead of night, they plastered the posters on electric poles, brick walls, and shop windows and on the public bulletin board at the main square. The students had scouted the locations ahead of time; the night before, one of them had ridden through town with a slingshot and shot out the streetlights above the selected locations. Still, they were nervous and one of the students later admitted to Tsegyam that he feared he had hung some of the posters upside down.

But Chinese authorities had gotten the message. Before dawn on Sunday morning, they dispatched the first cleaning crews out to scrub the walls. Tsegyam slept late, past ten A.M. By the time he went out for a stroll, the posters had disappeared. But people in town had seen them and were talking about them. He considered the mission a success.

Tsegyam lay low for almost a year. But by early 1989, the game was up. One of the students, who had been warned that the police were on to him, ran away from Ngaba and eventually escaped abroad. Another student, a young man named Dargye, was not so lucky. He was arrested and taken to the police station, where he was suspended from a beam by his wrists, kicked, beaten, and shocked with a cattle prod until he finally broke down and named Tsegyam as the one who drew the posters. One morning a week after Dargye's arrest, the police came for Tsegyam and drove him to the Ngaba county detention center.

They didn't have an arrest warrant, but otherwise Tsegyam felt he was fairly treated. Again, the police showed grudging respect for Tsegyam's position and education and his past membership in the Communist Youth League. But the interrogation sessions were exhausting. He was questioned from eight A.M. to noon, then from two P.M. to five P.M., and again from six P.M. to eight P.M. He readily admitted that he'd made the posters—he was rather proud of it, in fact—but they wanted to know more. They grilled him on his contacts with the Tibetan government in exile, wanting to know where he got the idea to put up the posters and how he decided to write the slogans. They asked him what he thought about socialism and capitalism and the political system of the Soviet Union. They wanted to know if he had studied psychology and asked him to explain some of the basic principles. It almost seemed to Tsegyam like the police were using him as their private tutor, trying to satisfy their own curiosity about the outside world.

During a break, one officer discreetly approached Tsegyam about becoming a government informant. He told Tsegyam if he revealed everything he knew, he would get money and a high-ranking government job.

"You're a teacher, a scholar. You're educated. Until now you have been looked after by the Chinese government. Now it's your chance to do something for us," he said. Tsegyam declined the offer.

By then, the euphoria of the post-Mao era was dissipating. Modern China has a bipolar personality with bursts of openness almost invariably followed by relapses of repression. For years, doctrinaire leftists within the Communist Party were seething over Hu Yaobang's reforms and plotting his comeuppance. They blamed his permissiveness for the public displays of discontent in Tibet and elsewhere in China. Hu had been removed as general secretary of the Communist Party in 1987, and although not exactly purged, he was nudged into obscurity.

In jail, Tsegyam somehow managed to get a transistor radio. He followed the political upheavals as best he could, tuning in to Chinese-language broadcasts because he couldn't understand Voice of America's Tibetan broadcasts, which were in the Lhasa dialect. Something shocking seemed to happen every day. Clashes had continued in Lhasa. On March 8, 1989, the Chinese government declared martial law in the city.

Hu Yaobang died on April 15, 1989. Thousands of students gathered in Beijing's Tiananmen Square with wreaths and mourning banners, praising Hu's commitment to freedom and reform. Over the coming weeks, the numbers swelled to more than one million as the gathering morphed into a demonstration for democracy, with spinoff protests taking place around the country. The students didn't leave Tiananmen Square until the tanks rolled into Beijing in early June. By the end of the day, June 4, hundreds, perhaps thousands, of people were dead.

Later that same year, the radio finally reported some good news. In Oslo, Norway, the Nobel committee had awarded the Dalai Lama the Peace Prize for his commitment to nonviolence. Tsegyam, who was by then out on bail awaiting trial, had to explain to Tibetans that it was the most important prize in the world. Although most hadn't heard of the Nobel, or for that matter Norway, they understood it was a great honor.

Shortly afterward, the police arrested Tsegyam again, this time with a proper warrant in which he was accused of counterrevolutionary propaganda and incitement. His trial took place in March 1990. The authorities hoped it would serve as an example for Tibetans on the perils of political activism, and so they opened the proceedings to the public. The courtroom was overflowing, with people cramming into the hallways. Loudspeakers broadcast the three-hour trial out on the street. Tsegyam wasn't allowed a lawyer, but he argued vigorously in his own defense, at one point shouting, "Long live the Dalai Lama."

The three judges deliberated fifteen minutes before finding him guilty. He was sentenced to another year in jail.

When Tsegyam got out of jail, he found himself unable to work. He had been fired from his job at the Middle School; the magazines that used to publish his poems and essays no longer dared. As a man of prodigious intelligence, he couldn't go back to raising crops with his parents. Unemployed and unemployable, he traveled and read books before sneaking across the border into India in 1992 with a former student who had become his wife. It was clear to Tsegyam that there was no place in Ngaba for somebody like him. He ended up working for the Tibetan exile government, eventually becoming the Dalai Lama's private secretary.

A PEACOCK FROM
THE WEST

Gonpo, her husband, and their daughters, in a taped-together photo.
The four were rarely together.

IT WASN'T UNTIL 1981 THAT GONPO AND XIAO TU WERE
permitted to leave their exile in Xinjiang. They had been married for
five years and had two young daughters. They settled in Nanjing,
Xiao Tu's hometown, 190 miles inland from Shanghai, up the Yangtze
River. Nanjing is one of the most congenial cities in China, with
broad, sunny avenues, shaded by parasol-shaped plane trees. Gonpo

and Xiao Tu were back in the bosom of China, embraced once again by family and nation, forgiven for the political sins of their past.

No longer barred from higher education, they both were accepted into teachers' college. Xiao Tu's mother was retiring from her job as a bureaucrat with the education department and, in keeping with the Chinese custom of the time, was permitted to pass her position on to her son. Gonpo was hired as a primary school teacher, assigned to teach music.

Gonpo was at home in Nanjing, accepted by her husband's family and her colleagues. She had mastered Mandarin Chinese so thoroughly that the school soon promoted her to teaching reading and writing to sixth graders. She remembered her father's advice to "behave as though you are a servant of the people." She was cheerful and cooperative, careful never to cause problems. After more than a decade on the farm in Xinjiang, she was accustomed to hard work and felt idle without it. She never complained when she was asked to sweep up the classroom at the end of the school day or clean up after a kindergartner who'd had a toilet accident. She was quick to volunteer to carry a sick child on her back to the doctor. She won an award as a model teacher.

At home, she kept a small portrait of the Dalai Lama, but there was nothing else in her behavior or manner that identified her as a Tibetan. Her soft, round features and dimples allowed her to pass as Chinese. In Xinjiang, she had even acquired a Chinese name, Yuqing (meaning "clear jade"), and although her colleagues knew she was Tibetan, she didn't make a big deal about it. The fact that she had spent years in exile in Xinjiang was nothing out of the ordinary since millions of Chinese had been sent away during the Cultural Revolution. It was bad form to dwell on traumas past. She didn't discuss her background with anybody other than her husband. Silence suited her. In adulthood, she had become painfully shy, the exuberance of girlhood long since shriveled under the weight of adversity. It was too painful to dwell on her losses. And although the Cultural Revolution was over, coming from a family of Tibetan nobility—with its connotations of slavery and serfdom—wasn't the sort of thing you'd boast about.

One day, while Gonpo was tidying up at the end of the school day, a colleague came rushing into the classroom to tell her something important. There was a man from the Nanjing municipality who had come to visit. He had a big black car and wanted Gonpo to come with him to the district office.

Gonpo was apprehensive. In her experience, if a government car came for you, it was bad news. But she dusted herself off and tried to pin her unruly hair behind her ears. A fellow teacher loaned her a change of clothes so she would look more respectable.

When she arrived at the district office, she realized that she had been recognized. No matter how much you tried to efface your personality, no matter if you changed your name, you could never completely hide in China. It turned out that a high-ranking Tibetan in the Chinese government, Ngapo Ngawang Jigme, was on a tour of Nanjing and had heard that the surviving daughter of the last Mei king was living there. Ngapo, as he was usually known, was one of the more famous—some might say infamous—Tibetan officials. He had been the Dalai Lama's delegate to the talks that resulted in the Tibetans signing away their independence with the Seventeen-Point Agreement. While other Tibetan cadres had subsequently fallen afoul of the Communist Party, Ngapo remained in its good graces and was a member of the National People's Congress. His position was senior enough that the district officials listened to his every word.

Ngapo put his hand on Gonpo's shoulder as he spoke. She tried not to squirm with embarrassment.

"You should take care of this young woman. She is a model teacher and a representative of her people," he told the Nanjing district officials.

That was the end of Gonpo's anonymity. She was named a delegate to the Nanjing People's Congress, the Nanjing People's Political Consultative Congress, and a women's association. These positions mostly entailed showing up at meetings, listening to long, dull speeches, and clapping politely at the appropriate moments. The Communist Party always liked to have ethnic minorities—preferably women dressed in

But she didn't really mind. Gonpo was not an angry person. Like so many other people who needed to survive in China, she had taught herself to forgive and forget. She didn't dwell on the persecution that had resulted in the deaths of both her parents. She didn't speak of the many years that she had toiled in the salt marshes in Xinjiang.

Still, at times she was overwhelmed by a sense of loss. Not just of her parents and sister, but of her own identity as a Tibetan, one of the last survivors of a once-distinguished dynasty. She had a sense that she had obligations that would put her far outside the life she'd built in Nanjing.

After Mao's death, the Communist Party had begun to rehabilitate the millions of people who had been purged during the 1950s and 1960s. The process, known as *pingfan*, was roughly the equivalent of a pardon to expunge political crimes. People who had been expelled from the Communist Party had their membership reinstated and in some cases were allowed to return to their former homes and jobs. Gonpo's father was rehabilitated by means of a letter that had been personally signed by Deng Xiaoping in 1978—too late to save his life, but Gonpo was pleased to see his legacy restored. In an official history later published by the Ngaba prefecture, the Mei king would be praised as a leader who "served the people," the ultimate compliment from the Communist Party.

Although Gonpo was the only living child of the king, she didn't get restitution for the properties that had been confiscated. All she would receive was a fox fur coat her father had worn for ceremonial events: it had been saved by a servant in an old leather suitcase she stashed above a wardrobe in her new apartment. However, Gonpo didn't covet the lost palaces, the lands, the jewelry or precious statues. She had taken socialism to heart, more seriously than many Chinese. What she wanted was to make sure her father had the proper Buddhist rituals for death.

Her mother's body had never been found and her death remained a mystery. It was assumed that she was pushed or had jumped into the

eye-catching headdresses and colorful robes—for the photo ops show
ing off Chinese diversity. The positions were mostly ceremonial, wit
no real power, but they did confer benefits.

The local government for her *qu,* or district, offered her an apart
ment—a major perk. Gonpo and her husband and their young daugh
ters had been living in various unsatisfactory accommodations—for
while part of a classroom at the school and then a shack with newspa
pers plastered on the walls for lack of wallpaper. The new apartmen
had two bedrooms, a living room, a gas line for a stove, and, best o
all, a bathroom with a toilet and shower. It was on the top floor of
relatively new six-story apartment building in a convenient residentia
neighborhood of Nanjing. Through concrete latticework on the fa
çade you could look out over a tree-lined intersection and small shops
Although it wasn't anybody's idea of luxury, even by 1980s Chinese
standards, it was the perfect home to raise a young family. Gonpo wa
thrilled with the idea of moving into an apartment, which to Chinese
of her generation was preferable to an old-fashioned house.

They were preparing to move in on a Sunday when they got noti-
fication from the city government that there was yet another apartment assigned to them. This one was similar, but on the fourth
floor—preferable since the building had no elevator. Gonpo had fallen
in love with the sixth-floor apartment, but her father-in-law advised
her to accept the new offer.

"Take what you can get when you can. The Party's moods are like
summer weather, changing by the hour," he advised. Her husband
agreed.

So in her thirties, Gonpo had achieved a more comfortable life
than she could have ever imagined. She had a husband who adored her
and whom she adored in return. She had in-laws who doted on her.
She had two smart, healthy daughters, a secure job in her chosen pro-
fession, and the status of her various ceremonial positions. Gonpo was
savvy enough to understand that she was being used by the Communist Party to whitewash their ethnic policies. She was the model
teacher, wife, and mother, a perfect propaganda tool for the system.

river at Lixian, but there were no witnesses. The king's death was clearer. His younger sister, Dhondup Tso, accompanied him on the trip to look for his wife and had seen him jump off a bridge at Wenchuan. Chinese villagers sitting on the banks of the river had also witnessed his suicide leap. A few days later, villagers downriver had fished out the body of a tall male in Tibetan clothing, assumed to be the king. The body was put in a simple coffin and buried locally.

In 1980, relatives from the king's family started petitioning Chinese authorities to exhume the body. They didn't get a clear answer, but the king's brother-in-law, a man named Jamphel Sangpo who was married to the king's younger sister, took charge of this familial obligation. He had a good relationship with a Tibetan official in the United Front Work Department, which manages the Party's relations with minorities, and was granted permission. When he finally went to exhume the body, it was the height of summer, making the task especially unpleasant, he later told an oral historian.

> I hired three people from the village and started digging around. We found it very hard to locate the corpse buried underground. When we finally found and exhumed the corpse, it was in a coffin. The flesh on the body had all decomposed. There was a shoe on one of the feet. The coffin also contained two enamel basins full of parched dead maggots.

Jamphel Sangpo said prayers, apologizing for the years it had taken to retrieve the body. "You had to remain in such a distant land for so long. Today, I am here to reclaim your body and take you back home." He bought firewood from a Chinese villager, and although it was drizzling, he managed to light a fire and conducted a do-it-yourself cremation. The next day, after the charred remains had cooled off, he hired a car to drive to Ngaba. On the way, the car broke down, and he walked the last fifteen miles carrying the remains. Once at Kirti Monastery, he stashed them away for safekeeping under a corner of the newly rebuilt congregation hall.

Gonpo tried to arrange funeral rites almost as soon as she moved from Xinjiang to Nanjing. After several failed attempts, she finally succeeded in 1984, when Kirti Rinpoche, the abbot, was visiting Ngaba. As head of the Kirti Monastery, he was considered the spiritual teacher for all the members of the former royal family, their "root guru," as Tibetans call it. He was also a cousin of Gonpo's mother. Kirti Rinpoche had fled to India along with the Dalai Lama, but during this brief period of unprecedented openness he had received permission to return for a visit.

Gonpo and her husband traveled again to Chengdu and then took a bus through the mountains. Each year the trip got a little quicker and easier. Engineers had bored tunnels through the mountain to straighten the stomach-churning switchbacks that had sickened them previously. Ngaba was in noticeably better shape than before, the town and the monasteries largely rebuilt. A taxi service had started up and visitors had fewer restrictions on moving around.

It was a relaxed visit. Gonpo and Xiao Tu took a taxi to see the palace where she'd spent her early childhood. It had been used as a government warehouse, but was now boarded up and padlocked. They couldn't go inside but posed for pictures out front. She visited Meruma, formerly headquarters of the king's military as well as the king's herds. She had lunch at the home of Delek, the boy with the runny nose whose father had been one of the king's generals. Gonpo and Delek were of the same generation, both in their mid-thirties now. Although she had been a princess and he merely a horse groom, they appreciated that they had experienced many of the same terrors from childhood onward.

"We had grown up in the same way and we struck a chord," Delek would later say of their meeting.

The funeral services for the king were held at Kirti Monastery. More than three hundred monks gathered to chant blessings. Family photos show Gonpo, Xiao Tu, and the aunt, Dhondup Tso, standing in front of the congregation hall with silky white *khatas* draped around their necks and dozens of monks in crimson bowing beside them.

As for the bones, the monastery initially had intended to place them in the great stupa, at Kirti, which serves as a reliquary for high lamas and other dignitaries. But the monks feared Chinese authorities might try to move the remains at some point in the future. Despite the permissive attitude of the moment, Tibetans knew they could never trust the whims of the Party.

They decided they would grind the bones into a fine powder and scatter them around the monastery. Some of the powder was turned into clay from which they made *tsatsa,* votive tablets decorated with raised figurines. In that way the king literally became inseparable from the monastery that was the spiritual passion of his life.

Gonpo had done the best she could for her father. It should have brought her a sense of closure, but she still felt uneasy. She was disappointed by her own conduct in Ngaba. She felt like a stranger in her homeland. She had known Kirti Rinpoche since she was a small child, but when she opened her mouth to speak to him, she couldn't summon up the words. They had to communicate through an interpreter since the lama did not speak Chinese. Whenever she heard her mother tongue, it conjured up memories and images, but she couldn't quite access specific meanings. What little Tibetan spilled out of her sounded like baby talk. When she met the monastery's official oracle—a high-ranking position—he asked if she knew who he was, and she couldn't remember his title in Tibetan and so she answered childishly, "You're the one who blows the horn."

The other Tibetans chuckled. It was funny, but Gonpo was mortified that she, the last offspring of the king, wasn't a better representative for her people.

Gonpo had tried to sew a chuba for herself, using a pattern somebody gave her. But the chuba from the Ngaba region is a very complicated garment. It is like a robe with oversized sleeves that slide off the shoulder to tie in back like a bustle and are held in place with a sash. Gonpo's effort was an epic failure. A relative had to bring her a simpler version of the garment from Lhasa.

SHORTLY AFTER HER FATHER'S FUNERAL, Gonpo got an audience to see the Panchen Lama in Beijing. The Panchen Lama, now in his fifties, larger than life by dint of his girth and his power, was now the most senior Tibetan religious figure in the Chinese political system. He had spent thirteen years in prison and house arrest after writing a petition excoriating the Party's treatment of Tibetans. Once rehabilitated, he had left the monkhood, married a Chinese woman, and assumed various ceremonial positions within the system. Like Gonpo, he existed in the overlap between the Chinese and Tibetan spheres, mixing language and culture. They spoke to each other in Chinese.

"You poor girl," the Panchen Lama chastised her. "You're a Tibetan, but you can't speak anything other than Chinese. You have to learn your own language. Your own culture," he told her.

The lama advised her to study the language in India, where the Tibetan government in exile had set up many schools. She could make a pilgrimage and get an audience with the Dalai Lama at the same time. He offered to arrange the paperwork.

"The next time we meet, we will speak in Tibetan," he promised.

With the Panchen Lama's help, Gonpo was able to get a Chinese passport and another for her older daughter, Wangzin, eleven, who had begged to come along. At that time, it still was uncommon for ordinary Chinese to travel abroad, especially to India, which had strained relations with China. But there was a thaw in 1988, when Rajiv Gandhi became the first Indian prime minister to visit Beijing, and that made it easier for Gonpo to get a visa. The Panchen Lama had advised Gonpo to fly through Hong Kong, but she was determined to make a pilgrimage through Tibet.

Gonpo and Wangzin left Nanjing in December 1988 with Ngaba as the first stop on their journey. One of the pieces of unfinished business was what to do with the family's property. They had no chance of recovering the main palace, which remained in the hands of the government, but the land returned to Kirti included a partially destroyed family house that had been used for royal pilgrimages. Gonpo readily agreed to a suggestion by Kirti Rinpoche that the house be renovated and used as a shrine to her parents. One of the family's most precious possessions, the statue of Avalokitesvara given to the king by the Dalai Lama, had been saved and would be the centerpiece.

Mother and daughter then headed southwest to Lhasa, a 1,200-mile trip. They intended to stop there just long enough for some sightseeing before heading farther west to the border with Nepal, which is the most convenient route into India. But a heavy snowfall blocked the mountain pass near the Everest base camp. They waited and waited for the snow to melt. Three months passed. It was just after the Chinese New Year and the beginning of the Tibetan New Year holiday, Losar, the time of year when families in both cultures come together. Gonpo felt terribly homesick and conflicted. She missed her husband and her younger daughter. She understood she had obligations to the family she had created in Nanjing and not just to the legacy of her parents and the defunct kingdom they once ruled. The living should take precedence over the dead, she thought. She decided she would return to Nanjing and made the travel arrangements. But the night before she was due to go home, she had a dream about a peacock. The bird was so enormous that when it spread its train the plumage filled the entire sky with iridescent blues and greens. The peacock was flying from the west, the direction of India.

It was an omen, Gonpo thought. The next morning she was filled with fresh resolve to keep going. Even though people warned her that the roads were still choked with snow, she hired a driver with a jeep and snow chains and they set off to the border with Nepal. They made it almost all the way before the snowdrifts came up to the hood of the jeep and they could go no farther. To the delight of Gonpo's daughter, they got out and trekked through the snow the rest of the way. The path was so icy that the guides had to attach ropes to keep them from slipping off. As they approached Dham, they saw smoke rising in the air. The border town was home to thousands of people from Ngaba—the traders who sold Chinese goods to Nepal and India. They had heard that the daughter of the last king of Ngaba was on her way and they had lit juniper branches as incense to welcome her. Gonpo was so giddy with excitement that she lost her footing and nearly slipped off the precipice.

What Gonpo didn't realize was that this would be a one-way journey. It was the fateful year of 1989, months before the Tiananmen Square massacre when the era of tolerance came crashing to an end. The crackdown would be felt from Beijing to Ngaba to Lhasa, marking the disappointing end of the halcyon decade of the 1980s. In January of 1989, the Panchen Lama dropped dead of an apparent heart attack. They wouldn't get to speak in Tibetan after all. A dispute over his reincarnation would add rancor to the relationship between Tibetans and the Communist Party. Gonpo and her daughter succeeded in reaching Dharamsala and getting an audience with the Dalai Lama, who would win the Nobel Peace Prize later that year. But the political climate in China made it unwise to return home. She was in exile once again.

PART THREE

1990–2013

CHAPTER

II

· · ·

WILD BABY YAK

Boy in Meruma, 2014.

BY THE 1990S, THE EXPLOSIVES HAD BEEN CLEARED FROM
the hills around Meruma village. Children played barefoot in the hills.
They liked to dart in and out of the crumbling concrete pillbox that
had been built by the People's Liberation Army in the late 1950s during
the battles with the last holdouts from the Mei king's army and where
a decade later self-styled Tibetan Red Guards on horseback were
mowed down by a hail of bullets. The children called it the *sokhang,*

the spy house. It was the perfect setting to play hide-and-go-seek and war games. The children knew little of the real wars fought by their fathers and grandfathers at this very same location. Only that people had died here and that they shouldn't stay after dark in case of ghosts.

This was an era when urban Chinese were eating at McDonald's and buying appliances at Walmart, but life in Tibetan villages like Meruma went on more or less untouched by modernity. Although the village had been electrified a decade before, the supply was just enough to power a lightbulb in every house and a radio or cassette player. There were few appliances. Women would squat by the stream washing their laundry.

There were plenty of children running around. One of the few advantages of being a Tibetan was that families were allowed more than one child. The children had none of the mass-produced plastic toys churned out by the factories of southern China. Instead, they would rummage through the garbage to find wood that could be fashioned into ice skates. They turned dried yak skins into sleds. In the summer, they would splash around the stream, one of the few times they'd get clean as it was not the custom for Tibetan children to bathe.

One of the boys in the pack was nicknamed Dongtuk, which meant "wild baby yak." He was small with ears that stuck out and a Dennis the Menace button nose. Dongtuk had had poor eyesight since early childhood but it didn't seem to keep him back; he was often a leader of the pack, seeking out the best picks from the garbage pile— like abandoned tires—and rolling them alongside the road.

Dongtuk grew up among females. He was born out of wedlock to a disabled mother. He lived with his mother, a younger sister, and his maternal grandmother in a mud-brick house protected by a walled courtyard strung with prayer flags. It occupied a prime location near the main road, facing south, but it was sparsely furnished because Dongtuk's mother was always strapped for cash. There was an armchair with the stuffing coming out and a wood-paneled hutch with chipped blue-and-white porcelain cups. A wooden bench lined one wall. The floors were bare concrete and the walls were lined with peeling vinyl paper that was actually shelf liners. A small room off the kitchen had a makeshift bed with a mattress of dried grass and twigs.

Dongtuk's mother, Sonam, had been the village beauty. She had high chiseled cheekbones and a dazzling smile that flashed so white her teeth practically glowed in the dark. But at thirteen she came down with a fever that left her paralyzed. When the fever broke, mobility returned to all but her left hand and her left foot. The village had no doctor and there was nobody to diagnose the illness.

"Evil spirits," said her mother.

Sonam viewed her misfortune as an omen that she should never get married. Tibetan wives are expected to carry a heavy household load, milking the animals, churning the butter, and collecting yak dung for fuel, as well as the cooking and cleaning. Her limp and paralyzed left hand made her an undesirable bride despite her good looks. Moreover, her father had died young, and somebody needed to stay home and take care of their mother, a duty that normally would have fallen to her older brother, except that he was the black sheep of the family, having run off with the family's savings.

Being single, however, did not mean being celibate. Although Tibetan women are exceedingly modest in their clothing, they are not prudish about sex (as long as it doesn't involve monks). Polygamy and polyandry were acceptable among rural Tibetans, particularly when it was a matter of practicality rather than lust. In Meruma, two brothers shared a wife, an arrangement that prevented the family's property from being divided and allowed one man to earn money trading while the other maintained the family's land and herds. Unmarried women frequently had children of their own; in fact, one anthropologist who studied a Tibetan village found that half of the unmarried women had given birth. Unlike Chinese women similarly situated, they weren't scorned as mistresses or concubines, but were treated as heads of households in their own right. That was especially true in Sonam's case since she had inherited her parents' house.

Sonam was the consummate single mother. She raised cows, yaks, and *dzomo,* the hybrid dairy cattle. With her useless left hand tucked into the folds of her cloak, she would go out to the mountains to scour the ground for herbs, the priceless caterpillar fungus, and the *beimu*. Dongtuk liked to boast that his mother could pick more with one hand than most people could with two. During the summer months, she'd pitch a tent in the pasturelands to take the animals to graze.

Before she even ate breakfast and started the day's work, Sonam visited the village's small shrine, which displayed three statues of Avalokitesvara, all draped with prayer beads that had been worn by Kirti Rinpoche. She fasted regularly to purify herself.

By the standards of rural women her age, Sonam was reasonably well educated. She could read and write in Tibetan, speak rudimentary Chinese, and do enough basic arithmetic to keep from being cheated when she sold her herbs. Still, it wasn't easy for a disabled single mother to earn a living and the family lived on the edge of subsistence. They ate a very basic diet of tsampa mixed with cheese and butter, or a soup of noodles shaped into squares called *thenthuk*. There was always a block of butter sitting out on the table, giving the house a slightly rancid aroma that to Dongtuk smelled comfortingly like home.

The children never had more than one pair of shoes, which they stuffed with grass for insulation. Sonam insisted that Dongtuk go barefoot in the summer to avoid wearing out his one pair. The family didn't have a television or radio. At night they would play a cassette tape with Buddhist prayer music. The rhythm helped them relax and ignore the noises of the night, the howling and barking of the dogs.

"Although we didn't have many things or furniture, I always had enough to eat," Dongtuk would later say. "I didn't feel poor."

Meruma didn't have the same cachet that it did in the days when so many residents were part of the king's court and army. Some of the children weren't even aware that their village was named for this fallen dynasty. But the elders knew who was who and they revered the heroes of old. One of Dongtuk's best friends was a boy a few years older, Phuntsog, who was the grandson of one of the resistance fighters from the 1950s, a man named Dhondor who had somehow survived eighteen years in prison, making him a local hero. The grandson too was one of the strongest kids in the neighborhood. He was a pale, broad-shouldered boy with a smile that stretched to his wide-set cheekbones. He loved lifting weights and wrestling; and although Dongtuk didn't enjoy that sort of thing, he liked hanging out with Phuntsog's large family—six boys and two girls—whose rambunctiousness compensated for the loneliness of having only one little sister.

Dongtuk's mother also enjoyed a higher status than one might expect of a disabled woman with neither a husband nor money. Sonam's uncle, who was born in the family house she now owned, had been recognized as the 15th incarnation in a minor lineage. Tibet has hundreds of such *tulku*s, or reincarnate lamas, from the world famous like the Dalai Lama and other senior Buddhist leaders to the abbots of lesser monasteries. Sonam's uncle, Alok Lama, was a relatively minor figure in the panoply of Tibetan Buddhism, but he nevertheless was held to be a bodhisattva who had taken rebirth for the benefit of others; he made Sonam's family akin to minor nobility and her home something of a shrine.

Dongtuk's house had a chapel off the courtyard that was dedicated to this uncle. It was the only room in the house constructed with real timber, which is precious on the plateau. The walls were decorated with renderings of various important lamas. An elaborate gilt-edged frame held a black-and-white photograph of Alok Lama, a thin pockmarked man with a goatee. A portrait of the Dalai Lama hung loosely from a nail in case it had to be hastily removed. In front of the photos were brass butter lamps. On a shelf below were small bowls for water, seven of them, each symbolizing offerings of drinking water, bathing water, flowers, perfume, food, incense, and music. The room had a narrow bed—a real bed with a wooden frame—which was supposed to be reserved exclusively in case a distinguished monk came to visit. It was kept locked with a padlock. But Dongtuk would sometimes take the key from the kitchen and let himself in to rest on the bed. It was the only time he was ever alone.

In 2000, a film crew arrived in Meruma to shoot a television drama based on the Long March. They had a big crew, dozens of good-looking actors, shiny cars, and trucks to transport the camera equipment and the horses. A famous actor, Tang Guoqiang, was playing Mao Zedong, complete with a fake mole on his chin, a khaki quilted coat, and a matching hat with a red star over the brim. He rode on a big white horse—a beautiful horse much nicer than any the children had seen in Meruma. Dongtuk and the others watched from afar, thrilled to see all the action. From their viewpoint, this was one of the most exciting things to happen in Meruma.

The adults weren't so happy. They had heard—and a few of the very old people still remembered—how the Red Army had come through Ngaba in 1935–1936, looting the monasteries and gobbling up the food supply. The Long March wasn't anything to be celebrated. They hated what would soon become a craze among Chinese tourists, who liked to follow the route of the Long March, visiting sites they considered monuments to the courage of the early Communists. ("Red tourism," it was called.) For Tibetans in Ngaba, these places were reminders of defeat and humiliation. When the television crew announced that they would shoot one scene at the small but picturesque Namtso Monastery, which is terraced into a hillside above Meruma, the monastery officials were upset. They dared not refuse since the crew came from Chinese Central Television. So after dark, they gathered together some of the teenagers from the village and handed them shovels. By the next morning, the dirt road leading up to the monastery was filled with trenches, making it impassable for the crew's equipment trucks. Victory, though, was short-lived. The film crew eventually carried up their equipment on foot.

The children didn't grasp why the older people were unhappy about the film crew. History was a taboo subject for the Tibetans. To the extent they were taught anything about Tibet in the twentieth century, it was about how the Communist Party had liberated Tibet from serfdom. Their parents tended not to talk about it. Maybe they didn't know themselves. Or they feared these stories of collective trauma might rouse anti-Chinese sentiments that could get the children in trouble later down the road. The surviving elders who knew firsthand—and who often still carried the scars on their bodies—disgorged their memories only sparingly. If they hadn't been half-starved and beaten, if they hadn't languished in prison doing grueling work, then they had done things of which they were now ashamed. You were either tormented or a tormenter. Nobody had escaped unscathed.

What little Dongtuk knew of history came from his grandmother. He used to sleep with her on summer nights when his mother was staying out in a tent in the pasturelands with the animals. He and his sister would snuggle next to her, warming their feet under her body, and beg to hear the stories. She told tales of brave warriors on galloping horses, but also told of death and defeat. She told them of the hunger of the 1960s. She whispered about how the female Communists tortured and humiliated monks, one particularly cruel activist forcing a monk to drink her urine.

"Did you do that, Grandma?" Dongtuk asked, wide-eyed.

"Of course not," she protested.

THROUGHOUT HIS EARLY CHILDHOOD, Dongtuk had only a passing acquaintance with his father. He was a blacksmith, or *gara,* which was one of the lowest castes, perhaps because it was associated with weaponry. But he elevated his trade with artistry, crafting silver belt buckles and earrings. On the occasions he came to visit, he would bring a gift of food for Dongtuk and his sister and some new trinket for Sonam. Dongtuk looked forward to those visits. "I always felt my parents really loved each other."

Dongtuk was aware that his father had a wife and another family, and eventually he started to visit them. They were a big brood, three boys and two girls. They lived in a shabby concrete house up the hill in a subdivision of the Meruma #2 village, a far less desirable location than Dongtuk's. His father, being a younger son, had started off without an established household or property; he had what Tibetans call a new family. But he was a successful herder with enough yaks and sheep to ensure that meat was always plentiful in his household. Dongtuk's father's wife, Wangmo, never behaved as a jealous stepmother; she went out of her way to treat Dongtuk kindly. She would pile his plate with extra portions of *momos*, Tibetan dumplings, fretting that he was so much scrawnier than her own children. Still, Dongtuk always felt a little on edge at his father's house, his antennae always attuned for slights. He feared that his father had more love for the children he had raised with his wife than for those of the mistress he saw only occasionally.

The youngest child of his father's family was a boy, Rinzen Dorjee, who was almost the same age as Dongtuk, although much taller. It was always assumed they would be playmates, although they had little besides paternity in common. Dongtuk was a chatterbox of a child; Rinzen Dorjee preferred the company of animals to people. He spent hours crouched by the edge of the stream, collecting frogs and tadpoles. He would talk to them as though they were his dolls. The boys liked to blow air into the bellies of the frogs so that they would expand like balloons—and although it was distinctly against Buddhist teachings, some would make them burst. But Rinzen Dorjee would just watch them get propelled by the release of the air. Dongtuk thought it was a stupid pastime and that his half brother was a little soft in the head. Just the same he appreciated Rinzen Dorjee's presence. Dongtuk was a scrappy kid—his big mouth sometimes got him in trouble—so it was advantageous to have a sturdy brother nearby for protection.

Every June, Dongtuk's father's family would pack up the essentials of their household—bags of tsampa, dried cheese and meat, blankets and cooking utensils—and head out to the pasturelands. They would erect a traditional black felt tent, made of yak wool, for a few weeks at a time before moving their herds to fresh grasslands.

The summer that Dongtuk turned seven, his father decided to bring him along. That meant he would need to ride a horse, a skill that, surprisingly for a Tibetan boy, he had not yet acquired. His father had more than a dozen horses. He selected the smallest, a grayish brown mare, for Dongtuk, but when he was hoisted into the saddle, Dongtuk tensed with terror. For the first time he could see the tops of the heads of his half brothers, and he didn't like the sensation.

The horse was walking alongside the others at first, well behaved enough, but then it picked up speed, galloping far ahead. The big brown dogs who protected the herd from wolves were barking behind him. He raced along the grassland toward the mountains, where the snow was still clinging. Dongtuk felt like he was running away. He would never see home again; he would go out into the wild and find his way in the world.

But then suddenly he was on the ground, landing smack on his bottom, sore and dazed. The dogs' barking was louder and louder until one of them, brownish gray like his horse, caught him by the shin, the teeth digging into his flesh.

The first person to reach him was his stepmother, Wangmo, who dusted him off, muttering prayers. The children were laughing, but she hushed them. It was lucky, she said, that the bite was only a surface wound and that Dongtuk's foot hadn't been caught in the stirrup. He could have been dragged to his death.

His father never spoke to him about the incident. It was clear that this nearsighted boy who couldn't ride a horse wasn't cut out to be a nomad.

CHAPTER

I 2

. . .

A MONK'S LIFE

Kirti Monastery, 2014.

DONGTUK WAS ELATED WHEN HIS MOTHER SUGGESTED
he become a monk. He wasn't old enough to think through the vows
of celibacy and sobriety, but he knew of no greater honor. He'd grown
up watching how visitors to his home would prostrate themselves before the portrait of his uncle, the reincarnate lama. One devotee was
so overcome with reverence she burst into tears. The community of
monks and nuns, the *sangha,* is one of the "three jewels" that are most

treasured by Tibetan Buddhists, the repository of learning and spirituality for the society. As far as Dongtuk was concerned, monks were
demigods. And being a monk wouldn't require him to get back on a
horse.

"The monk's life is good. You will get an education," Sonam told
her son. "You won't have responsibility for supporting a family. You
will not have the same suffering as the others." Dongtuk didn't need
further convincing.

A single mother like Sonam was not expected to sacrifice her only
son to the monastery. More often, families with multiple sons would
designate one to become a monk, which would gain the family spiritual merit, ensure that one family member would be literate, and re-
duce the competition to inherit the family property. Without a
husband and as a disabled woman, Sonam was badly in need of a young
man to help her with the animals and the household. But she put her
own needs aside, recognizing that her son was ill suited for life in the
village. Moreover, she saw that he possessed a spark of intellectual
curiosity that would allow him to thrive in the monastery.

Many families in Meruma belonged to Kirti Monastery because of
its long association with the Mei rulers. Since Kirti is on the west side
of Ngaba and Meruma to the east, it truly felt like Sonam was sending
her son away. Tears welled in her eyes as she delivered him by taxi to
the monastery.

When Dongtuk arrived, he removed his threadbare clothing and
bathed in a large vat of steaming water. The monks scrubbed seven
years of nomadic dirt from his skin until it was pink and raw. They
cleaned under his fingernails and shaved his hair. It was the first bath
of Dongtuk's life and it was in effect a baptism. He was assigned a new
first name, Lobsang, meaning "noble minded," which is part of the
name of all Kirti monks. He put on a clean crimson robe, which to
Dongtuk was a symbol of manhood.

After Kirti was rebuilt in the 1980s, it was larger than before,
sprawling over hundreds of acres. The golden roofs added in the 1990s
seemed to reflect the glinting sunlight throughout Ngaba. There were

libraries and fields, classrooms, art studios, and residential compounds. The tallest structure on the grounds—in fact, the tallest in Ngaba—was the 161-foot-high stupa, a tower-like shrine with the lower level gleaming white and round like the body of a Buddha squatting on a square throne. Chapels on each level contained paintings and statues. Near the top was a platform with a railing; along the wall were painted the giant almond eyes of Buddha looking out over Ngaba. From that vantage point, one could see from the river in the south to the mountains in the north and the road leading out to Golok, the Wild West.

The most important ceremonies took place at the big assembly hall, a two-story building with a large verandah and a gilded slanting roof. Over the entrance hung split door curtains decorated with a dharma wheel and two stags facing each other, a popular symbol in Buddhism. A portrait of Kirti Rinpoche hung above it. Although he lived in exile in India, he remained the head of the Kirti monasteries inside Tibet, the original monastery in Dzorge as well as the now-larger branch in Ngaba.

In front of the assembly hall was a large flagstone quadrangle that served as the main gathering place for public events. During ceremonies and debate the monks would fill the courtyard wearing bright golden hats that looked like cocks' combs, the symbol of the Gelug school. Next to a small stream that ran through the monastery grounds was a general store well stocked with candy, crackers, and ice cream.

A monastery sounds like an austere environment, but for Dongtuk it was an oversized playground. Near the stupa was a gigantic heap of dirt left from an unfinished construction project. The boys were happy that nobody had bothered to shovel it away. You could slide down if you paid the older boys—who appointed themselves guardians of these mountains. Since they didn't have money, they used empty packets of juice from the general store as currency. The chapels, dimly lit and redolent of incense and butter lamps, had nooks and crannies to explore, walls filled with paintings of bodhisattvas and deities. Other paintings depicted fearsome demons with glaring red eyes. The mysteries were infinite. Behind the congregation hall was the chapel dedicated to the king, displaying the statues he'd been given by the Dalai Lama during his visit to Lhasa in 1956. Across the stream was a small chapel dedicated to Palzel, the deity who was the protector of Kirti and its monks and who was believed capable of teleporting himself anywhere in the world in a blink of an eye. To a Tibetan boy, it was like having your own personal superhero to watch over you.

So many Meruma boys were sent to Kirti that Dongtuk didn't have to miss old friends. Phuntsog had arrived a few months before him. They didn't hang out much—Dongtuk had developed a taste for basketball and Phuntsog liked to lift weights—but Dongtuk found it comforting to see familiar faces from the village. His half brother, Rinzen Dorjee, arrived a little later. It was at the monastery that they finally were able to bond. Dongtuk had always been somewhat jealous of his brother's easy athleticism and the obvious affection he enjoyed from their father, but at the monastery, Dongtuk had the advantage of being the better student. It brought balance to their relationship.

MONASTERY SCHOOLS ARE OFTEN criticized for their old-fashioned ways. Students are instructed by rote memorization and are disciplined with the rod when their eyes invariably droop from the tedium. Kirti, however, was more like an elite boarding school. The school, which had opened in 1994, taught math and science as well as the traditional subjects like Buddhist philosophy and Tibetan language. The Dalai Lama, frustrated by the inadequacy of his own education as a young monk, had called for Tibetan monasteries to offer a more modern curriculum. Many Tibetan writers, filmmakers, and academics were monastery-educated. Kirti itself produced notable figures such as the vice president of PEN International's Tibetan Writers Abroad, Lobsang Chokta Trotsik, and Go Sherab Gyatso, an essayist and blogger.

The young monks engaged in a ritualized form of debating, as integral to their studies as it is among Talmudic scholars. One group of monks would be assigned to defend a thesis, and the others to challenge it—punctuating the question with a sharp clap of the hands. If one took too long to answer a question, the other monks would protest with a round of three claps, indicating disapproval. A successful defense of a thesis would be approved with a vigorous round of stomping on the pavement, the monastic equivalent of a high five. The subject itself might be existential—what is the meaning of the Buddhist dharma or the impermanence of worldly phenomena—but it was carried out with such gusto to make it exercise for the body as well as the mind. The debates took place outdoors in the large courtyard in front of the main assembly hall, where members of the public could watch. Sometimes the debates lasted until eleven P.M. Dongtuk would tumble into bed past midnight, exhausted and exhilarated. He loved it. He was one of the best debaters in his age group, which gained him status not usually afforded to a short, unathletic boy with poor eyesight.

When she came to visit, Dongtuk's mother commended herself on her decision to send Dongtuk to the monastery. It was a place where he would be safe and happy. Sonam was too busy making a living to pay attention to politics, and so she wasn't aware of the extent to which Kirti was in the crosshairs of leftists within the Communist Party.

Tibet policy was handled by the United Front Work Department, a Soviet-inspired organization designed to coordinate relations between the Party and outsiders, including ethnic minorities. At a meeting in 1994 known as the Third National Forum on Work in Tibet, the Party directed the United Front to rein in Tibetan religious life. "The struggle between ourselves and the Dalai clique is not a matter of religious belief nor a matter of the question of autonomy; it is a matter of securing the unity of our country and opposing splittism," read an internal version of the statement produced at the forum. The monasteries, they claimed, were breeding grounds for activism.

The new policy criminalized many aspects of Tibetan culture and religion. In the past, Communist Party members had been prohibited from visiting temples and monasteries and keeping shrines in their homes, but now the ban was extended to all government employees. That was a large slice of the workforce in a Communist system and included teachers, bus drivers, conductors, and the millions who worked for state-owned enterprises. All monks and nuns were also targeted for what was called "patriotic education," indoctrination sessions to foster loyalty to the Communist Party.

At first these new policies applied only to what the Chinese designated as the Tibet Autonomous Region, centered around Lhasa. As part of Sichuan province, Ngaba was still enjoying the intellectual and cultural renaissance that had begun the decade before. But by the late 1990s, the United Front decided to expand the campaign, and their first target was Kirti, as one of the largest and most influential monasteries in the region.

It started so abruptly and dramatically that monks remembered the exact date: June 15, 1998. A work team of officials from the United Front and the State Administration for Religious Affairs showed up at Kirti. They set up a long table and chairs at the entrance to the assembly hall, a long gold-peaked building raised three feet off the ground, which gave the impression of being on a stage. All of Kirti's monks, some of them quite elderly, were directed to sit cross-legged on the pavement in front like children—a breach of etiquette that was shocking to the younger monks who had never seen anybody position themselves above their seniors in that way. They also were appalled by the way the Communist Party officials were chain-smoking. Tibetans don't smoke as much as Han Chinese and certainly never in a monastery.

In the morning, the Party officials were shaded by the elegant wooden eaves in front of the assembly hall, but by noon, the sun shifted so that it was shining directly on the table. Then came a flash, a bang, and flames licking the white tablecloth. A cigarette lighter that belonged to a chubby-faced, chain-smoking official had exploded. The monks erupted. They clapped and cheered and laughed so hard that they were rolling on the pavement. The Communist Party controlled China, there was no doubt about that, but the sun was aligned with the Tibetans.

Kirti's monks were to undergo these patriotic education lectures intermittently for most of the following decade. Loudspeakers were set up inside the congregation hall to broadcast denunciations of the Dalai Lama. The essential message: "You must love your nation first before you can have religious freedom." A sample essay question was "How can one become a model monk or nun abiding by the principle of loving one's country and loving one's religion and respecting the law?" And another pamphlet insisted that "the so-called Tibetan Independence is a creation of the imperialist forces with the evil aim of dismembering the People's Republic of China."

The sessions lasted from nine A.M. to six P.M., while senior monks were called in after hours for private chats that turned into interrogation sessions. The Communist Party demanded that the monks get registration cards, obtainable only after they signed what were in effect oaths of loyalty to the government and denunciations of the Dalai Lama. Many refused and quit the monastery.

Kirti became a hotbed of unrest. The young monks became restless and angry. They pulled tricks on the Communist Party cadres that started as pranks and eventually turned into sabotage. The work team members used to park their cars and motorcycles in front of the general store. One day, they finished the patriotic education session and found all the cars had been vandalized or stolen. The monks managed to scale high concrete pillars where the cadres had installed loudspeakers for their propaganda. The loudspeakers were removed; in their place, they attached "Free Tibet" stickers. They also scrawled slogans on the *lungta*—the square paper prayer flags—and scattered them through the monastery grounds. Soon there were thousands of the pieces of paper wafting around the monastery grounds. The strong winds lifted them into the juniper bushes and onto rooftops. They stuck in the mud and floated in the stream. It was impossible to remove them all.

These activities had begun a few years before Dongtuk arrived at Kirti, and at first he was oblivious. He was too preoccupied with playing, exploring, and learning. But in 2002, just a year after he arrived, the government declared that his school would be closed. This was a huge blow to Kirti and to Dongtuk personally. The ministry also began enforcing a long-standing but frequently ignored rule that nobody could be a monk under the age of eighteen. The rationale was that the monasteries were not to interfere with secular education, but it went against the age-old tradition of sending boys for their education at age seven. Despite the ban, the underage monks remained in the monastery, but they had little to do, no classes to attend, no debates.

The monastery was in theory self-regulating, with a management committee made up of senior monks who were supposed to follow the orders of the religious affairs administration. There were occasional inspections to make sure that underage monks were not in the monastery. Often enough, somebody on the committee would get a tip that an inspection was imminent. It was in everybody's best interest to avoid a confrontation that would disrupt the "harmonious" atmosphere that the Chinese government claimed to maintain.

The young monks kept a set of extra clothing in their rooms so they were prepared for occasions when they had to vacate the monastery in a hurry. It was like a fire drill: Put on your jeans and T-shirts as quickly as possible. Stash your crimson robes under the floorboards. Grab some money and head into town. Across from the Tibetan Middle School were sports fields where the boys could play basketball.

Dongtuk remembered one surprise inspection. He was in his house studying when he heard the voices coming down the alley. He realized immediately that it was too late to slip away. The monks at Kirti didn't live in traditional dormitories. They were assigned to narrow two-story earthen houses owned and maintained by their own families. When those families came in from the countryside to make pilgrimages or shop, they would stay in the houses. Young monks usually lived with relatives—in Dongtuk's case, he lived with a cousin. The houses had kitchens, and the monks generally did their own shopping and cooking. Almost like townhouses, the buildings stood close together, lining both sides of rutted mud alleys that twisted and turned like a maze. It was easy to get lost, but hard to escape. The houses had no backyards, only a courtyard in front with a single gate.

Dongtuk was terrified of what might happen. He had heard rumors that if the Chinese caught you at the monastery they would force you to go to a Chinese school, which as far as he was concerned was the equivalent of being sent to prison. He looked around for a place to hide. There was a crawl space under the floorboards of the kitchen where food and supplies were kept. Dongtuk climbed inside, lowering the boards over his head. He heard the sound of two men coming into his house and through the gaps between the uneven floorboards he got a glimpse of heavy boots of the type that belonged to soldiers or police. He squeezed his eyes shut in the way of young children, feeling irrationally that if he couldn't see others, then they couldn't see him. He was so frightened that he remained curled up that way long after the inspectors had moved on.

CHAPTER

1 3

· · ·

COMPASSION

Worshippers sitting outside Kirti Monastery, 2014.

AFEW BLOCKS AWAY FROM KIRTI LIVED A WOMAN NAMED
Pema who ran a stall in the market selling socks and counterfeit Nike
sneakers. It would be a stretch to say that she was unusually pious
since Buddhist devotion was the norm for so many Tibetans in Ngaba,
but she was nonetheless a constant presence at the monastery.

Pema would go to the monastery to circumambulate by six A.M.,
when it was often still dark, the result of a decree by Mao Zedong to

set all of the clocks in China to Beijing time, a thousand miles to the east. Along the way, she would encounter neighbors heading in the same direction, but at that early hour, people didn't chat; they would just nod their greetings. The circumambulation route was enclosed by a series of long, low-slung covered corridors that protected the prayer wheels. Worshippers would recite the mantra of compassion, *om mani padme hum,* while turning the wheels, a ritual called the *kora.* With each turn, the prayers would be exponentially multiplied, in effect released to the world for the benefit of all sentient beings. The entire circuit ran for nearly a mile, turning hundreds of the wheels. The wheels at Kirti are colorfully painted vertical cylinders. You had to go clockwise only using your right arm, which would ache before long. Pema navigated at a brisk pace, often passing the older worshippers, many of whom were supported by walking sticks or crutches, or were dragging along their grandchildren. Pema could complete the circuit in less than ninety minutes, and then she would do it again, and sometimes a third time. She tracked her progress by counting her prayer beads.

Pema lived around the corner from Kirti, in what was known as the *thawa,* a Tibetan term for the neighborhood adjacent to a monastery. She and her neighbors were the audience for the rituals and provided help as needed. She had been one of the many volunteers who helped with the monastery's rebuilding in the 1980s, transporting bricks and construction materials, even when she was pregnant and then, afterward, with her newborn son strapped to her back.

The monastery was an everyday carnival of color, a joyous celebration of spirituality. Although Pema was too poor for jewelry, many of the women draped themselves in beads of coral and turquoise, braids tied behind their backs. Both men and women wore ribboned hats as fanciful as those at an Easter parade. Each prayer wheel was a work of art, intricately painted with mantras and Buddhist symbols. Off the main corridors were separate niches containing prayer wheels the size of merry-go-rounds that required several people to turn. They chanted and sang in unison as they pushed. Exhausted by their efforts, the elders would pass the rest of the day on wooden benches that lined the courtyard in front of the congregation hall. They spun hand-held prayer wheels on little spindles and gossiped among themselves, sometimes pausing to watch the spectacle of the monks debating.

Pema worked at the market, so she couldn't linger with the elders. But she usually returned at seven P.M. for another round. Pema believed her devotion would give her merit, ensuring the likelihood of a favorable reincarnation and disseminating good karma to all beings. But even in the here and now of this impermanent life, it was the ritual that gave meaning to her existence.

"I wasn't tired when I did the *kora*. That's when I felt happiest and calmest," Pema said.

Pema had grown up on the less desirable south side of the river. She moved into the monastery neighborhood in 1983, when her father arranged her marriage. She was eighteen years old at the time, an exceptionally diligent girl with a meek, unthreatening beauty. She was barely five feet tall with full, round cheeks sloping down to an evenly spaced smile of tiny white teeth like Chiclets. Her hair was parted low on her forehead with two long braids that fell down her back. These attributes should have set her up for a decent marriage, but for reasons she wouldn't learn until much later, the man selected as her groom was decades older with a chronic breathing ailment that left him gasping for breath. And he was already married. Her father was well aware of this—the first wife was his older sister, Pema's aunt.

Although the government didn't do anything to stop it, polygamy wasn't exactly legal, and Pema's father seemed sheepish about the match. The tradition was for the bride to be escorted to the new family's home by her father, but Pema's father sent her teenaged brother instead. The family didn't even bother giving Pema the customary wedding clothes—she wore a robe of the cheapest hybrid fur—and was served a meager wedding meal of fried bread and barley beer.

Pema's bridegroom turned out to be even poorer than her own family. He had no yaks or sheep, so there was no butter or cheese, no dung for fuel. He and his first wife, the aunt, lived in a single room, barely two hundred square feet, bare of furniture except for wooden benches along the walls. They didn't have quilts or blankets, so they wrapped themselves at night in their sheepskin robes. Pema, who had been informed of the impending nuptials only a few days earlier, spent the first weeks of her marriage in tears, cowering in the corner of her little house trying to avoid intimate relations with her husband.

Pema's husband had been assigned three *mu* of land—about half an acre—in 1982 when the cooperatives were disbanded, but his lung condition left him unable to do heavy labor. His first wife was lame and almost an invalid. That left Pema alone to farm the family's barley. She would rise at dawn, drink black tea, and go out to do the plowing and weeding, come back at noon for a lunch of *thukpa,* a Tibetan noodle with a meatless broth, then go out to work again. At harvest time, she had to cut the barley with a scythe, load it into a wheelbarrow, and push it up a dirt path to unload it at the family's home.

When Pema started feeling weak and nauseous, she went to the hospital, thinking she was suffering from exhaustion. She was in for a shock. She had not been entirely successful in avoiding her husband and nobody had explained to her that sex could make you pregnant.

The birth of her first son provided a respite. A boy brought honor to the family. Pema finally figured it out: she'd been given to the childless older couple to breed. Her father sent Pema's sister to help out with the baby. The family served her tsampa, this time with cheese, as a reward for the success of the mission. With money from other relatives, they were able to expand the house into a second floor.

Soon the neighborhood got electricity. The road outside their house was paved and renamed Tuanjie Lu, meaning Solidarity Street, a favorite Communist Party moniker attached to streets and parks throughout the country.

Then there came in rapid succession another boy and a girl—and five years later, when she thought her body was too depleted for any more, yet another boy. That meant more expenses, since the school, nominally free, required cash for books and supplies that amounted to roughly $15 per year per student. She managed to get her two older boys into Kirti Monastery under the sponsorship of her youngest brother, a monk, but that left two more.

Pema realized there was no way she could afford schooling costs on top of her husband's medications. The barley she cultivated was just enough to feed the family. So she decided to abandon her little plot, which like much farmland in China would soon go fallow, and start in business. Her husband had a friend who was a wholesaler of fur hats, and they arranged for Pema to sell them at the market near Kirti. She couldn't afford space on the sidewalk, so she set up a wooden cart on the grating over the sewer. It was a little smelly, but Pema wore one of the face masks that had become ubiquitous in China.

One night in 2005, Pema's husband woke up gasping for breath and she brought him to the Ngaba People's Hospital, where she was told he needed to go to a larger hospital in the prefecture capital of Barkham. As she was trying to borrow money for the journey, he died. He was carried to a hillside above Kirti Monastery for the traditional sky burial, his body picked apart by vultures so that it would be returned to nature without a trace. Then Pema, a dutiful wife to the end, carried his crushed bones to Lhasa to be blessed.

Pema was devastated. Although she had been forced into the marriage, her husband was a kind man who appreciated the sacrifices she'd made for him. His disability prevented him from drinking, womanizing, and gambling, unlike some of the husbands of her friends at the market.

And yet after a few months, Pema had to admit that her standard of living had improved. As a widow, she received a stipend of about $20 a month plus rations of rice and flour. She no longer had to pay for her husband's medicine. Her second son had been recognized as the reincarnation of a lama—not a very famous lama, but it was enough to raise her status. She expanded the little mud house to three rooms, adding a shrine with portraits of the Dalai Lama and Kirti Rinpoche. She got a black-and-white television.

It was after her husband's death that Pema began making the daily visits to the monastery. She had free time now, being no longer obliged to make breakfast for her husband.

Pema continued to run her stall at the market. But she switched to selling socks and shoes. The Dalai Lama in 2006 had called for Tibetans to stop wearing clothing trimmed with fur in order to avoid participation in the trade of endangered wildlife. To the dismay of the Chinese government, Tibetans responded by torching all their furs in big bonfires. Pema was among those who answered the call, burning her entire stock of fox fur hats. Each hat sold for the equivalent of $50, so the sacrifice consumed much of her life savings. But her new business, selling counterfeit American sneakers, better reflected modern Tibetan fashion trends. With other merchants, she would go every few months to Chengdu, where she could buy her shoes wholesale for 24 yuan ($3) and then sell them for 35 ($5).

IN HER FORTIES, PEMA in effect became a foster mother. One of her cousins, a relatively well-to-do man who owned a bar and shop in Lhasa, came to confide in her about the difficulties he was having with his twelve-year-old daughter, Dechen. The girl was the only child from his first marriage, which had ended badly. Now he was remarried and the girl was always fighting with her stepmother, a woman Pema knew from the market. The cousin offered Pema financial assistance if she would help him with this troublesome child. He warned that the girl was stubborn and argumentative. But even without the money, Pema was willing. With her husband dead, she needed somebody to care for; and her heart went out to this scorned child.

Dechen was as tiny as Pema with a downy heart-shaped face, wispy baby eyebrows, and bangs that hung in a curtain over her eyes. She wore her hair Chinese-style, pulled back in a ponytail. Dechen attached herself quickly to Pema, pouring out her woes. Her own mother had been sent away by her father soon after Dechen was born, leaving Dechen to be raised mainly by the hated stepmother. Dechen saw her mother just once afterward when she was about ten years old and her friends brought her to the village where her mother was living to arrange a reunion. Her mother, who had a younger child in her arms, burst into tears when she saw Dechen. She cried and cried and couldn't stop. Dechen wasn't able to ask her any of the questions she'd intended. So after thirty minutes of watching this sobbing stranger, Dechen went home.

In Ngaba, it was common for children to be raised by a single mother, but not for a child to be motherless. Dechen's unusual situation, along with her small size and scrappy personality, made her a magnet for bullies.

"*Mei you mama,*" they taunted her. You have no mother.

Dechen attended the Ngaba #2 primary school, which taught only in Chinese and had mostly Chinese students. By that time, parents in Ngaba had the option of sending their children to a Tibetan-language primary school, but Dechen's father had chosen the Chinese school, thinking his daughter might land a secure government job if she spoke fluent Chinese. Working in the civil service was the preferred career path for Tibetans who didn't want to be farmers or herders, since large private employers were mostly Chinese and tended not to hire Tibetans. Dechen was a strong-willed girl who didn't always take direction from her father, but on this point she agreed. Besides, Dechen was relieved to be studying Chinese rather than Tibetan, which she thought far more difficult with its intricate writing system and grammar.

Also, Dechen was, by her own admission, a television junkie and there was limited programming in Tibetan. All her favorite cartoons were in Chinese. She also loved the war movies, thinly disguised Communist Party propaganda that were a staple of Chinese television. They usually featured tales of dashing People's Liberation Army soldiers battling the Japanese or some other capitalist enemy. Dechen had a sweet spot for those handsome men in uniform. Whenever one of the Chinese soldiers was killed onscreen, Dechen would mutter a Tibetan prayer. Otherwise she showed little affinity for Buddhism or Tibetan tradition. She didn't like to wear Tibetan clothing or jewelry.

At school, her friends were both Chinese and Tibetan. When the class sang patriotic songs ("Without the Communist Party, There Would Be No New China"), Dechen sang wholeheartedly.

It was hard to generalize, though, about the younger generation. Pema had another young relative who was just as opinionated as Pema, but whose views veered in the opposite direction.

Lhundup Tso was her husband's niece and a few years older than Dechen. She studied at the Tibetan Middle School in the same class as Pema's youngest son. Lhundup Tso's family came from a village too far out of town for the girl to commute, so she boarded at the school. When she wanted a good home-cooked meal, she would pop in to Pema's house. Pema was always happy to serve a meal to Lhundup Tso, especially since she thought the girl looked poorly fed. She was tall and lanky with that slapped-cheek ruddiness of many Tibetan children. Her arms and legs protruded from too-small hand-me-down clothing. Her parents were barley farmers who were even poorer and more tragedy-prone than Pema. They had four daughters, the oldest of whom had been killed in a freak car accident. Another daughter had gone to India to study.

Lhundup Tso was the baby of the family. She was high-spirited and an incessant talker, which alternately amused and irritated the others. She would ask questions most people were afraid to ask. She grilled her grandparents about what life was like during the Cultural Revolution, touching on all the forbidden subjects. Lhundup Tso wanted to know everything about the Dalai Lama.

"His Holiness," as she referred to him. "I don't understand why he had to leave Tibet. Why can't he come back? Why aren't we independent?"

Pema didn't always agree with her niece, but she appreciated that the girl thought about things other than money, clothing, and electronics, the obsessions of her oldest son.

"This freedom you're talking about; how are we going to get it under the Chinese?" Pema challenged her niece. "The Chinese are too strong. They won't allow it. Anyway, you shouldn't talk about these things. Our family doesn't have money or position. They can't help you if you get into trouble," Pema scolded the girl.

These kids didn't understand how her generation had suffered. Pema thought back to the times that they had had to recite their prayers in silence and how she helped her father carve a niche in the wall so they could hide their butter lamp. A neighbor next door was caught with a lamp and received a three-year prison sentence.

These days, Pema felt satisfied. The Chinese government was providing her with food aid and money. She had the three jewels, as Buddhists call them—Buddha, the dharma, and the *sangha* (the clergy). By her thinking, it was enough freedom that she didn't have to whisper her prayers. She could go to the monastery every day. Still, Pema realized she couldn't take anything for granted. The atmosphere in Ngaba had grown tenser with the arrival in 2007 of a hard-line Communist Party secretary for the prefecture. People thought the secretary, Shi Jun, disliked Tibetans, passing them over for government jobs, promoting cadres who spoke not a word of Tibetan. She worried about Kirti Monastery, which she felt was as much a part of herself as her own home. The crackdown had had a direct impact on her family. Her second son, the reincarnate monk, had been enrolled at Kirti, but left for India at the age of fourteen in order to continue his studies. There was nothing political in his decision to leave the country, but Pema feared his proximity to the exile government might make him unable to return home.

Another worry was a Chinese construction project in the mountains forty miles northwest of Ngaba. The Chinese government had long eyed Tibet's glaciers and alpine lakes as a solution to the chronic water shortages elsewhere. Now they were drawing up plans to divert water from the glacial lakes of Nyenbo Yurtse (Mount Nianbao in Chinese) to more arid regions. It was one of many ambitious water projects under way in China that embodied Mao's exhortation that "man should remake nature." This was completely antithetical to the reverence for nature that grew out of the animist strain of Tibetan Buddhism. Nyenbo Yurtse was revered as a sacred mountain, and believed to be the birthplace of the Golok tribe, who were closely related to the people of Ngaba. Runoff from the mountain lakes fed the Ngaqu River, which ran through Ngaba and provided the irrigation for the barley and vegetable fields in the valley. The Ngaqu was already too shallow, with islets of sand appearing in the dry season between the braided channels of water. Chinese crews sometimes quarried the sand for construction. Ngaba residents feared their town would disappear if the river dried up.

Pema saw this activity as an existential threat. She had grown up near the southern banks of the river—she had done laundry in the river as a girl. Her family had land in the same area where surveyors had started working in the 1980s. Her relatives had been told they couldn't plant barley on their land or build any new structures. One Tibetan family that had disregarded the ban had their house demolished without compensation. An improbably large new bridge across the river was also under construction. Pema recognized the signs that something very big was coming. Tibetans complained they couldn't get a clear answer about what was on the drawing board. She too had heard the rumors that the government would build apartments for 60,000 workers, some of whom she'd heard would be working on the water diversion project.

"There are too many people in mainland China. They need our land to give themselves more room to grow," Pema complained to her friends.

Pema was conflicted about the Chinese. She was a devout Buddhist, who took seriously not just the ritual but the obligation to behave with compassion toward all beings, including Chinese migrants. Many of them ran their own stalls at the market, and she could appreciate that they were hardworking women, some of them widows who like herself were struggling to survive. But they had no religion for their comfort, no belief in the afterlife. They would die, thinking that was the end and that they would merely turn into dust. She felt more pity than hostility toward these Chinese. Still, she didn't want more of them in her town.

CHAPTER

14

· · ·

THE
PARTY ANIMAL

Dancers and models in Tibetan costume, Jiuzhaigou, 2007.

TECHNOLOGY MOVED FORWARD. HISTORY SLIPPED BACKWARD.
In 2001, Beijing was named as the host country for the 2008 Summer Olympics, affirming China's status as the world's new superpower. In anticipation of the games, the government embarked on a manic building spree. Not just stadiums but also airports, railroads, towers and bridges, dams and water diversions, ring roads, overpasses

and underpasses, townhouses and condominiums. Every provincial capital became a megacity. No feat was beyond the genius of China's finest engineers. The world's highest-elevation railroad was inaugurated in 2006, traversing more than one thousand miles of the Tibetan plateau, part of it permafrost, to connect Lhasa with Qinghai province. Each passenger had a personal oxygen supply. China was building new airports at a rate of four per year. In Ngaba prefecture alone, a new airport had opened in 2003 in Songpan; another was planned in Hongyuan, only thirty miles from downtown Ngaba, at the edge of the marshlands. It was as though the engineers were bending the laws of physics, time and distance shrunk, closing the divide between Tibet and the heartland of modern China.

Just when life should have become more convenient for Tibetans, it became more controlled. With economic development came more Chinese troops and paramilitary, the *wujing,* or armed police. Chinese paratroopers had been conducting airborne exercises with motorized hang gliders in the marshlands since 1999, and the presence of the military was increasingly obtrusive.

An enclave to the west of Kirti Monastery just off the busy main road had been designated for the military and was off-limits to Tibetans. A checkpoint erected outside the base became notorious for harassing Tibetan drivers. If you had a broken taillight or didn't fasten your seatbelt—and happened to be Tibetan—you'd be stopped and extorted for money. A monk from Qinghai province who frequently traveled to Ngaba to buy supplies for the monastery remembers being in a van in 2007 when the driver made a wrong turn and ended up at the entrance to the military base outside Ngaba. The soldiers ordered everybody out of the van, kicked them, and made them empty their pockets and bags. Unfortunately, the monks were carrying 3,000 Chinese yuan (roughly $400) of the monastery's money, which the soldiers pocketed. The monastery had connections and lodged a protest, recovering about half the money. But the shakedowns continued.

On another trip the monk was in a van that was stopped by the armed police for inspection. One passenger was found to have a medallion with a portrait of the Dalai Lama. The policeman grabbed it and threw it into the dirt, threatening to destroy it if the man didn't pay him 2,000 yuan. The man paid up.

By the mid-2000s, many Tibetans had phones with cameras, so police took to inspecting the phones to make sure Dalai Lama photos weren't lurking within.

Checkpoints proliferated. It had always been a challenge for Tibetans to obtain passports to leave the country, but now they had trouble simply traveling inside China. It was a throwback to the day when you weren't allowed to leave your commune. The rules varied from place to place and month to month, but you could never be assured of the ability to get where you wanted to go. Chinese authorities required special permits to travel to Dham, the last Tibetan city before the border with Nepal, effectively killing off the livelihood of many traders. Travel permits were often required for Tibetans to go to Lhasa. Sometimes you needed a permit just to travel within Ngaba prefecture. A young man from Hongyuan told me that in order to get a travel permit to bring his ailing father to consult with a doctor at the Ngaba People's Hospital, he needed a letter of permission from the county police, who in turn needed a letter from the village police as well as the village head and the doctor at the hospital confirming the time of the appointment.

The bureaucratic requirements were challenging for Tibetans raised in a nomadic culture that wasn't strong on paperwork. You couldn't get a travel permit—or for that matter a railway ticket or a plane ticket—without a *hukou,* the household registration document required of all Chinese citizens. Many Tibetan babies weren't registered either because their parents feared falling afoul of family size limits or simply because they were born at home and their families hadn't bothered. One nomadic family with fifteen children said they'd been trying to get their paperwork straightened out for years, but were told they couldn't get documents unless all fifteen showed up at the same time, which was impossible since they were adults scattered around the country.

Despite the new airports and the new rail lines, Tibetans continued to roam the plateau as they always had, on horses or the modern-
day equivalent, motorcycles, which could travel off-road and bypass
the checkpoints. Or they got off their overloaded vans and walked
around the checkpoints. They chafed at the restrictions that seemed
to apply only to them. They longed for the same freedoms as their
Chinese counterparts. Their discontent spawned a new generation of
dissidents.

IN HIS FORMATIVE YEARS, Tsepey was into partying, not politics.
He was born in 1977 in Charo township, a nomadic community at the
far eastern edge of Ngaba county, beyond Meruma, where his father's
family had settled in the 1940s after fleeing the atrocities of Muslim
warlord Ma Bufang. Tsepey was the ninth of eleven children, a large
brood even by Tibetan standards. His father was frequently away on
business and his mother out with the animals, so each child was responsible for raising the next younger one. The grass around Charo
was some of the best quality on the plateau, so the yaks and sheep
grew strong, giving the nomads abundant food, but their lifestyle was
far more primitive even than in villages like Meruma. At the cusp of
the twenty-first century, Tsepey's family lived as though they were in
the nineteenth. They had no telephone and no electricity, not even
candles; they relied on lamps made with their own butter. They had
only animals for transportation. The nearest government school was a
day's ride on horseback, while the center of Ngaba was two days away.
Tsepey was a teenager before he went to town and saw shops. He had
no idea who was the president of China. Nowadays, the land is fenced
off and families assigned their own pastures, but during his childhood
the family moved every few months so that the animals could graze on
fresh grass.

Like his brothers, Tsepey was sent to a monastery as a child to be
educated, but he stayed for only two years. Tsepey was not a studious

boy—he learned elementary reading skills, not much else—but he had something else going for him: he was exceptionally good-looking. As he grew into adulthood, he shot up to over six feet tall and his chest filled out. He had a cleft chin and sculpted cheekbones, and when his hair turned prematurely silver, he looked like nothing less than a Tibetan George Clooney.

Tsepey's looks and charm went far. A friend who was a well-known folk singer helped him sign on with an entertainment troupe that performed at Jiuzhaigou, a resort and national park at the northern end of Ngaba prefecture.

The resort was developed in the 1990s and had modern, Western-style hotels, a Sheraton and a Hilton among them, and was popular with Chinese package tourists who flew into the new airport in Songpan. With more disposable income and freedom to travel, newly middle-class Chinese were keen to see the exotic Wild West of their country. Besides the spectacular waterfalls, sparkling aquamarine lakes, and karst peaks, the resort offered tour groups a sanitized glimpse of Tibetan culture. Chinese tourists would dress up in Tibetan costumes to pose for photographs and buy souvenir versions of prayer beads.

The resort offered nightly galas with Tibetan dancers—or Chinese dancers dressed as Tibetans. Sometimes Tsepey would sing and dance, but mostly he announced the other performers and strutted the runway in fanciful Tibetan costumes, chubas in dazzling colors, felt hats with streaming ribbons, swashbuckling sashes and swords.

Tsepey's family disapproved. His father said that only beggars performed for money. But Tsepey loved the job. The pay was good; the lodgings comfortable, the food and drink abundant. Tsepey hadn't cared for the sobriety and celibacy associated with the monastic lifestyle. He liked to drink beer and smoke cigarettes with his coworkers, most of them Chinese or Qiang, an ethnic minority related to the Tibetans but considered closer to the Chinese.

The nightly shows extolled the unity of all peoples in the motherland and the happiness of the Tibetans living under Chinese rule. "The Tibetans and Chinese come from a single mother," they sang.

"Oh, these Tibetans, the minute they open their mouths, out comes a song. They move their feet and it is a dance," the emcee would tell the audience.

Eventually, the condescension got on Tsepey's nerves. He found he was constantly biting his tongue, fearful he might lose his friends or his job if he said what he really thought. The tipping point came in 2003 when a high-ranking Chinese official, Zhu Rongji, who was then premier, visited the resort. The Chinese performers were buzzing with excitement. After he left, they took turns sitting in the chair he'd sat in, posing for pictures. One of them remarked on Tsepey's obvious disinterest.

"If it were some Tibetan lama who came to visit, you couldn't wait to sit in the chair and fall at his feet," Tsepey's coworker chided.

Tsepey replied that there was nothing sacred about a Communist Party official. The coworker took offense and launched into a tirade.

"After everything the Chinese government has done for the Tibetan people. They built houses. They brought electricity. They're building roads." He mentioned the new airport and the railroad to Lhasa.

The men bickered. Tsepey said that the Chinese were building for themselves, not for the Tibetans, and that they were taking the Tibetans' land and natural resources.

"The Chinese government treats us like little children. If we cry, they give us candy," Tsepey retorted.

It was more of a debate than a fight. No one cursed anyone else. No punches were exchanged. Still, the next day Tsepey was called into the boss's office and given a quiet warning. "You need to behave more like the others," he was told.

Tsepey never felt the same pleasure again performing for Chinese tourists. He quit his job before they got a chance to fire him. He had been sending most of his salary back to his mother, but he had a little saved for himself and he used the money to acquire the tools he needed to explore. He bought a new cellphone, a camera, and a motorcycle and started traveling around the plateau, documenting the transformation of the landscape.

Tsepey's own village was close to Tsenyi Monastery, where Tibetan troops under the command of Gonpo's grandmother had battled the Red Army in the 1930s. It lies at a strategic point along the pass leading up from the Min River, just above the tree line that demarcates the beginning of the plateau. Once dense with spruce and pine, the pass had been clear-cut by Chinese logging companies. State-owned enterprises were laboring under artificially high quotas set by the government, harvesting so much lumber that Chinese forestry officials were complaining it was not sustainable. From the 1950s to the 1980s, 60 percent of the prefecture's forest cover was removed, according to Chinese forestry journals. People from Ngaba considered the forest behind Tsenyi Monastery to be their own repository of lumber, but they harvested sparingly, since trees were scarce on the plateau. And the mountain passes, like the lakes, were alive, inhabited by deities. Tibetans often said prayers to those deities as they crossed their territory—lest some inadvertent offense cause a freak accident, such as a falling boulder or a lightning strike.

As Tsepey headed west into Qinghai province, he saw more desecration from mining. Chinese companies had long been mining coal, aluminum, and uranium. More recently the demands of the tech industry had created a modern-day gold rush for lithium, needed for the batteries that power electric vehicles and cellphones.

As he roamed the plateau, taking in all the new development, Tsepey couldn't help but compare the living conditions for the new Chinese migrants with the way he had grown up. Many Tibetans were still living with only sporadic electricity and water. In Jiuzhi (Chigdril in Tibetan), a town in Qinghai province just across from Ngaba, brand-new Western-style townhouses sported carved stone balconies and elegant front gates. The billboards advertising these choice properties were entirely in Chinese, making clear—if it wasn't otherwise obvious—that these would be Chinese homes. For Tibetan nomads, who were being pressed into giving up their herds and settling into permanent houses, Chinese construction crews were building squat two-room cement houses with dirt floors.

Tsepey's political views were slowly coming into focus. He rehashed incidents from his past, slights that he'd laughed off back in the days when he prided himself on being an easygoing party guy. He thought of the lack of schools and utilities during his childhood. There were the checkpoints and arbitrary arrests, fights in which the police invariably took the Chinese side. A Tibetan dared not quarrel with a Chinese shopkeeper for fear of being arrested or beaten. Tsepey remembered attending a friendly basketball game between the staff of the Tibetan Middle School and the local Chinese police. One of his friends who was playing for the Middle School accused a Chinese player of repeated personal fouls.

"We're playing by the rules. This guy keeps grabbing the ball and pushing us," the friend complained.

Another policeman grabbed him, punched him, and accused him of being anti-Chinese. The friend was arrested after the game on subversion charges, although it had nothing at all to do with politics. It was only basketball.

What upset Tsepey most, though, were the affronts to his religion. Although he'd been an indifferent student at the monastery, squirming through the recitations of mantras, he now studied Buddhism on his own. He was a slow reader, so he educated himself by listening to recordings of teachings delivered by the Dalai Lama.

One of Tsepey's friends had started a small business burning the Dalai Lama's teachings and lectures onto CDs. He asked Tsepey's help in distributing them. One of the CDs concerned what should have been an arcane doctrinal debate about a deity called Dorje Shugden. The Dalai Lama had discouraged worship of this deity, provoking a backlash from Dorje Shugden followers. Tsepey believed that the monasteries worshipping Dorje Shugden were supported by the Chinese government and that the Party was perpetuating the feud as a way of dividing the Tibetan people.

Other recordings concerned a long-festering dispute about the Panchen Lama. A six-year-old boy, Gedhun Choekyi Nyima, was identified in 1995 as the reincarnation of the 10th Panchen Lama, who had died in 1989. Beijing refused to accept the boy, who had been endorsed by the Dalai Lama, and named its own candidate through a dubious method dating back to the Qing dynasty that used a name drawn from a golden urn. The first boy disappeared (along with the lama who was head of the search committee) and has not been seen since. Human rights groups referred to him as the world's youngest political prisoner. The Chinese government claims he is living a normal life and wants his whereabouts to be kept secret.

Tsepey knew the disappearance of the original boy boded ill for the future of the Dalai Lama's lineage. It was obviously a dress rehearsal for Beijing to install its own choice of Dalai Lama into office when the current incarnation passed away. In 2007, the State Administration for Religious Affairs issued an order that said in essence that one needed advance permission from the Chinese government in order to be reincarnated. The order was much ridiculed for its absurdity (really, how could the resolutely atheistic Communist Party decide the transmigration of Buddhist souls?), but it was clearly intended to tighten control over Tibetan Buddhism.

These were unmentionable topics inside China. The Chinese Communist Party had effectively criminalized any public displays of affection for the Dalai Lama. Photos, medallions, books, and recordings of the Dalai Lama weren't sold openly, but there was always an active under-the-counter trade and people sold these items privately. There was a secret thrill in collecting Dalai Lama paraphernalia. Chinese authorities didn't have a consistent policy about it. At some times in some places, you could get away with hanging up a portrait of the Dalai Lama—even behind the counter of a shop or restaurant. Sometimes you couldn't. It was like a color-modulating mood ring that reflected the Party's insecurity at any given moment. Most Tibetans kept a portrait of the Dalai Lama, but were accustomed to hanging it loosely on a nail so that it could be hidden away in a hurry when the mood turned sour. And it inevitably did.

IN 2006, LOCAL OFFICIALS started conducting "patriotic education" meetings in Charo, Tsepey's home village. Each household was required to send a family member to attend lectures on the dangers of Tibetan nationalism and on the evils of the Dalai Lama. During one of those sessions, somebody fingered Tsepey for distributing Dalai Lama recordings in the village. He was arrested, quickly tried, and given a three-year prison sentence for inciting separatism. He was sent to the prison in Wenchuan, down the river toward Chengdu. Tsepey's father had some money saved from his trading business and knew whom to pay off. Tsepey was released after serving one year.

The experience was supposed to teach him a lesson to deter him from future activism. But by the time Tsepey got out of prison, he was not so much chastened as angry and ready to fight.

THE UPRISING

*Lhundup Tso,
Pema's niece.*

DECHEN LIKED TO SLEEP LATE ON SUNDAY MORNINGS WHEN she didn't have school, but on this particular day, March 16, 2008, her grandmother shook her awake before dawn. She had spent the night at her grandmother's house instead of at Pema's so that she could carry a large cushion to Kirti Monastery for her grandmother first thing in the morning. The monastery was holding a special prayer service, and her grandmother didn't want to aggravate her rheumatism by sitting on the cold paving stones in front of the congregation hall. They needed to get there early to secure a good spot.

Dechen was obliging but silent as she tried to shake the sleep out of her eyes. She had no intention herself of attending the prayers. She had absorbed the anti-religious teachings of the Chinese primary school she attended and sneered at the old people who wasted their waking hours in prayer. She figured she would either go back to sleep afterward or watch television.

Her grandmother—like Pema, a few doors down—lived on Tuan-jie Street, which ran along the river parallel to the main street, just around the corner from the market and the monastery. Normally at six A.M., before the stores were open, the streets would be quiet save for the intermittent barking of stray dogs and the shuffling of elderly worshippers heading to the monastery to circumambulate. This morning, though, as Dechen and her grandmother headed past the shuttered storefronts, they were surprised to encounter columns of Chinese military marching in formation. The paramilitary, or *wujing,* were a familiar presence in Ngaba. They were part of a force one million strong tasked with subduing domestic unrest. Often when Dechen saw them, though, they'd be chatting with each other or with passersby, especially kids like herself who spoke fluent Chinese. As a girl raised on Chinese television war movies, Dechen thought the young police—who looked like regular military personnel in their green uniforms with red epaulets—were dashing characters. She would giggle and say hello when she passed. Now, though, the soldiers seemed unfriendly. She heard them before she saw them, boots stomping in unison on the pavement, the clap of rifles as they switched position with precision. They chanted as they marched, a grunt that sounded like "Hey ho, hey ho, hey ho."

"Why are they doing that?" Dechen's grandmother asked.

At thirteen, Dechen was the family expert on all things Chinese, since she had the best command of the language and many Chinese friends.

"I don't know, Grandma," she said. "Strange."

Had Dechen or her grandmother been following the news, they would have known that the Chinese military was on heightened alert. Protests had broken out in Lhasa the week before, on March 10, a symbolic date for Tibetans. It was on that day in 1959 that the uprising that led to the flight of the Dalai Lama had begun. Tibetans consider that date to be the beginning of their exile—a tragedy that for Tibetans is roughly the equivalent of the way religious Jews see the fall of the Second Temple in 66 C.E. Every year on this date, Tibetans in exile stage demonstrations; a few brave Tibetans inside China will sometimes stage a protest too.

This year, Tibetans were feeling emboldened. It was just months before the opening of the Olympic Games. Nerves were on edge. The Chinese government, always concerned with not losing face, wanted to make sure that nothing would spoil their $50 billion party. That meant rounding up dissidents and deploying extra troops in trouble spots, like Tibetan towns. At the same time, Tibetan advocacy groups abroad wanted to seize the opportunity to put the Tibetan cause back in the news. They had demonstrations planned along the 85,000-mile route that the Olympic torch would travel from Greece to Beijing.

Among Tibetans at home, the thinking was that the Chinese government would be on its best behavior, more tolerant of peaceful protests and less inclined, for example, to allow troops to shoot live ammunition into a crowd.

So it was that in Lhasa on the morning of March 10, a few hundred monks from Drepung, one of Tibet's great monasteries, tried to stage a peaceful march to the center of town. Police quickly blocked their route and arrested the leaders. Fears that the arrested monks were being tortured brought more and more Tibetans out until the streets exploded with anger. The uprising would prove to be the deadliest since the protests of the late 1980s, when the Chinese imposed martial law. But that wasn't known yet to Dechen or her grandmother.

By the time Dechen headed back from the monastery on the 16th, having left her grandmother to pray, the sun was coming up. More people were up and about, and they gave uneasy sidelong glances to the soldiers as they passed. Dechen could sense the tension in the air, but she felt it didn't have anything to do with her. She didn't pay much attention to current events. She ducked back into the walled court-yard adjacent to her grandmother's house. She planned to spend the day curled up watching television. Her favorite show was on: a Chinese version of *American Idol*.

PEMA TRIED TO MAKE it to the monastery daily, but she avoided days when it was crowded, and she happened to have a busy schedule that particular Sunday. She was expecting guests for lunch. And she didn't want to close her cart on special prayer days at Kirti, when people would come in from the countryside; that was when she enjoyed her best sales.

On the way to the market, she noticed the columns of Chinese paramilitary. She'd never seen so many in town. They made her nervous. She didn't understand why they couldn't do these exercises at their own base on the outskirts instead of making so much commotion right smack in the middle of town where everybody could see them. She knew their presence would make people angry. I hope nothing happens, she told herself.

Pema worked until noon, when she threw a plastic tarpaulin over her cart and closed up. On her way home she stopped to buy vegetables to fry up with some leftover rice for lunch. Her oldest son and her husband's niece Lhundup Tso would be there; both were students in the Middle School and although seven years apart in age they were close friends, as well as cousins. Over lunch, Pema remarked that the kids were uncharacteristically quiet. Even the usually garrulous Lhundup Tso tucked into her meal in silence. Pema figured they were tired after the weekend. Middle School students had a half day on Saturdays and then returned to school by five P.M. on Sundays. They didn't discuss the unusual deployment of Chinese military out in the streets and, Pema would later recall with much regret, she did not tell the teenagers to be careful.

After they finished their lunch, Pema gave 30 yuan to Lhundup Tso and told her to buy bread and snacks on her way back to school. The girl was too thin; Pema was always urging her to eat. The girl hugged her aunt and left. Pema's son was supposed to go back to school as well, but he was stalling, fussing with his clothing, and ended up staying home. Pema suspected he was nervous and didn't want to admit as much in front of the girl.

DONGTUK, THE YOUNG KIRTI MONK, woke up on the morning of March 16 with a vague sense of anticipation. He felt sure something was stirring, but he didn't know exactly what. He was only fourteen years old, so he was often excluded from the more serious discussions at the monastery. He would see the young men whispering conspiratorially and feel he was missing out. Underaged monks also were barred from some of the ceremonies. But today, he would be part of the *puja,* a prayer festival marking the end of the holiday. Outside the assembly hall, some monks were doing a ritual debate and worshippers from town were gathering with their cushions and folding chairs. Inside, the monks were gathered for prayer. Almost the entire population of the monastery was there, some three thousand monks, the younger ones sitting cross-legged on the floor, intoning the chant *om mani padme hum*. Dongtuk soon felt himself lost in the recitation, repeating the same chant until the rhythm was knocked off course by a murmur of voices at the front of the assembly hall. People were gesturing toward one of the monks in his twenties who was holding something, a large color photograph of the Dalai Lama, above his head. In the background of the photograph, Dongtuk could see the red and blue stripes of the Tibetan flag.

"Long live His Holiness the Dalai Lama," the monk yelled. Dongtuk was surprised. This wasn't something you did—not just because you could get in trouble from the authorities, but because they were in the middle of the prayers. He suspected that this monk was slightly deranged. But then he heard others yelling the same—"Long live His

Holiness!" and "Tibet for the Tibetans!"—and soon the voices shouting slogans drowned out the prayers.

The monks rose to their feet. The assembly hall was in an uproar. The monks surged out into the courtyard and from there into the alley leading to Ngaba's main street.

Dongtuk found himself swept into the crowd, following the older monks without question. They threw their heavy crimson outer robes onto the pavement, a gesture that signaled they were prepared to fight. Above the crowd, more photos of the Dalai Lama and the snow lion Tibetan flags appeared and were hoisted aloft. The monks surged toward the gate of the monastery. Dongtuk started to follow, although on the other side of the gate he could see a menacing gray cloud—tear gas, he realized, although he had never witnessed anything like it before. The Chinese paramilitary also seemed to be firing bits of gravel at the protesters. Although Dongtuk was not in the front of the crowd, a lump of something sizzling—a stick of dynamite? he wondered—fell at his feet. With a childish curiosity, he reached down to grab it, imagining that maybe he could toss it back at the soldiers, but it exploded first, singeing the bottom of his robe and his fingers. Just then, a hand grabbed the collar of his robe, pulling him backward. It was a senior monk, one of Dongtuk's teachers.

"You little kids don't belong here," he said. Dongtuk was indignant—he didn't think of himself as a little kid—but he was in no condition to protest. He was retching and crying, trying to rub the grit out of his eyes. He meekly followed the monk back toward the dormitory.

DECHEN HEADED TO HER father's house because he had the best television in the family. She and her cousin, a boy a few years older, settled onto a sofa and watched a succession of shows. Typical of even modest families, her father had a compound built around a courtyard with separate rooms for the grandmother and other relatives. The gate was often propped open and people would pop in and out. Around noon, a girl from school stopped by to tell them about the excitement in town.

"There are bombs going off. Real bombs, not television. You need to come see," she told Dechen and her cousin.

Dechen didn't want to leave the safety of the television room, but her cousin insisted. They made their way down Tuanjie Street, then around the corner toward the main street.

The soldiers she had seen marching earlier that morning were out in full force by now. They wore blue-black uniforms and full riot regalia. Shiny black helmets obscured their faces. They carried curved Plexiglas shields. Dechen almost giggled when she saw them—they looked like *Star Wars* characters—but she didn't want to get too close. She and her cousin ducked into a stairwell. Upstairs on the second floor was a small Tibetan tea shop that afforded a view of the action. Dechen could see a small, rowdy crowd of Tibetans approaching the paramilitary, throwing rocks that bounced off the riot shields. She was horrified and a little embarrassed. She recoiled and turned to her cousin.

"How can Tibetans be so rude to throw rocks at the soldiers?" she asked.

Her cousin gave her a look of disgust. "You don't get it, do you?" he said. "The Chinese are always killing Tibetans."

Dechen started to cry and asked to go home.

AS PEMA WAS CLEANING UP from lunch, she could hear the rush of a crowd past her front gate, the agitated footsteps, and the pitched voices of an excited crowd. Her son was still at home. Good, better that he stay inside, she thought. But Pema couldn't contain her curiosity. She left the dirty dishes and went out, locking the gate and tying about it a shiny white *khata*. The ceremonial scarf was usually bestowed on guests, but it would also serve as a signal, in case things turned ugly, that this was a Tibetan home.

Tibetan protests often unfold in such a similar manner that it almost feels like the choreography of a classical ballet. Monks and nuns come out first, sacrificing themselves for arrest since they don't have responsibility for spouses or children. But the monastic community is sacred to Tibetans—they are, after all, among the three jewels—so the laypeople feel it is incumbent upon them to offer their protection, so they follow in protest, especially if the monks have been arrested. That had been the sequence in Lhasa the week before and it would happen the same way in Ngaba.

When Pema emerged, she saw people from the neighborhood streaming toward Kirti. Some held portraits of the Dalai Lama high above their heads. They pumped their fists in the air and shouted out loud.

"Long live His Holiness
the Dalai Lama."
"We want Tibetan independence."

Some were crying.

At the corner the crowd split. Some people headed north toward the monastery. Others went straight ahead toward an administrative building where a makeshift jail had been set up for the detention of monks who were being arrested. People shouted demands for their release. A cordon of police and paramilitary were protecting the building, cowering behind their riot shields. Since Ngaba was always in a state of construction, plenty of projectiles lay within easy reach of the ground—bricks, chunks of concrete, stones. For lack of other weapons, people picked up shovels and axes. Some carried slingshots—which were in widespread use to scare away vicious dogs. Projectiles were flying in all directions.

People found targets everywhere to vent their anger. Teenaged boys ran wild through the market, overturning Chinese stalls and opening cages of chickens and ducks. It was an extension of a Buddhist tradition of releasing animals to gain merit. At the Ngaba People's Hospital, the doctors, all of them Chinese, were afraid that they would be punished if they took in Tibetan patients, so they closed the emergency room and locked the gates. This angered Tibetans, who pelted the façade with stones.

By midafternoon, all the shops were closed, the steel security gates slammed shut. To her dismay, Pema noticed that gangs of young men had pried open some of the gates and were looting the inventory— televisions and appliances and clothing. Pema was embarrassed, but there was one attack that she quietly cheered. The Yonganli Department Store, the biggest store in town, located at the main intersection, had been cleared out, the display cases smashed and the building set on fire. The store was owned by Peng Yongfan, the former PLA officer whom the Tibetans called "Brushhead." They complained that he was rude to Tibetan customers. If a Tibetan came in looking at appliances he couldn't yet afford, Brushhead would kick them out. If you crossed him, he'd ask his friends in the police to beat you up. Many Tibetans boycotted his store, even though it was the only place in town to buy washing machines and refrigerators. He deserved it, Pema thought.

By midafternoon, it felt like all of Ngaba was embroiled in the melee. In the crowd of protesters, Pema saw many of the women from the market—vendors like herself, ordinary women, most of them middle-aged or older, not troublemakers or loudmouths. They were bent over the pavement scooping up stones and bricks to deliver to the young men who were throwing them. A Hui Muslim woman at the market had a stall that sold buckets, and one of the Tibetan women rushed over to grab them. The Hui woman didn't dare say no. The buckets soon got passed around to other women who carried them to a spigot at the market where they filled them with water so the protesters could wash their eyes to clear the tear gas and gravel. Pema didn't want to throw rocks, but she was happy to help with the buckets. The women formed an assembly line, conveying water to the front lines; on the way back came information. There were protests at the prison. Protests at the police station. Now the Chinese were shooting at protesters with live ammunition. People were mentioning names of those who had been shot.

A woman spoke Lhundup Tso's name, and then turned to Pema. "Isn't she your husband's niece?"

Pema dropped her bucket and headed for the Middle School.

IN CHARO TOWNSHIP, TSEPEY had slept late and was planning on a lazy day at home. He was still on probation and rarely went out, fearful of getting himself into trouble. But he had a mobile telephone now, as did most of his friends, and it wouldn't stop buzzing with calls and texts about the protests that were popping up all over. There was a protest in Labrang, another in Dzorge, yet another in Repkong. In the township, somebody had removed a sign from the Public Security Bureau and taken down a Chinese flag. Then a call came in from Ngaba. Things were going crazy in the center of town. He couldn't resist.

He jumped on his motorcycle and roared toward Ngaba. A distance that used to take two days on horseback now took about an hour. Other men from the village followed on Tsepey's trail, a posse of motorcycle avengers. The police had set up a checkpoint at the entrance to the city, so the riders parked their bikes at Se Monastery. The melee that had started near Kirti had rolled like a wave two miles down the road to where they now stood. Tsepey saw police scuffling with some Tibetan men. In the distance, he heard bursts of gunfire and explosions that sounded like bombs.

He felt the adrenaline seeping out of him. This was more than he'd bargained for when he came in for the protest. He'd been thinking maybe he would go yell a few slogans, throw a couple of rocks. Nothing too extreme. He wasn't up for gunfire. Still he wanted to see what was going on in the center of town. Tsepey approached via the parking lots and fields just behind the main road, making his way slowly because he was unsure of what he was getting into. Between the Middle School and the headquarters of the traffic police he cut through to the main road.

That's where he saw her. There was something about the unnatural angle of the body in the street that caught his eye. It was a young woman lying on her side, one leg dangling into a drainage ditch. She wore a traditional Tibetan cloak, a chuba, but no other adornment. Tibetan women usually wore jewelry, coral necklaces or earrings, but the girl's clothing was so plain he thought she must be a student. She was no older than twenty, he thought. Her hair was cut shoulder length and matted with blood. More blood, thick and pasty, covered her forehead. A gash ran vertically from her hairline to her nose, which he figured must be a bullet wound.

Although Tsepey was a large, intimidating man, he was not a fighter by nature. He was an emotional man who cried at sad movies, prompting the ridicule of his friends. He couldn't bear to see an animal slaughtered. Tsepey had always been frightened of dead bodies. It dated back to the death of his grandmother when he was young; he had this childish terror that they would turn into ghosts and snatch him away. Now he had to swallow his fear. He knew he couldn't leave the dead girl lying there on the street. People were gathering around, most of them senior citizens. He was the only one strong enough to lift the body. He carefully removed her from the ditch and laid her down on a patch of grass away from the street. He adjusted her cloak to cover her face. He told the elders to take care of the body—to keep the police away so that her family could conduct a proper Buddhist burial. Tsepey had important things to do. He was ready to fight.

Tsepey returned to the path behind the main road, hopping from courtyard to courtyard, heading past the police station, toward Kirti. By then the crowds had thinned; many of the protesters had prudently returned home. None of the Tibetans had guns, but they knew how to fight with whatever was available. Tsepey pulled out a pocketknife and joined forces with about ten other Tibetan men who had captured a courtyard behind the police station. Chinese police were hurling smoke bombs over the wall. The Tibetan men would pick up the bombs as soon as they landed and throw them back over the wall.

Whether it was the fumes from the smoke or the image of the dead girl, Tsepey felt himself transported by rage. Until then, his anger at the Chinese government was vague and unfocused. He hated the way they condescended to Tibetans. He hated the Chinese companies that were cutting trees from Tibetan land and mining in sacred hills. He hated that you could be sent to jail for reading a banned book or pamphlet, that Tibetans were forced to learn the language of their oppressors, and that they had to go to lectures in which the Chinese government defamed His Holiness the Dalai Lama. But Tsepey hadn't felt anger toward the Chinese as individuals—he had many Chinese friends and had dated Chinese women. He was a Buddhist who respected human life. Now he fought with abandon. He didn't care if he lived or died. He found himself surrounded by four police officers and he swung at them with his knife, whirling like a dervish until he got himself tangled in his chuba, which he would later admit was not the right garment for urban warfare. He fought on, dazed and confused, a gash on the back of his head dripping blood down his back.

"I lost my fear. I was a wild man," Tsepey would later say. "The feeling of revenge overtook me. There was something so powerful about seeing such a young girl dead."

PEMA WALKED AS FAST as she could toward the Middle School along the main road. As she was walking there, she saw a group of Tibetans coming the other way, carrying a makeshift stretcher of wooden beams taken from a construction site and blankets. The ambulance service wasn't picking up that day because the hospital wouldn't admit Tibetan patients. It wouldn't have made any difference since Lhundup Tso was already dead and they were bringing her body straight to the monastery.

Later Pema learned that Lhundup Tso had dropped off her bags at her dormitory before heading out with a dozen other students who wanted to join the protests. School authorities had tried to lock the students inside, but they snuck out anyway. They'd just arrived at the police station when Lhundup Tso was killed by a single gunshot to the head. It is likely that the body Tsepey saw was Lhundup Tso, given the location and the nature of the wounds, but years later he was unable to make a positive ID when shown her photo. She was the only young female reported killed that day in Ngaba.

How many died in Ngaba? Exact numbers are hard to come by in China, a country with a penchant for statistics but a political culture that prefers not to publicize them when they present an inconvenient truth. The official Chinese news service, Xinhua, initially reported that there were four people killed that day in Ngaba, but it later removed the story from its website and issued another reporting no deaths. Tibetan exile groups put the death toll at twenty-one. The higher number seems more likely given witness accounts. Not all the dead were taken to Kirti, but Dongtuk personally saw a dozen bodies near the assembly hall used for funeral prayers and rituals.

For a small town like Ngaba, twenty-one dead was a catastrophe, the equivalent of the Tiananmen Square massacre. Everybody knew somebody who was shot. Dechen was incredulous. She knew three of them. Besides Lhundup Tso, a classmate from her primary school, Louri, was also killed that day. He was a very straitlaced, serious kid, so responsible that he'd been selected as a hall monitor. Another boy in the neighborhood, only six years old, was shot in the leg. His parents had to bring him all the way to Dzorge, a six-hour drive, for medical treatment.

Still glued to the television, Dechen watched the news on CCTV, the state television network. The same footage from Ngaba was broadcast repeatedly, a three-second clip of a police car on its side and on fire, against the backdrop of a snow-covered mountain. A crowd of about a dozen men mills about gathering stones, and then one of them rushes forward and hurls a big chunk of concrete at a building covered with metal shutters as smoke billows from a second-floor window. Over and over it was replayed.

"Tibetans engaged in looting, rioting, smashing," declared the news anchor. "Local government officials state that there are sufficient facts to prove these events were instigated by the Dalai clique."

The report did not include mention of any Tibetan casualties. The anchor only told one side of the story. Dechen suddenly realized how childish she had been to believe what she saw on television.

MARCH 2008 SAW PROTESTS throughout the region. Men on horseback stormed a township near Labrang Monastery. Police opened fire on protesters in at least one other town in Sichuan province, Kardze (or Ganzi in Chinese). But Ngaba's protest was the deadliest outside Lhasa, cementing the town's reputation as a hotbed of discontent. "There's a saying that when there is a fire in Lhasa, the smoke rises in Ngaba," the head of an exile association told me a few years later. Although the uprising in Lhasa was for the most part peaceful, it was marred by some nasty personal assaults that strayed far from the Dalai Lama's teachings on nonviolence. Tibetan gangs attacked random Han Chinese civilians riding motorcycles on a main street in Lhasa and torched shops belong to Hui Muslims, the result of a long history of Buddhist-Muslim tensions in the area. At least twenty were killed, including members of one entire Hui family, burned in their shops. The facts remain unconfirmed because there has never been an opportunity for independent reporting. According to the Tibetan Center for Human Rights and Democracy, which obtained some leaked autopsy reports, at least 101 Tibetans were killed by security services that opened fire on demonstrators.

Ngaba's Tibetans more closely adhered to the nonviolent ideal. They did not vent their anger against Chinese civilians, only against the police and military. Although there was some looting, for the most part Tibetans spared Hui shops from attack—testament to the long history of congenial relations with Muslims in Ngaba. And in this deadly day of fighting, there were no reports of serious injuries sustained by Chinese in Ngaba.

CHAPTER

16

. . .

THE EYE OF
THE GHOST

Monks under arrest in Ngaba, 2008.

TSEPEY BARELY GOT OUT OF NGABA ALIVE. HE'D BEEN HIT
on the back of his head with a shovel. He was dizzy from the impact
of the blow and from all the tear gas and smoke he had inhaled. It was
almost nightfall when he left town, sneaking through the marshy path
alongside the river until he reached Se Monastery, where he had left
his motorcycle. He arrived back home later that night, his hair and

clothes matted with blood. His father took one look at him and figured it all out.

"You were involved in the uprising. You have to run away before
they come and arrest you," his father said.

Tsepey swallowed a painkiller and got back on his motorcycle.
Somehow he made it to Chengdu, where his head was stitched up.
Still, he didn't feel safe in Sichuan province. His friends told him the
police were looking for him, so he headed farther south, ending up in
Shenzhen. Bordering Hong Kong, Shenzhen is the city where the
Chinese government first experimented with market capitalism in the
1980s, and it remained a brash, pulsating city, perfect for hiding out in
the crowd for few months. But one day that summer Tsepey was at a
cybercafé chatting with some friends on QQ, a popular instant messaging service, when his computer suddenly froze. Two policemen
grabbed his backpack and checked his travel documents. He had borrowed a friend's identity card for just such a purpose, but unfortunately he had his real ID in the bag too. One of the policemen
cross-checked his name on a list.

"It's him," he announced.

Tsepey was held for a week in the local lockup. Then, four policemen arrived from Ngaba. They had flown two thousand miles, all the
way to Shenzhen, to pick him up and bring him back. Even the jailers
in Shenzhen were amazed at how far they had traveled for one suspect.

"The Communist Party has control of the sky and the earth. You
can't run away," one of the Ngaba policemen told Tsepey. They were
clearly proud of the way they had tracked him through the Internet.
It was a novel use of technology for that time.

In the end, Tsepey escaped through old-fashioned brute strength
and cunning. The police were required to remove his handcuffs before
going through airport security, so they wrapped his hands instead
with duct tape, fingers touching opposite elbows. In the waiting
room, the policemen lit cigarettes and read the newspaper. The senior

officer took off his shoes. The atmosphere was relaxed. Tsepey had already spent several days in their custody, chatting with them and being his charming self. He had offered no resistance. While they waited in the airport, Tsepey asked to use the bathroom. Two junior policemen were sent to escort him, skinny young guys a head shorter than him. They were unprepared when he wriggled out of their loose grasp and bolted for the escalators.

The waiting room was on the third floor. Tsepey ran down the escalator steps, struggling to keep his balance with his hands immobilized. He could hear people shouting behind him, but he didn't look back. He made his way to the exit, dodging past a security guard who hit him with a truncheon, bloodying his nose. The blow stung his eyes. Still, he just kept running, straight out the door, through the traffic, and across a low highway bridge that spanned marshy fields. He jumped. He landed in a bog, where he managed to use twigs to loosen and remove the tape. After dark, he walked through a cornfield until he stumbled into a populated area. He told an older couple that he had passed out drunk and had lost his phone and wallet. Tsepey was convincing. He had done enough acting at the Chinese resort to play the role of the amiable drunk, and with his muddied clothes, he certainly looked the part. The old man allowed him to use his telephone to call a friend to pick him up.

AFTER THE MARCH 2008 PROTESTS, Chinese authorities put Kirti Monastery under what amounted to a siege. They barricaded the main entrance to the monastery and, shortly afterward, the five smaller entryways that led in from the mountains to the north. The high mud-brick walls that enclose the courtyards around the monastery are somewhat labyrinthine and suggest secret routes in and out of the compound, but now every alleyway was blocked off. The monks couldn't leave, not even to do their shopping at the market. Visitors couldn't get into the monastery either. Even the elders were not permitted to spin the prayer wheels. Of greatest consequence, however, was that deliveries to the monastery, including deliveries of food, were prohibited.

At first it was merely an inconvenience. Tibetans tended to steel themselves for hard times with stockpiles of tsampa and other grains. But the blockade dragged on for weeks and then months. Monks' families tried to deliver care packages, but were blocked at the gates. Telephone signals were blocked as well—effectively preventing the monks from contacting Tibetan advocacy groups or anybody else who might report the abuse. The monks complained that there was no security rationale to prevent them from shopping for food, but their complaints went unanswered. Cutting off the food supply was purely punitive. It was as though the government forces were trying to starve them into submission.

Whatever food there was was shared, but there was never quite enough. Dongtuk didn't eat fresh vegetables or meat for the rest of the year. Fortunately, his mother had stocked his kitchen with instant ramen noodles. In his flights of self-pity, Dongtuk thought he might have starved without them.

After a while, some families managed to bring in tsampa, butter, and cheese—the staples—but other families couldn't even get into the center of Ngaba because they didn't have the right ID cards. Tibetans without *hukous*, or residency permits, showing they were registered in the town center could not enter. Checkpoints went up on either side of the main road—one near Se Monastery to block traffic coming from the east and another near Kirti to block traffic coming from the west. They were to become semipermanent fixtures in Ngaba. Sometimes they were left open and unmanned, but they were never taken away.

After a few weeks surrounding the monastery, Chinese security forces moved inside the gates, erecting bunkers at strategic locations. Next to the largest of the yellow buildings housing the prayer wheels, they erected a guardhouse with windows on four sides. They piled sandbags around the sides.

Then came the closed-circuit television cameras. They were white metal boxes—about the size of cigarette cartons—tucked under the eaves of the roofs and on lamps and utility poles.

"There's the eye of the ghost," Tibetans would say when they passed one.

One of the cameras was installed directly across from Dongtuk's house, just a few feet from the window. It would blink red when it was filming. Dongtuk wondered if anybody ever reviewed the security footage or if it was just there to intimidate people. He once threw a stone at it but nobody seemed to notice. He hung up a robe that partially covered the window, but after a while he learned to ignore the camera. There wasn't much to see: he spent most of his time playing cards, since classes were suspended and prayer schedules sharply curtailed.

Chinese authorities searched every nook and cranny of the monastery. Under orders from Shi Jun, the Communist Party secretary for the prefecture, they confiscated a cache of rusting knives and broken muskets that had been turned over to the monastery as part of a tradition by Buddhists to show they had renounced violence. The authorities claimed these weapons were proof that Tibetans were planning a rebellion.

Nearly six hundred men were arrested—more than one-fifth of Kirti's monks. Some monks returned after a few days, looking bruised and subdued. Dongtuk didn't know at the time what they had experienced, but he later heard the stories. The men had been put into a locked room that was so crowded nobody could sit or lie down, making it impossible to sleep. Some were beaten, others were not, but they all had to endure humiliating treatment. In most of the holding centers, there were no toilets; the monks had to urinate and defecate where they stood. The monks had been paraded through town in an open-back truck, bent over at the waist, their arms straight behind them in a stress position known as the airplane that harked back to the struggle sessions of the Cultural Revolution. They wore placards around their necks with their names and their crimes.

"Separatist," read some, the favored term used by the Chinese government for the Tibetan independence movement. "Subversion of state authority," read others.

Those who weren't arrested were hauled off to attend more patriotic education lessons. They were similar to the lectures introduced at Kirti a decade earlier; the basic message was that it was permissible to practice Buddhism as long as love for the Communist Party came first. But this time it was an effort less to convince than to intimidate.

On one exam, the Kirti monks were given this multiple-choice question:

> If somebody is guilty of endangering state security, what will be the prison sentence?
>   (1) three years' imprisonment
>   (2) ten years' imprisonment
>   (3) lifetime imprisonment

The propaganda fixated on the Dalai Lama. According to Chinese authorities, the Dalai Lama had directly incited and orchestrated the protests. The propagandists strained to come up with increasingly vituperative language with which to denounce the Dalai Lama.

"The Dalai is a wolf in monk's robes, a devil with a human face but the heart of a beast," Zhang Qingli, the Communist Party secretary in the Tibet Autonomous Region, was quoted as saying. He called the struggle against the Dalai Lama a "life-and-death battle between us and the enemy."

Although human rights groups in Dharamsala, India, acted as a clearinghouse for information about the protests, the Chinese produced no evidence of incitement to violence. To the contrary, the Dalai Lama had given a strongly worded unequivocal condemnation of the attacks on Chinese civilians in Lhasa. "If the Tibetans were to choose the path of violence, he would have to resign because he is completely committed to nonviolence," his spokesman Tenzin Taklha said.

Monks had to make statements—sometimes videotaped—in which they disavowed their support for the Dalai Lama. Samples of the statements included "I oppose the Dalai clique," "My thinking is not influenced by the Dalai clique," and "I will not keep the Dalai's photo in my home."

Now the photo policy was zero tolerance. Traditional paintings that depicted the Dalai Lama were torn up or defaced, his face scratched out. A large portrait in the prayer wheel house was ripped out and destroyed.

Chinese inspectors started searching the monks' rooms for illegal portraits. The Chinese took these inspections deadly seriously. They were carried out by a unit called the *tejing,* literally "special police." They carried rifles and were clad head to toe in black uniforms, their faces covered with black balaclavas. Dongtuk thought they looked like jihadists. They would barge in for surprise inspections and order the monks out of the room at gunpoint. They pulled clothes and dishes, linens and books and food, out of the cupboards, leaving everything a mess. Often money and valuables disappeared during these searches. Although smartphones weren't in common use at that time, monks kept photos of the Dalai Lama on their cellphones; sometimes the entire phone would be confiscated. But the real offense was the disrespect shown to the Dalai Lama. The monks complained that they were often forced to tear up the portraits or stomp on them.

It is not like burning a Koran, exactly, but Tibetan Buddhists have strong feelings about any desecration of the Dalai Lama's image. Tibetans who weren't interested in politics, who didn't know much about the exile government, and who weren't necessarily anti-Chinese couldn't help but be infuriated when the Chinese insulted the Dalai Lama. He was first and foremost their spiritual leader, the reincarnation of Avalokitesvara, the bodhisattva of compassion and the traditional patron of all Tibetans. In Buddhist art, the physical image is an aid to meditation and a reminder to the faithful that they too can achieve enlightenment. The more intent the Chinese became about removing any trace of the Dalai Lama, the more Tibetans were reminded of his importance. The Chinese campaign couldn't have been more counterproductive. It led to a cycle of bitterness and misunderstanding.

The pressure to denounce the Dalai Lama put the monks under enormous stress. Many refused and tore up the exams. In most cases, that meant they had to resign from the monastery, in effect giving up the only way of life they'd known. Throughout Kirti and other monasteries, there was a string of suicides, including that of a seventy-five-year-old monk who had survived the crackdown of 1958 as well as the Cultural Revolution but couldn't take this latest affront. A young partially blind monk in his twenties hung himself at Kirti. A monk in his twenties left behind a suicide note reading, "I do not want to live under the Chinese oppression even for a minute, much less live for a day."

For the Kirti monks, it felt like the world as they knew it was collapsing. Previously unseen dangers surrounded them. Their sense of foreboding was compounded by the earthquake that struck Sichuan province on May 12, 2008. It was a national disaster of epic proportions, the largest earthquake that had stuck China since 1976. Nearly 70,000 people were killed. The epicenter was about 150 miles away in Wenchuan, which is part of the same Ngaba prefecture. Although Ngaba county was spared extensive damage, many people had relatives and friends killed, including some who were held in prisons near Wenchuan. The roads between Ngaba and Chengdu were impassable for months because of landslides. The only good to come out of it was that the authorities temporarily lifted the restrictions on religious ceremonies at the monastery so that the monks could pray for the dead.

For Dongtuk, it was a period not only of crisis but of awakening. From early childhood, he had heard stories from his grandmother's generation about the persecution of monks, but he hadn't paid much attention. These were the reminiscences of old people whose experiences, it seemed, had little to do with his own. Now he saw his situation as part of a continuum of the oppression inflicted by the Chinese on Tibetans.

In his spare time, which was abundant, Dongtuk started listening to Tibetan folk songs known as *dunglen,* literally "strumming and singing," a style of music popular in Amdo. It was slow, hypnotic music in which the singer lamented some long-lost love or homeland, sometimes referring obliquely to the Dalai Lama. The songs were Dongtuk's political education. The albums were illegal. In some towns, shopkeepers would sell them discreetly from behind the counter, not daring to put them on public display. Dongtuk was lucky to know someone who was good with computers and would burn CDs for his friends.

Dongtuk's personal favorite was Tashi Dhondup, who had recorded a song called "1958–2008" comparing that darkest year to the current situation.

> *The year nineteen fifty-eight*
> *The year when the bitter enemy arrived in Tibet*
> *The year when venerable lamas were imprisoned*
> *We live in terror of that year. . . .*
>
> *The year two thousand and eight*
> *The year when innocent Tibetans were tortured*
> *The year when the citizens of the earth were killed*
> *We live in terror of that year.*

The song would earn Tashi Dhondup a fifteen-month prison sentence for inciting separatism.

CHAPTER

17

· · ·

CELEBRATE
OR ELSE

Chinese police marching in Ngaba, 2011.

FOR A YEAR AFTER LHUNDUP TSO'S DEATH, PEMA WAS SO
depressed she could barely leave her house. She blamed herself for not
insisting that her impetuous niece stay inside during the protests; she
replayed constantly what she did or did not tell the girl during their
final lunch. When she finally dragged herself out of bed, Pema had no
place to go. She was confined to within a few blocks of her home, cut
off by all the checkpoints. Pema couldn't open her stall because the

market area near Kirti Monastery had been cordoned off and closed. There were no customers anyway, since people from the villages weren't permitted to enter the center of town. Pema suspected that the closures were a form of collective punishment for *tawa,* as the neighborhood around the monastery was called.

Normally when Pema was feeling stressed, she could comfort herself with her ritual circumambulations, but now no outsiders were permitted on monastery grounds. She had no choice but to stay at home and worry. She felt anxious even reciting her mantras at home, remembering the prohibitions from her childhood. She removed the portrait of the Dalai Lama that she'd kept lovingly draped with a silk scarf as the centerpiece of her shrine. She placed it in a secure cupboard along with her Dalai Lama medallion. She'd heard rumors that you could be thrown into prison if you were caught with the photo.

DECHEN BECAME THE FAMILY'S go-between. She was small for her age and could pass as an elementary school girl. That gave her an advantage navigating the obstacle course that was downtown Ngaba, since children were stopped less often at checkpoints. And if she was stopped, she could usually get through with the flash of a smile and a friendly *ni hao.* After a few weeks, Dechen got to know a few of the soldiers and would chat with them. She realized that some of them were teenagers, not much older than her. Some of them, she could tell, were nice people. When Tibetans tried to sneak into the monastery to deliver food to the monks, they would turn their heads and pretend they didn't see. She actually felt sorry for them standing on patrol all day.

Sometimes she would bring them food. The soldiers were crazy about animal-shaped cookies that were sold in a bakery on the other side of town. They would give her money for the cookies—and pay three yuan for a three-wheeled pedicab to take her there. She became a courier for both sides. She shopped for the Tibetans and the Chinese across enemy lines. She felt like a double agent.

In the fall of 2008, Dechen started at Tibetan Middle School, where her loyalties would be tested. Since Tsegyam taught in the 1980s, the school had become more conventional, following the Party line, especially when it came to teaching history. Although the students could still study Tibetan language and literature, the other classes were taught in Chinese.

After the protests, the school redoubled its campaign against expressions of Tibetan nationalism. Banners went up in all the classrooms: "Fight Separatism," "Fight Against the Dalai Clique." At the school assembly, the principal lectured the students on the evils of the Dalai Lama and denounced the participants in the protests as hooligans. Extra lectures about Mao and the exploits of the Red Army were scheduled for Sunday evenings. Although Dechen had loved old Chinese war movies, she slumped in her seat during the lectures, barely able to keep her eyes open.

Dechen wasn't the only student transformed by the shock of the 2008 uprising. Lhundup Tso had been a popular student and her death roused her classmates out of their apathy. Once aspiring to civil service jobs, which would require fealty to the Communist Party, many of them now professed a renewed interest in all things Tibetan—language, food, clothing, religion. Some of the older students had started a campaign to speak pure Tibetan, banishing from their vocabularies the many words borrowed from the Chinese. Although the students all spoke fluent Chinese, they promised not to speak Chinese at home. When they went home for weekends, they put a coin in a jar as a fine if a Chinese word slipped into the conversation. For computers, the familiar Chinese word *diannao* was replaced with *lok-le*. They banned the use of *shouji,* cellphone, opting instead for *khapar.*

Another trend that caught on among Dechen's classmates was the Lhakar movement. *Lhakar* translates as "White Wednesday" and refers to the auspicious day of the week for the Dalai Lama. On Wednesdays, they made an extra effort to observe Tibetan traditions. Students would wear Tibetan clothing on Wednesdays. For Dechen, it was the first time she'd regularly worn a chuba. The students promised not to shop in Chinese stores or eat in Chinese restaurants. And to make themselves into better Buddhists, they didn't eat meat on Wednesday—although ironically the Dalai Lama himself is not a vegetarian. (When I interviewed the Dalai Lama in 2015, he told me he gave up the vegetarian diet on the advice of his doctor because he had developed jaundice.)

By the end of 2008, controls had relaxed around Ngaba. The Communist Party was basking in the success of the Beijing summer games. The markets reopened. The blockade around Kirti Monastery was lifted. The checkpoints leading in and out of town were left unmanned, although the guard posts were left in place. One never knew when the storm would strike again.

In early 2009, a new grassroots campaign to boycott the Tibetan New Year had begun. Losar is the most important holiday in the Tibetan calendar. Although the date varies from year to year and place to place, the fifteen-day holiday usually falls around China's lunar New Year. Traditionally, Tibetans eat *momos* and make a fried dough pastry called *khapse*. They burn incense and light firecrackers. This year, Tibetans vowed they would forgo the celebrations and use the holiday as a mourning period in memory of the people killed the previous year.

A peculiarity of Chinese rule over Tibet is the government's insistence that Tibetans are happy, so happy that they while away their days singing and dancing. This ruse grows out of the Chinese Communist Party's historical posturing as the defender of the oppressed. To absolve themselves of the sins of imperialism, it was essential that they show the Tibetans' enthusiastic acceptance of Chinese rule. To this end, government propagandists devote inordinate effort to disseminating photographs, pamphlets, and books that show Tibetans with smiles stretched across their faces. State television regularly publicizes supposed polls that claim Lhasa is China's "happiest city." A few years ago, Chinese propagandists were caught making fake Twitter accounts to post upbeat stories of life in Tibet. ("Tibetans hail bumper crop of highland barley," read the headline of a posting in 2014.)

The "No Losar" campaign, therefore, infuriated the Chinese, hitting them exactly where it hurt. Chinese authorities countered with their own campaign of forced merriment; local governments organized concerts, pageants, fireworks, horse races, and archery competitions. Officials handed out money for dinner parties. The message was in effect: celebrate or else. And they enforced it with massive arrests.

In Meruma, a group of villagers gathered outside on the first day of the holiday. They arranged themselves in a line and sat on the ground, their heads bowed in a display of mourning. They went home for a simple meal of tsampa—without butter, which they were giving up for the occasion. They returned the next day to renew their silent protest, but this time the police were waiting for them. All were arrested.

Arrests only led to more resistance. Silent protests and fasts spread throughout Ngaba. Teenagers were quick to pick up on the trend.

One day Dechen arrived for classes dressed in trousers, her customary attire, and was approached by a group of older male students. They told her there would be a special commemoration and that all the girls should put on chubas. At lunchtime, students reported to the cafeteria as usual, but instead of eating they were instructed to throw their food—a hot pot cooked with sausage—into the garbage. They gathered in the courtyard and sat cross-legged on the ground and began the chant *om mani padme hum*. Dechen could see Chinese cameramen outside the gates taking videos. A few of the older students picked up pebbles and threw them toward the gate.

The Tibetan teachers were in a panic. They knew that they would be held accountable by Chinese authorities for the students' insurrection. And the parents would blame them if the students were arrested. They begged the students to stop their protest.

"Please, please, eat lunch," the teachers said. "If you don't, it will be difficult to explain."

Dechen remembers being torn about what to do. Her stomach was growling, and she didn't want to get her teachers in trouble. But she was also afraid to disobey the older students who had organized the fast. As a compromise, she and a few of her friends went to a small shop inside the school to buy snack food, but the boys saw them and started jeering and whistling. Then the headmaster saw the girls walking off by themselves and tried to question them about who had told them not to eat. The girls were in an impossible position.

A few days after the fast, the three older students who had organized the protest were removed from the school. One by one, they disappeared without explanation. After a few months, the students returned to school. They refused to talk about what had happened to them, and the other students were advised not to pry into the matter.

"You better not ask any questions, or you will be arrested too," Dechen's teacher warned.

Dechen obliged. She was terrified.

ONE OF THE HIGH POINTS of the Tibetan calendar is a three-day prayer festival known as Monlam that takes place toward the end of the New Year season. A giant scrolled tapestry of Tsongkhapa, founder of the Gelug school, is displayed on a wall of the monastery. Monks beat drums, perform in masked dances, and distribute sweets to the public. As Monlam approached in 2009, the monks anticipated that the authorities might scale back the festivities, but they were dismayed when word circulated through the monastery that the festival might be cancelled entirely. This wasn't entirely a surprise. Monlam had been banned throughout the Cultural Revolution. And because the date on the Tibetan calendar often fell close to the March anniversary of the Dalai Lama's flight to India, it was frequently an occasion for protests.

As the holiday approached, Dongtuk could feel the collective anxiety. Some monks warned they would protest if the prayers were cancelled. More troops were called in to surround the monastery. It felt like both sides were gearing up for a confrontation.

A few days before the scheduled start of Monlam, Dongtuk went to the market to buy vegetables for the day's meals. On the main street he saw a tall, lanky monk a few years older than himself loitering around a police car. Dongtuk recognized the monk on sight—he had a long face and the hunched posture of a teenager who'd grown too quickly—although he didn't know his name and had never spoken to him. The monk peered into the police car, putting his face practically up to the passenger's side window, and kicked the tires in disgust before striding off. The police officer sitting in the car did not react. But the Tibetans walking by looked on with concern, as did Dongtuk.

"This guy is very brave, really macho," Dongtuk said to himself. "He's looking for trouble."

On February 27, Kirti's monks dressed in their best robes and cloaks in the hope that the Monlam festival would begin. They had taken out the bright yellow cock's-comb hats reserved for ceremonial occasions. The *puja* prayer in which all the monks would participate was supposed to start at two P.M. Then it was pushed back to three P.M. Dongtuk heard the blowing of the *gyaling,* a double-reed instrument used to signal the beginning of the prayers, but when he arrived at the assembly hall, he heard that the festival had been cancelled after all and that there was trouble again.

A monk had set himself on fire. It had happened on the main street next to a police car. The name was unfamiliar, but in the excited chatter of his classmates, Dongtuk realized it was the monk he'd seen two days earlier who'd kicked the police car.

Dongtuk's curiosity got the best of him and he tried to get to the market to see for himself, but he couldn't get out of the gates. This time it wasn't the police who were blocking the monastery, but a large crowd of elderly Tibetan pilgrims. They had been on their way to the prayers and, as was often the case, wanted to protect the younger monks from harm. They yelled at Dongtuk to go back inside.

The monk was named Lobsang Tashi, a name he had been given when he joined the monastery, but everybody called him Tapey. He was easily recognized by his elongated face and quizzical eyebrows. He came from the *tawa,* the area surrounding the monastery. Video footage of the immolation shows a tall, thin figure in crimson stumbling around a white police car parked on the main street near the crossroads to the monastery. He appears to be gesticulating wildly as though trying to say something. He is dancing inside a fast-moving ball of fire. Flames shoot straight from his head and from his waving arms. A sudden puff of white envelops him—a fire extinguisher, perhaps—and then he rushes away from the police car. It is unclear why he changed direction, although Tibetan human rights groups later said that the police shot him three times.

The Kirti monks gathered again in front of the assembly hall. The tradition after a death was to carry the body to the family home for prayers. In this case, they didn't have a body—Tapey had been surrounded by police and taken away—but they proceeded anyway. They chanted their prayers and cried, still in a state of shock, as they walked in procession. Tapey's family lived in a traditional Tibetan house with a walled courtyard out front, and they crammed inside, some of the monks spilling outside the gate. As best they could, they conducted the prayers without the body, comforting the weeping family, and then headed back to the monastery. On their way, they discovered that the police had blocked all six entrances to the monastery. It was only after hours of arguing and persuasion that the monks were allowed back inside. And then they discovered yet another surprise in a day that already held too many of them. Tapey, the man whose death they had just prayed for, whose family was grieving his loss, was not in fact dead. He had survived the self-immolation. He would later be used in propaganda videos on Chinese television, in which—appearing drugged—he claimed he had been manipulated into burning himself by classmates at Kirti who mocked him for not participating in the 2008 protests.

The entire incident was baffling. Self-immolation has a long history among Chinese Buddhists, who have seen it as an assertion of their devotion. It was a not infrequent phenomenon in India among Buddhists and Hindus alike. But among Tibetans, self-immolation and suicide in general were taboo. The body was impermanent, to be sure, but suicide was thought to be cheating the natural cycle of death and rebirth. It was also an act of violence against the microbes living in one's own body.

In 1998, a Tibetan exile in New Delhi, Thubten Ngodrup, burned himself to death as Indian police were breaking up a hunger strike by members of the Tibetan Youth Congress. Another Tibetan in India burned himself, but survived, to protest a visit by China's then-president, Hu Jintao, in 2006. These were random, rare occurrences that seemed unlikely to inspire a trend.

After Tapey's experience, nobody in Ngaba expected it to happen again.

NO WAY OUT

Checkpoint in Ngaba.

BY 2009, DONGTUK FOUND HIMSELF SUFFERING NOT SO MUCH from oppression as from the chronic teenaged affliction of boredom.

He had been a rising star at the monastery, a top student and debater. Now he was an aimless fifteen-year-old with a fresh outcropping of acne and a bad attitude. After the self-immolation, the checkpoints tightened again like a noose squeezing out the life of the town. But Dongtuk had become more skilled in the art of deception. He learned how to bypass the checkpoints and lie to the teachers at the monastery. He and his friends would skip morning prayers and loiter around town. Sometimes they'd hitchhike or take a bus out of town. Once they wandered as far as Lanzhou, a city in Gansu province two hundred miles away. But they ran out of money quickly enough, couldn't thumb a ride, and had to beg on the streets for the bus fare home.

Although Ngaba was a small town, there were plenty of temptations to lead a young monk astray. A KTV bar, short for "karaoke television," had opened just down the main street from the monastery. The neon lights at night bathed the sidewalks in a garish rainbow that rivaled the bright crimsons and yellows of the monastery, which was no longer the most colorful structure in town. Chinese men would pull up in black cars with tinted windows. People whispered that prostitutes plied their trade inside. Dongtuk was too young and too poor to test his monastic vows, but he succumbed to lesser vices. An Internet café had opened between the bus station and the Middle School. Although the Chinese censors blocked many websites, the kids could message their friends with QQ or play games. Billiard parlors were popular among Tibetan men, even though the lamas denounced the pockets as the six circles of hell.

Like many young Tibetans, Dongtuk was crazy about basketball. It was the most popular sport in Ngaba and young people would play on packed dirt if they couldn't find a proper court. Dongtuk would team up with some of his childhood friends from Meruma, like Phuntsog, the biggest and most athletic of the old gang. Short and nearsighted, Dongtuk wasn't a natural at basketball, but he made up for his deficits with enthusiasm. He knew all the players of the NBA. Kirti Monastery didn't have a court, but the boys would wander into town to play at the school courts.

Dongtuk also developed a taste for movies. Ngaba no longer had a movie theater, but restaurants and tea shops turned themselves into informal cinemas, showing DVDs on a large screen. While his friends favored war movies and kung fu, Dongtuk had gentler taste and preferred Tibetan music videos. The shops charged a small admission fee.

Dongtuk once stole a bag of cheese from an older monk, sold it at the market, and used the money to watch movies and videos.

These antics gave Dongtuk a bad reputation. The senior monks were constantly calling his mother, Sonam, to complain that he'd run away, skipped prayers, or quarreled with a teacher. It wasn't enough to get him expelled, but the family predicted he would soon renounce his vows and drop out.

So the family was surprised when it was not Dongtuk, but his half brother, Rinzen Dorjee, who decided to leave the monastery. Rinzen Dorjee had always been the model son, sweet and respectful, so quiet that you would often forget he was in the room. Admittedly he was not the most brilliant student, but his placid temperament seemed to fit in with the monastic life. But one day, he came back to Meruma wearing lay clothes and simply announced, "I am no longer a monk."

It is not uncommon for boys enrolled as novices to leave the monastery when they reach puberty. Sometimes it's because they discover their sexuality or are rebelling against other strictures of the monastic life. Often, boys will leave because their families need them to work. It is a terrible sin to break one's vows while still a monk, but acceptable enough to leave the monastery to return to lay society.

Rinzen Dorjee offered no explanation. His parents asked him if he had a girlfriend, but he shook his head no. He just didn't want to be a monk anymore. His father tried to talk him out of it, but he knew it was hopeless. Rinzen Dorjee, although obedient, had a stubborn streak. He wasn't one to change his mind, not like Dongtuk, who was considered more volatile.

Rinzen Dorjee went back to work for his father, herding the yaks and the sheep. He built a small coop next to his father's house to raise pigeons. Sometimes he talked to his birds.

Traditional families from Meruma usually wanted one son to be a monk—it elevated the family from a religious standpoint, and also provided a room in which to stay when they went to town.

Now their father was convinced Dongtuk would be the next to quit. "He's the naughty one," he said.

Dongtuk, though, had no intention of leaving the monastery. On the contrary—his brief period of rebellion made him realize how much he missed his monastic studies. Dongtuk was not particularly athletic; he could barely ride a horse. He couldn't play the guitar or sing like his idols. He realized that studying was what he'd wanted to do all along. He thought back to the times as a small boy when he'd sneak into the locked shrine room in his mother's house. What else could he do but be a monk?

Dongtuk talked to his mother. It was impossible, he told her, to continue his studies in Ngaba. He wasn't yet eighteen, so his opportunities to participate in the monastery were limited. He wanted to go to India, the birthplace of Buddhism, to advance his studies. His mother scoffed at the idea.

"What's the point?" Sonam told him. "Only people who are learned scholars of Buddhism go to India. What's the point of sending an ignorant boy like you?"

She was still angry over the trouble he'd caused her with his frequent absences from Kirti. A trip to India would cost at least 20,000 yuan, about $3,000. As a disabled single mother, Sonam was always strapped for money; Dongtuk's father rarely had anything to contribute. Sonam examined her finances. Despite her lack of education, she was competent at managing money. She had even rebuilt their house a few years before, taking out a bank loan for the construction, but a trip to India for a boy who had been so poorly behaved did not seem like a prudent investment.

Dongtuk pestered her for months. He cajoled and he threatened. If she wouldn't let him leave for India, he would run away again, try to work to raise money, and go on his own. Sonam knew he was serious since he had bolted so often from the monastery. She started to work her contacts. Neighbors in Meruma promised to chip in. Sonam was popular in the village; people appreciated how hard she had worked to overcome her disabilities, but they had little money themselves.

She turned to a monk living in India who had a connection, albeit an unusual one, to her family. As a boy, he had been identified as the reincarnation of her late uncle—the goateed lama whose portrait graced the wall of her shrine room. He promised to help with the money and also to secure a place for Dongtuk at a branch of Kirti Monastery that had been established in Dharamsala in 1990.

IN THE AFTERMATH OF the Dalai Lama's flight from Lhasa in 1959, about 80,000 Tibetans followed him to exile in India. Another wave followed in the 1980s. Some were activists fearing arrest or recently released from political prison. Others were pilgrims who wanted to receive a blessing from the Dalai Lama. Others were young people with wanderlust. Perhaps the largest category were the roughly 24,000 Tibetan students who sought educational opportunities that were unavailable for them in China. More than seventy schools run by the Tibetan government in exile offered young Tibetans the chance for a modern education that was steeped in neither Chinese Communist propaganda nor religion, a middle ground between the government and the monastic schools. They could learn their own language and history, as well as English and sometimes Chinese. Other schools were run by charities and monasteries.

For decades, Tibetans had trekked through the Himalayas over an ancient pilgrimage and trading route, the Nangpa La pass, which lies just to the northwest of Mount Everest. The topography and persistent border disputes between China and India made it most practical to cross first into Nepal, where refugee organizations were set up to receive them. At an elevation of 19,000 feet, it was a treacherous route. Many refugees suffered from frostbite, snow blindness, and altitude sickness. In 2006, a Romanian mountaineer on a hiking expedition to Cho Oyu Mountain near the pass captured footage of Chinese soldiers opening fire on a column of refugees, killing a seventeen-year-old Buddhist nun.

It had always been difficult for Tibetans to get out of China, but nonetheless, at least 1,000 used to make it to India every year. Since the protests of 2008, the numbers have dropped to the dozens. Even the Nangpa La pass was blocked.

The Chinese government had adopted a policy that effectively prevented Tibetans from leaving China. The government created a two-track system in which residents of predominantly Tibetan prefectures as well as the Uighurs (the Muslims of the northwest) had to go through an impossibly cumbersome process to apply for a passport. Human Rights Watch found that 36 of the 339 prefectures in China had been designated as "areas where passports are not supplied on demand" and that those were prefectures populated by minorities.

"Getting a passport is harder for a Tibetan than getting into heaven," a Tibetan blogger complained.

As for the few lucky Tibetans who had gotten passports in the past, the government confiscated them on various pretexts, claiming they needed to be turned in for "safekeeping" or replaced with newer passports with biometric data on embedded chips.

The purpose of the policy, never fully articulated, was to keep Tibetans away from the influence of the Dalai Lama. If they couldn't leave the country, they couldn't visit him in Dharamsala or attend any of the innumerable lectures the peripatetic monk delivered around the world.

The unfairness rankled Tibetans. This was precisely the time that upwardly mobile Chinese, flush with cash, were spreading their wings, arriving by the planeload in Paris and Venice to enjoy the splendors of the wider world. Their children were headed to prep schools and universities in the United States, where they'd become the largest overseas student population. The Tibetans wanted no more, no less than other Chinese citizens.

AS HE EXPLORED HIS OPTIONS to travel to India, Dongtuk almost lost his nerve. The expenses were prohibitive, the obstacles seemingly insurmountable. It would require navigational skills he did not possess—not just a matter of finding the route through the Himala-yas, but maneuvering through Chinese bureaucracy. He hardly spoke any Chinese. He didn't even have a Chinese identity card.

Dongtuk managed to get to Lhasa, which is on the way to the bor-der with Nepal. He stayed initially with one of his mother's relatives, but after her home was inspected by police looking for unauthorized visitors, the family had to move him into a hotel owned by an ac-quaintance. Since the troubles in 2008, the authorities had required Tibetans to get a permit to visit Lhasa; and the permits were scarce for Ngaba people, who had a reputation as troublemakers. Without pa-pers, Dongtuk was scared to walk around Lhasa. More soldiers pa-trolled the streets here than even in Ngaba. The narrow stone streets of the old Tibetan quarter were sectioned off with checkpoints. Snip-ers were stationed on rooftops.

Dongtuk had been advised that monks attracted more scrutiny than laypeople, so he put aside his robes and bought blue jeans. He stopped shaving his head. His hair grew back spiky and jagged. He tried to dye it blond but it turned out red. He bought large sunglasses to protect his eyes, weak since childhood, from the blinding glare of Lhasa's high-altitude sun. Now he looked like a punk rocker, but this guise was more tolerable in the eyes of Chinese authorities than that of a monk.

The plan had been for Dongtuk to get a travel permit to the border with Nepal, but he didn't have the paperwork he needed to apply. Dongtuk and a friend met a smuggler who told them that for 20,000 yuan (about $3,000) each he could get them a car to the border. That was Dongtuk's entire budget for the trip, and he had spent half his money already just on living expenses in Lhasa. He telephoned his mother to consult.

Sonam said she could raise the money, but then she consulted a monk who performed a divination for her, and he advised against it. She told Dongtuk to come home.

Defeated, Dongtuk returned to Ngaba. He lived for a few months back at the monastery, skipping away most days to play basketball, although he no longer enjoyed it. He was depressed. So he moved back in with his mother, moping around the house all day. Sonam was distraught. After opposing her son's dream to go to India, she was convinced now it was the only way for him to fulfill his destiny as a monk—in fact, the same oracle had told her so—and she resolved to help him. She went deeper into debt so that she could accompany Dongtuk on another trip to Lhasa to investigate.

She wasn't much more successful than Dongtuk, but together they got one important tip: They were told they needed documents from the Public Security Bureau in Ngaba—among them a letter guaranteeing that Dongtuk didn't have a criminal record. They were advised to visit the administrative offices after the Chinese and Tibetan New Year's holidays, when the senior officials were still on vacation, leaving their more compliant underlings in charge.

And so it was that Dongtuk was back in Ngaba in early 2011. Just when he thought he had extricated himself from a bad situation, he had returned at a time that was more dangerous than ever before.

CHAPTER

19

. . .

BOY ON FIRE

The monk Phuntsog.

MARCH 16, 2011. IT WAS A BRIGHT DAY ON THE CUSP
of spring. Tufts of grass pierced through the snow, which would soon
begin its annual retreat up the slopes of the mountains. Dongtuk took
a minivan rideshare into Ngaba hoping to get a travel document he
needed for his trip. His mother and sister had accompanied him. When
they arrived at the entrance of town, they found the checkpoint

closed. This time, the police weren't even inspecting identity cards; they just waved the van away with a dismissive gesture. Tibetans know better than to start an argument at a checkpoint, so the driver backed up the van to turn around and return his passengers to the villages.

But Dongtuk said no, he would get out and walk the rest of the way. Before his mother could object, he hopped out of the car in front of Sinopec, the town's only gas station, near the eastern checkpoint.

As he proceeded on foot, he could see there was trouble in town. Although it was midafternoon, shops were closed, their metal shutters down. Police cars cruised back and forth between the checkpoint and the center of the town. Instinctively, Dongtuk got off the main road and took a detour favored by the locals when they wanted to avoid the police. He cut behind the People's Hospital and the Public Security Bureau, where the parking lots devolved into uncultivated fields. It was better to trudge through the mud than walk in plain view on the sidewalks. Other Tibetans were doing the same. Dongtuk didn't want to ask, but he tried to eavesdrop on the conversations and the story eventually revealed itself.

There had been an incident. A fire. Somebody had lit a fire. Lit himself on fire. It was a monk from Kirti Monastery. Again.

Dongtuk knew he ought to hurry back to the checkpoint and catch another car back to Meruma. He was in a precarious situation. Ngaba was a small town—he didn't want to be recognized. Many people knew that he had been trying to go to India, which was in itself a crime. His mother had warned him to keep a low profile. Even Tibetans he knew well could be informers who'd point him out to the police. He was seventeen years old now—no longer a kid. He could be arrested and sent to jail.

He was thankful that he had changed his appearance in Lhasa. His hair had grown out now into a reddish bouffant and he was wearing large tinted glasses that made him look less like a punk than like a middle-aged Chinese woman. He reflexively pulled his thick black-and-white scarf over the lower part of his face as he headed to the center of town. He felt himself sweating. Although it was only March, the sun was punishingly bright. Or maybe the town was on fire with intensity.

He cut through an alley between the storefronts on the main street to reach the market area with its clutter of carts stacked with fruits and vegetables, sneakers, hats, and scarves—usually the most crowded place in town, except today everything was closed.

He realized he was at the very spot where the self-immolation had happened. There was a cordon of police surrounded by a crowd of Tibetan onlookers. On the sidewalk stood a gaggle of old women, traditionally dressed in big chubas and black braids, with fat beads around their necks; it looked as if they had come from the monastery. They were crying and yelling, praying and screaming—calling at one moment for compassion and the next for revenge.

"Om mani padme hum." They chanted the mantra calling for compassion.

"Chinese bastards."

"Eat dirt."

"May dust fill their mouths!"—a favorite curse in Ngaba.

Tucking his face further into his scarf, Dongtuk jostled between the women to get a better look. In front of a small shop that made metal stoves and across from a bar called Chomolungma (the Tibetan name for Mount Everest), he could see a trail of white foam caked onto the pavement—probably the residue from the fire extinguishers. He backed away, and as he did he looked down and spotted a cardboard matchbox with wooden matches spilling onto the pavement. He reached down before anybody could notice and tucked them into his pocket. He wondered if these were the very matches that the monk had used to light himself on fire.

Dongtuk still couldn't believe it. He'd been sure that nobody would try to burn themselves after what had happened to Tapey, the monk who survived a self-immolation two years earlier and was left a mangled invalid imprisoned in a Chinese hospital, trotted out for propaganda on Chinese television. Who could be so idiotic as to try it again? Who could be so brave?

The people around him seemed to be milling about in a state of shock. And something else was astir. After the monk burned himself, the police and military had stormed Kirti Monastery in search of somebody to blame. Twenty-five monks were arrested and were being held at the police station. The older people who were the self-appointed defenders of the monastery moved on from the site of the self-immolation to the sidewalk across from the station, holding a vigil to wait for the release of the monks. A younger, more boisterous crowd gathered directly in front of the police station. Dongtuk had learned enough about the choreography of protests from 2008 to realize that all the actors were in position for a repeat performance.

At this point there was no practical reason for Dongtuk to remain in Ngaba. The public security office where he'd hoped to get his papers was closed. He could almost hear his mother pleading for him to return to Meruma. But he was consumed by the same curiosity that had sent him to town when obviously he should have turned back at the checkpoint. He couldn't look away. He had some money for the administrative fees—just enough to rent a room for the night. Ngaba was full of cheap hotels that catered to villagers who came into town to shop or sell goods. He picked a hotel across the street from the police station so that he could see what was going on. Naturally, the hotel was abuzz with talk of the self-immolation and the arrest of the monks. Dongtuk was reluctant to engage in the conversation since he was traveling incognito, so he loitered around the lobby and eavesdropped.

At first, he thought he'd heard it incorrectly, but people kept repeating the name: Phuntsog. Many Tibetans have the same name, but this was Phuntsog from Meruma, from the Jarutsang family. That Phuntsog. His friend. Phuntsog was a few years older, but assigned to the same teacher as Dongtuk at Kirti—which was like being in the same homeroom or residential college. Dongtuk was always a little intimidated by Phuntsog, not because he was a bully in any way, but because he was an excellent athlete and student, equally talented in both aspects. Although Phuntsog's father was a blacksmith of the same lowly social class as Dongtuk's, the Jarutsang were a large, respected family. Dongtuk recalled that Phuntsog's grandfather, Dhondor, had been one of the anti-Chinese resistance leaders in the 1950s. It was all beginning to make sense—like grandfather, like grandson.

Phuntsog was a strong young man with a radiant smile. As a teenager, he had developed a passion for weight lifting; he liked to show off his six-pack and flex his impressive biceps. Phuntsog was very proud of his body—a quality perhaps incongruent for a monk headed for a lifetime of celibacy and asceticism. Only later did Dongtuk think that perhaps Phuntsog had lavished so much attention on his body so that it would be a worthy offering when it was consumed by fire.

Dongtuk's emotions flitted between revulsion and respect. He tried to imagine how much it would hurt—he remembered how painful it was when sparks from a smoke bomb burned his hand. He wondered how it was that Phuntsog, the same age, the same upbringing, from a family much like his own, could have made the decision to douse himself with gasoline and light himself on fire. Dongtuk fingered the matches he'd picked up on the street. He wondered if he would ever have the courage to do something like that. Probably not, he had to admit. But outside the hotel, as he watched the angry crowds gathering like storm clouds in front of the police station, he thought that for sure there would be protests and for sure this time he would join in as an adult. "At that moment, I had no doubt, no doubt at all, that I was ready to die," he would later recall.

At midnight, the Ngaba police released the monks who had been arrested earlier in the day. Somebody high up must have ordered that the authorities show restraint, at least for the time being, to prevent another uprising.

Phuntsog was more successful than Tapey. He died at three the next morning. His funeral was one of the largest anybody in Ngaba could remember. It took place on a hillside about two miles from Kirti, the same place used for sky burials, but in the case of Phuntsog, he was cremated because he had drenched himself in gasoline, making the body unsuitable for consumption by the birds. Long lines of

mourners made the slow climb up the hill chanting mantras and dragging a long, white rope made of *khata*s, the ceremonial scarves.

Dongtuk's mother didn't allow him to attend. When he'd returned
home to Meruma, Sonam was so worried that she wouldn't let him
out of her sight. She had one son and she wasn't going to let him burn
himself to death or get shot protesting. She told Dongtuk that he
could mourn his friend properly by chanting mantras in the privacy of
his own home, and for once, he had to admit that his mother was
right. But he remained in the same volatile state and couldn't stop
flirting with trouble. A horseback riding festival was planned for the
summer. Dongtuk decided that Tibetans should not participate in
anything so festive, and so from his home he started a campaign to
stop it. When his mother went out, he got some white typing paper
and wrote out his message by hand:

> I URGE THE PEOPLE OF MERUMA TO REFRAIN
> FROM LAVISH FESTIVITIES LIKE WEDDINGS AND
> HORSE RACES OUT OF COMPASSION FOR THE
> MARTYR PHUNTSOG WHO SELF-IMMOLATED FOR
> OUR CAUSE. WE MUST STAND IN SOLIDARITY.

He posted the notices at three locations in Meruma—on the bridge,
on the window of a restaurant, and at a small shrine near the stream.
When Sonam found out what he'd done, she was furious. By now, she
had invested most of her savings and more in the plan for him to study
in India. She wanted him out of Ngaba for good; there was no chance
if he got himself arrested. She spoke to Dongtuk's father and they
agreed to send Dongtuk to live with Rinzen Dorjee, his half brother,
to herd yaks for the rest of the year.

SONAM WAS RIGHT TO get him out into the mountains and away
from Kirti.

Although Chinese authorities had avoided provoking the crowds the night of Phuntsog's death, they were not prepared to let his death go unpunished. In the following weeks, three hundred monks were arrested. The monastery was barricaded once more, encircled by armed soldiers, barbed wire, dogs, and armored personnel carriers. The food supply dwindled. The local government put out a pamphlet saying the reeducation program was necessary because "some monks in the monastery had visited prostitutes, got drunk, and kicked up rows and engaged in gambling . . . and some disseminated pornographic videos"—a claim that nobody in Ngaba believed.

It's impossible to prosecute somebody who is already dead, so the authorities searched for novel legal theories in order to inflict punishment. They charged three people with homicide in connection with his death. After immolating himself, Phuntsog had been picked up in a van and transported to Kirti Monastery, all of which had been captured by closed-circuit cameras. The monks said they had taken the dying monk to prevent him from being mishandled by the Chinese police. The Chinese police had beaten and kicked Phuntsog as he lay on the ground.

The Chinese court, however, ruled that the monks' action was tantamount to homicide because Phuntsog was still alive and should have gone to the hospital. "They were well aware that Phuntsog had sustained serious injuries from the burns, and they moved him when he should have received emergency medical care," the Maerkang (Barkham, or Ngaba prefecture) People's Court found in its ruling.

Phuntsog's uncle, who was one of those who handled his body, received an eleven-year prison sentence. Two other monks got lesser sentences. Phuntsog's father and one of his brothers were sentenced to six years.

So began a pattern that would persist over the next few years. Anybody who had anything to do with a self-immolation could face criminal charges for homicide and subversion. In December 2012, China's top court issued an opinion saying that anybody urging self-immolation should be charged with "intentional homicide" and, furthermore, that their motivation was to "split the nation . . . endanger public safety and social order," according to the Dui Hua Foundation, a human rights group. Among those prosecuted were people who overheard a comment in advance, people who sold kerosene or even the plastic jugs in which kerosene is carried, people who took photos and videos on their cellphones, and people who gave information about the self-immolators to human rights organizations.

If the policy was designed to deter further self-immolations, it backfired. In mid-August, a monk in Kardze (Ganzi in Chinese), another tense part of Sichuan province, distributed leaflets calling for the Dalai Lama's return before drinking petroleum and setting himself on fire in front of the county administrative offices. On September 26, Phuntsog's younger brother, Kelsang, also a Kirti monk, along with an eighteen-year-old classmate, repeated his brother's self-immolation in nearly the same location. Just eighteen years old, Kelsang was a dead ringer for his brother; he had the same wide grin and dimpled cheeks. Kelsang and his friend survived, and like Tapey ended up as cautionary tales on Chinese television.

After that incident, the self-immolators improved their technique to ensure they died. They swaddled themselves in quilts and then coiled wire around the quilts so that they couldn't be easily removed to extinguish the flames. They not only drenched themselves with gasoline, but drank it as well so that they burned from the inside. The self-immolators were determined to perish; they were better off dead than locked in a Chinese hospital with their limbs amputated.

On October 7, two former Kirti monks, Kayang and Choepel, who had been forced out during the crackdown, did a joint self-immolation on Ngaba's main street. The two boys, both about eighteen, held hands as they went up in flames. Both were taken to the hospital, but died soon after.

Ten days later, a twenty-year-old Tibetan nun self-immolated in front of the Mamey Dechen Choekorling nunnery, about two miles west of Kirti and also politically active. Nuns had marched to town during the 2008 protests, and one had been shot to death. Relatives later released a photograph of the nun who self-immolated, Tenzin

Wangmo, whose beauty was all the more striking for her shaven head. She was the first woman to self-immolate.

It was getting harder for Chinese propagandists to claim that Tibetans were happy. One self-immolation led to another and then another. There was no stopping it.

CHAPTER

2 0

...

SORROWS

Photos of self-immolators, Dharamsala.

NGABA HAD NEVER BEEN SO FAMOUS. THIS NOTHING LITTLE town that had just gotten its first traffic light, a place few people even in Sichuan province had heard of, let alone visited, was now putting Tibet back in the headlines. The undisputed world capital of self-immolations, it was on the front page of newspapers around the world.

It was discussed in white papers, congressional hearings, and academic conferences. The U.S. ambassador to China, Gary Locke, tried to investigate, requesting permission to visit Ngaba, but was allowed only as far as Songpan, which is part of the same large Ngaba *prefecture* but one hundred miles from Ngaba *county*. Chinese authorities had never welcomed foreigners in Ngaba, but it had never been a tourist destination anyway. Now the curious were determined. Foreign television crews tried to slip by the cordon of checkpoints. A favored technique was for the foreign correspondent to scoot down in the back seat with cameras pointing out the window, trying to capture images that would bring clarity to the confusion.

It wasn't only the journalists and diplomats trying to gain access. Tibetans from elsewhere were coming for the express purpose of self-immolating. The main street, identified on Chinese maps as Route 302 or Qingtong Lu, Tibetans now renamed Pawo Road, street of the heroes or martyrs. To keep people out, cameras were mounted over the roads leading into town, photographing all cars and their occupants with a blinding flash. Tank traps and high slanted barricades of reinforced steel closed off all the entrances to town and were erected on almost every block. Interspersed among the pedicabs and peddler carts were futuristic vehicles displaying state-of-the-art riot control technology. One white armored vehicle had cameras on top that pivoted to point at bystanders. Another in camouflage was mounted with machine guns. A long white vehicle had a turret in the back. Oversized buses with flashing police lights carried personnel into action. There were also conventional vehicles—canvas-covered troop transport trucks, jeeps, and police cars. An armored personnel carrier was stationed in front of the Yonganli Department Store, the one owned by "Brushhead" that had been gutted by protesters in 2008.

In 2011, China's domestic security budget, at $95 billion, surpassed defense spending for the first time. The budget for what the Chinese called "stability maintenance" in Ngaba prefecture increased sixfold from 2002 to 2009, and was roughly five times the level for non-Tibetan areas of Sichuan province, according to an analysis by Human

Rights Watch. It was hard to tell who was military and who was police, as there is a blur in the functions in China, but there was such
variety of uniforms and insignia that it almost looked like a military
parade. The special police wore black and carried riot shields as they
marched double file down the street. The armed police, or *wujing,*
wore khaki or bright green with red epaulets. The security forces carried rifles, shields, spiked clubs, and fire extinguishers—the newest
and most indispensable tool in the arsenal.

Witnessing a self-immolation was risky. In every case, at least half
a dozen people were arrested. Many of the arrests resulted from skir-
mishes over the bodies. As soon as someone burned, Tibetan bystanders would rush in to claim the body for a traditional prayer service and
funeral. If the person was still alive, they'd be taken to a quiet sanctu-
ary to die. Horror stories had emerged about the torment inflicted on
dying burn victims in Chinese hospitals.

In Meruma's administrative center, a man named Kunchok Tsetsen
immolated himself at two P.M. on December 23, 2013. It was shortly
before school let out for the day, so there were a number of parents
nearby heading to pick up their children. When they saw the burned
man, they rushed to help load the body into a van. Closed-circuit
cameras captured the scene. All the parents who participated were arrested. A former monk told me that his sister, who had gone to pick
up her daughter, was arrested that same afternoon. She received a
three-year sentence.

Over time, the Tibetans in Ngaba became more resentful of the
extraordinary security cordon around their town. Ngaba's gas station,
the Sinopec, near Se Monastery, was cordoned off with police tape.
You could only buy gas with an identification card. It was also forbidden to buy gasoline or kerosene in canisters, which posed a problem
for the rural Tibetans who needed to stock up on their infrequent
visits to town. People without electricity still used kerosene for lamps.

A woman who ran a small general store was arrested after she sold
kerosene to a monk who later immolated himself. "It was a family
business. They had a lot of children. The husband begged the police to

take him instead, but they said, no, she was the one who sold it," a neighbor told me. Somebody had to be punished.

The greatest inconvenience, though, was that communication to Ngaba was almost entirely severed. Landlines, mobile phones, and 3G were all affected. From 2011 to 2013, it was difficult even to call a government office in Ngaba from Beijing. The police station and post office had the Internet for a while, but then it was unplugged entirely, not just censored as it is in most of China. This spawned an entirely new phenomenon of "Internet refugees." Ngaba residents had to travel across the border to Qinghai province, where Internet cafés were still operating.

Business people—some of them Chinese—appealed to government officials to have communication restored. Economic life was strangled without telephones and Internet, but the authorities were insistent. If they couldn't stop the self-immolations, they could at least keep people from finding out about them. A self-immolation without publicity would be like a tree falling in a forest.

As it happened, very little transpired in Ngaba that didn't end up on a camera of one sort or another. The Tibetans were early adopters of technology—after motorcycles and solar panels, the first thing they bought was an iPhone or a Samsung Galaxy. Between the phones and the ubiquitous closed-circuit cameras, many of the self-immolations were captured on video and made public, the first of the social media age. There are close to a dozen of them on YouTube, all gruesome in their own way. For the most part, the self-immolators did not achieve the composure of the Vietnamese monk Thich Quang Duc, who managed to maintain a perfect motionless lotus pose throughout. In the videos from Ngaba, one streaks down a dimly lit gray street like a fireball. Another twitches and crumples like a piece of paper thrown into a fireplace. Those whose bodies are completely consumed shrivel as small as children, blackened and twisted. The worst is the screaming coming from the onlookers—a high-pitched keening, like an animal being strangled.

The self-immolators often left goodbye notes and videos on the hugely popular texting app WeChat. One of the most articulate was an eminent reincarnate monk, Lama Sobha, who left a nine-minute recording in which he said, "I am giving away my body as an offering of light to chase away the darkness to free all beings from suffering." Another announced his self-immolation on a WeChat group popular among Tibetan businessmen that was dedicated to nonviolence.

By November 2011, the Dalai Lama was being asked regularly to weigh in, and his statements often sounded muddled. "There is courage—very strong courage. But how much effect?" he told the BBC. "Courage alone is no substitute. You must utilize your wisdom." He would later explain that he was trying to discourage self-immolation, but did not wish to offend the surviving families by condemning the deed. "The reality is if I say something positive, then the Chinese immediately blame me," he said. "If I say something negative, then the family members of these people feel very sad. They sacrificed their life. It is not easy."

The Dalai Lama was in a bind. The young men and women who were killing themselves did so in his name—carrying his photograph and chanting for his long life. Most of the self-immolators who made statements in advance referred to their desire for the Dalai Lama to return to Tibet. At the same time, the self-immolations were an implicit rejection of his policies. His call for nonviolence, for patience and cooperation with the Chinese, wasn't working; by burning themselves, Tibetans were highlighting his failures.

Tibetan advocacy groups were also in an awkward position. They couldn't be seen as encouraging young Tibetans to kill themselves, but the self-immolations brought publicity to a cause that had long since disappeared from the headlines. On a world stage losing interest in the rights of self-determination of other peoples like the Kurds and Palestinians, and now consumed with the fresh horrors of the news cycle, the Tibetans were off the map. The self-immolations brought them back.

In Paris, the Collège de France hosted a two-day conference in May 2012 entitled "Tibet Is Burning: Self-Immolation: Ritual or Political Protest?" The scholars uncovered many contradictions in Buddhist attitudes toward suicide. "Self-immolation is viewed differently according to the period and the school of Buddhism to which one refers," Katia Buffetrille, a French Tibetologist and one of the conference organizers, wrote in a journal published afterward. "It seems one can always find the answer one wants to find in one text or another."

For everyone who argued that Buddhism prohibited suicide, many more countered that the self-immolators had become bodhisattvas, giving up their lives for the enlightenment of others. Some invoked a story that the Buddha, in an earlier incarnation, had fed himself to a starving tigress so that she wouldn't have to eat her newborn cubs. Looking for doctrinal justification for self-immolation, others turned to the Lotus Sutra, an important Buddhist scripture compiled around the first century C.E. in which a bodhisattva known as the medicine king sacrifices himself by fire.

As researchers delved into the history of self-immolation (or auto-cremation, as it was more technically called), what became clear was that the Tibetan Buddhists were novices when compared to the Chinese. Chinese Buddhists had been burning themselves with regularity since the fourth century. A Buddhist scholar, James Benn, who researched the phenomenon, found hundreds of cases of monks, nuns, Zen masters, scholars, and hermits who had, in Buddhist terminology, abandoned or left their earthly bodies in order to advance their path to enlightenment. At times, it was a spectacle for invited guests, a veritable sound and light show. Before the sixth-century monk Daodu immolated, his monastery was bathed in multicolored rays of light and the environs echoed with mysterious sounds. A few were described—by perhaps unreliable chroniclers—as having spontaneously combusted. As a method of suicide, it is believed to be particularly painful, although the pain is reported to subside quickly as nerve endings are destroyed.

In his classic 1897 study of suicide, the French sociologist Émile Durkheim distinguished between four types of suicide: egoistic, anomic (in which an individual suffers moral confusion), fatalistic (somebody who has no other options, for example, a person in prison or suffering from a fatal illness), and altruist (somebody who kills himself for the benefit of society as a whole). "The term suicide is applied to all cases of death resulting directly or indirectly from a positive or negative act of the victim himself, which he knows will produce this result," Durkheim wrote. A scholar quoted in *The New Yorker* offered a cogent explanation: "Fire is the most dreaded of all forms of death," he wrote, so "the sight of someone setting themselves on fire is simultaneously an assertion of intolerability and, frankly, of moral superiority. . . . This isn't insanity. It's a terrible act of reason."

At least initially, most of the self-immolators were in their teens and twenties, the age group thought most vulnerable to "cluster" suicides. Psychologists sometimes refer to the "Werther effect," after the 1774 novel *The Sorrows of Young Werther,* by Johann Wolfgang von Goethe. It tells the story of a young man who kills himself after a failed romance; the book was blamed for inspiring countless copycat suicides in Europe.

Although Tibetans in Ngaba were not all that attuned to international affairs, many had heard about the Tunisian fruit vendor Mohamed Bouazizi, whose self-immolation in 2010 after the confiscation of his electronic scales set off a chain of events that led to the Arab Spring. More than a few Tibetans imagined that it might happen the same way in China. Jamyang Norbu, a U.S.-based Tibetan intellectual and an eloquent Tibetan commentator, wrote on his blog in November 2011 that the self-immolations could be "the ultimate sacrifice to rouse the Tibetan people to action, in much the same way that Mohamed Bouazizi's self-immolation woke up the oppressed people of the Middle East from many, many decades of fear, apathy, cynicism, and weariness."

The self-immolations thrust the Chinese leadership into a panic. It was not merely the obvious loss of face. Beijing was already on edge over the imploding of the dictatorships in Tunisia, Egypt, Libya, and Syria. Young Chinese were organizing pro-democracy demonstrations in Beijing inspired by events in the Middle East; although only a few Chinese dared to show up, the gatherings were well attended by the international press corps and publicized accordingly.

Chinese state media went on the offensive, trying to dig up dirt and discredit the self-immolators. Under the headline "Self-Immolation Truth," Xinhua, the official news service, claimed that the teenagers failed to get good grades and had killed themselves because they couldn't stand the competition. One woman was caught in a feud with her alcoholic husband. Another felt guilty over 8,000 yuan he had stolen. The lama, Xinhua claimed, was having an affair with a married woman.

One monk told me that family members were under pressure to say that self-immolators were suffering from depression. A man he knew in Dzorge lost his wife when she self-immolated. "You should say that your wife killed herself out of grief," authorities told the man. "If you do, you will get money in compensation for her loss." The man refused and was arrested for complicity in her death.

As of November 2019, 156 Tibetans had self-immolated and about one-third of the cases were in Ngaba or its surroundings. Thirty of those were former or current Kirti monks and most of those came from Meruma. The rest were almost all from Amdo and Kham, the eastern reaches of the Tibetan plateau. Even the single self-immolation that took place in Lhasa, in front of the Jokhang Temple, was a former Kirti monk from Ngaba.

The reasons why Ngaba led the plateau in self-immolation were obscure. Ngaba was not the worst-off town under Chinese rule. Its residents were wealthier than some others. The public facilities and infrastructure were much better than in many Tibetan towns in Qinghai province where sewage ran through open gutters of the streets and former nomads had been resettled in concrete boxes. Testifying before a U.S. congressional commission in 2011, Kirti Rinpoche suggested the reason was that Ngaba was the first place where Tibetans encountered the Chinese Communists in the 1930s. "The people of this region have a particular wound causing excessive suffering that spans three generations. This wound is very difficult to forget or heal," Kirti Rinpoche testified.

Daniel Berounský, a scholar who contributed a paper at the Paris conference, also pointed to the high level of political awareness at the monastery. "When taking into account the historical outline concerning the kings of Ngawa [Ngaba] and the Kīrti masters, it becomes apparent that the monks are strongly affected by their past history, which is seen as a golden time."

A Tibetan Party official who penned a rare open letter published (and quickly removed) on a public forum blamed Shi Jun, the Party secretary for Ngaba prefecture. "Some called him the Lord of Demons, because he escalated small incidents into huge confrontations in order to secure his own advancement and to try to win brownie points," wrote the official, who used his Chinese name, Luo Feng. He complained that Tibetan-speaking officials were excluded from promotion and that out of six hundred Party officials who had been recently promoted, only twenty spoke Tibetan. If you were Tibetan, you were an object of suspicion, Luo Feng wrote.

Discussions about self-immolation took place in every Tibetan tea shop, home, and tent, although people usually spoke in lowered voices. To talk about it implied firsthand knowledge, which could get you arrested. A monk in his seventies who lived on a windswept mountain in a village six miles to the west of Ngaba told me that suicide is permissible in Buddhism under certain circumstances.

"It all depends on your motivation. If somebody does this to benefit the Tibetan people, if it will help the Dalai Lama return to his land, if it will build support from America and the European Union to help us become an independent country, then it is worth it, no?" he said. One of the monk's relatives, a woman who was a few years younger, disagreed. She was upset about a young man who had self-immolated in a nearby town. "His father is blind in both eyes. His mother has tuberculosis. We are trying to help the family with some food and money, but there is nobody to take care of the parents now."

At least initially the self-immolations were confined to monks and nuns, who are understood by Tibetans to have absolved themselves of responsibility for their families, but the laypeople were another story. One self-immolation that elicited widespread disapproval was a thirty-two-year-old widowed mother, a woman named Rinchen. Her husband had died the year before. She had four children, the youngest a baby less than one year old. Rinchen was reported to have shouted for the return of the Dalai Lama to Tibet before lighting herself on fire in front of the army barracks in Ngaba at six thirty A.M. on the morning of March 4, 2012. Little more has emerged about what else in her life might have led her to self-immolation. In the one blurry photograph that was published, she appears to have been an attractive woman with full lips, black hair swept slightly off-center, and a necklace of stone beads.

One thing that made the Tibetans proud of the self-immolators was that they had so thoroughly incorporated the Dalai Lama's teachings about nonviolence that they hurt nobody but themselves. One self-immolator, a middle-aged man named Neykyab, had been involved in a dispute with a neighbor; just before he immolated himself in his own courtyard on April 15, 2015, he explained on a WeChat group dedicated to nonviolence that he would take his life rather than be tempted to commit violence toward this neighbor. In conversation, Tibetans frequently contrasted the self-immolations with the violence in Xinjiang, the northwestern territory where periodic attacks by Uighurs with knives and homemade explosives had been killing dozens of Han Chinese each year. Tibetans in the past had been fierce fighters against the Red Army, but in self-immolation, their violence was turned inward.

With the exception of a firefighter, there were no reports of any Han Chinese being seriously injured by a Tibetan in Ngaba—not during the self-immolations, not even during the protests of 2008. Not even, say, in a random bar fight did I hear of a Chinese person beaten or stabbed by a Tibetan. It's almost impossible to believe it didn't happen at least once, but if so it was not reported.

THE
ZIP LINE

A monk in Kodari, Nepal, looking at the border with Tibet, 2014.

PEMA INADVERTENTLY WITNESSED THE FIRST OF THE self-immolations. She had been working at her stall in the winter of 2009, selling her counterfeit sneakers, when she saw an eerie flash of light streaking through the market. Although she didn't realize it at the time, it was the monk Tapey, on fire. Chinese soldiers surrounded him, then spun around as though fearful of being ambushed, their guns facing outward toward the stunned onlookers. There was no place for Pema to run and hide, so she stood frozen in place. She was close enough to see the monk's charred crimson robes and blackened face; only his nose was left curiously untouched by fire. Then she watched as the Chinese soldiers picked him up and tossed him into the back of a truck.

"Like an animal, they threw him in," she told her family later.

The scene haunted her for months. She became increasingly fearful of leaving home. She trembled when she saw the police vehicles with their guns and cameras protruding from the turrets. It was like living in a war zone. She was afraid to go anywhere that would require her to pass through a checkpoint—no matter that she had a new identity card for which she'd been fingerprinted and had her eyes scanned. She was always watching over her shoulder, convinced that the police were after her. So many people had been arrested over the preceding year—monks, neighbors, students, nomads, women from the market—that it was hard to relax. Her heart would race when she thought back to the death of her niece, Lhundup Tso.

In the past, Pema had always prided herself on her composure in the face of the misfortunes in her life—her arranged marriage to an impoverished, already married man and then, after finally learning to love him, losing him when she was still in the prime of life. Her faith told her that was her karma. Now she found her resilience strained beyond the breaking point. Her relatives said she was suffering from wind disease, a term for anxiety used colloquially by Tibetans.

Pema's young cousin, Dechen, was also faring poorly. Her adjustment to the Tibetan Middle School had not gone well. The school was seething with tensions, some political in nature and some run-of-the-mill teenaged angst. After the first immolation in 2009, school authorities locked the gates for weeks to prevent students from organizing or joining protests. Some of the braver students escaped by jumping out windows, but Dechen was too timid.

Abandoned by her mother, shunned by her father and stepmother, Dechen was an angry girl. She wasn't being bullied as she had been in elementary school. Now she had her own gang of friends, five tough girls who vowed to protect each other. They often got into fights with another gang. One day the girls in her group jostled a boy in another group, and then one of the boys pushed back and then a girl who was known to be rowdy slapped one of the boys. Later that evening, Dechen had already forgotten what the fight was about, but when she undressed, she realized that the back of her jacket had been slit open. Down her back was an inflamed red wound where she had been grazed with a knife.

Although Dechen remained ambivalent about her identity as a Tibetan, events of the preceding year cooled her enthusiasm for her original plan to perfect her Chinese and apply for a civil service job. The last thing she wanted to do was work for the Chinese government.

Dechen started to cut school and neglect her homework. On weekends, when Middle School students were allowed to go home, she would sneak out at night to meet her friends. In the past, they'd hang out at the Internet café, but the Internet was shut off and they could only play computer games. An Internet café without Internet couldn't stay in business for long and soon it closed, leaving the kids no choice but to go to the pool hall or the karaoke club.

Her family was horrified. Dechen's stepmother telephoned her father and he rushed back from Lhasa to speak with his daughter. The most obvious solution for dealing with a rebellious teenager, the same the world over, would be to send her away to boarding school. But the Chinese government had closed down many of the Tibetan boarding schools nearby, fearing they would be breeding grounds for nationalism. So Dechen would have to go to India, where the schools run by the Tibetan exile government and by various charities offered young Tibetans a good education at nominal cost. She could learn English and improve her Tibetan and even her Chinese.

Dechen didn't know much about India. Although she prayed to the Dalai Lama as the bodhisattva of compassion, she hadn't quite appreciated that he was a real person who lived in exile in India. But she immediately agreed to her family's plan to send her away, realizing she had to get out of Ngaba.

"I want to go to India. I think I can learn to be a better person there," she told her father.

Since Dechen was only fourteen and admittedly not the most mature teenager, she would need a chaperone. The family came up with the idea of sending Pema with her. Pema was unwell, that was clear, but she would be a responsible chaperone. Pema had taken Dechen under her wing in the past and was willing to help out.

The decision was finalized when Dechen's father realized that the Chinese government had stopped issuing Tibetans passports. He had initially assumed his family would have no problem since they were resolutely apolitical, uninvolved in the protest movement or anything else deemed criminal by the Chinese. They were successful enough in business that they had the money to grease the wheels, if necessary. Now it was impossible and they would have to go overland.

Even that proved difficult. The trip still required a series of permits; it was not like 2006, when Pema had been able to catch a bus to Lhasa on her own to bury her husband's ashes. Chinese authorities were now restricting travel permits, especially for people from Ngaba. Although Lhasa is southwest of Ngaba, they headed first in exactly the opposite direction, into Gansu province, where the family had contacts who would help them with the paperwork. Along the way, they stopped off at monasteries, making offerings of money and lighting butter lamps. Good karma and the right documents would be needed for the journey.

In Lhasa, Dechen stayed with her father, hardly venturing outside the apartment. Her father had a permit to live in the city, but the privilege was not automatically conferred on a child, so she had to lie low. Pema stayed with another relative and also remained mostly indoors. Only on Sundays, when the swarms of people circumambulating the Barkhor, Lhasa's old Tibetan quarter, were so large that you could get lost in the crowd, did they feel safe enough to venture out and see the splendors of the city.

After three months, Dechen's father managed to secure the coveted permits for the women to visit Dham. With the permits in hand, it should have been easy to get to the border, since there is a direct road running the entire five-hundred-mile route through the snowy mountain passes with stunning views of Mount Everest to the south. But every hour or so, the car was stopped at a checkpoint and the occupants questioned. At the third checkpoint, Pema and Dechen were taken into separate guardhouses for interrogation. They were grilled about their friends, their family, the relatives they were visiting in Dham. The officers posed their questions with such detail that Dechen wondered if they had advance intelligence about their plans.

"You are heading to Nepal, right? You're going to India, right?" they kept pressing.

Dechen had been well coached and didn't crack, but she was sure that her answers didn't match what Pema was saying in the other room. In the end, the Tibetans turned her over to a Chinese soldier, and Dechen was sure she was finished. But the Chinese soldier just winked and gestured that she could get back in the car to proceed on the journey to the border. Dechen couldn't figure out if he was just being nice or if he had been bribed.

Dham was the gateway between Nepal and the People's Republic of China, the last stop for truckers hauling cheap manufactured goods from China—rice cookers, mobile telephones, DVDs, sneakers, and clothing. Chinese president Xi Jinping likes to refer to these trading routes as the New Silk Road. Back in the 1980s and 1990s, Ngaba's entrepreneurs, Norbu included, were big players in Dham, controlling much of the trade, but by 2010 when Dechen and Pema arrived, the shops were mostly Chinese-run. Their trucks crossed the border over the steel-arched Friendship Bridge, part of the Friendship Highway built in the 1960s and named to commemorate ties between China and Nepal.

Dechen and Pema wouldn't be able to take the bridge since they had no passports and their travel documents were only valid as far as Dham. They waited three days, again not daring to leave the house, until two men came to drive them to the border, bumping along a rutted dirt path. After the car couldn't proceed any farther, they scrambled through the forest thick with pines and a dense, prickly underbrush, sliding down on their bottoms when it was too steep to walk. Their palms were bleeding. They had been advised in advance to buy gloves, but leaving the house was too risky.

Finally the path came to a dead end at the edge of a cliff. In the ravine below was the Sun Kosi River, which runs along the border. It is not a deep river, but it is fast, with white water cascading loudly over jagged rocks that point upward as though stating a challenge: I dare you to try to get across this trench.

On the other side, they saw men using a long hook to pull a rope out of the water, which they stretched until it was tight. Their guide pulled another length of rope out of his bag. Dechen trembled with fear as the man approached her, pulled the rope between her legs, over her shoulders and around her waist, before looping it again over the rope that stretched across the river. He'd made a harness. She understood now: it was a zip line that was supposed to pull them across the river. There was no way she could do that, no way at all.

"No, no, no. I'm not going!" she screamed.

"Come on, little girl," the men coaxed her. Pema had already crossed quietly and the men were growing anxious, urging Dechen to keep her voice down.

Dechen planted her feet firmly on the ground, digging in her heels. Like a stubborn mule, she was not going to budge. But before she could yell again, the guide gave her a shove. She lost her footing, tumbling toward the edge of the ravine. She could see the water crashing white as milk over the rocks below. She screamed. She was still screaming at the top of her lungs by the time she reached the other side. The man with the rope caught her in his arms and immediately clapped a hand over her mouth.

THEY WERE NOW ON the Nepal side of the river, but they could not yet relax. They were entirely dependent on the human smugglers, gruff men who spoke a Sherpa dialect of Tibetan that was barely intelligible to them. Pema was sure they were about to be robbed and raped. She and Dechen hadn't eaten since they left Dham and wanted to buy instant noodles, but she was afraid to open her purse to show the smugglers that she was carrying cash. And they still needed to worry about the long arm of China. The border areas were crawling with undercover Chinese police, big men in black T-shirts who spoke Mandarin loudly on the streets, not bothering to disguise their presence. Cameras were affixed to trees and rocks. China has surpassed India as impoverished Nepal's main benefactor in recent years, building countless infrastructure and tourism projects, including a $3 billion tourist park in Lumbini, the birthplace of Siddhartha Gautama, the historical Buddha. They've also talked about a tunnel under Mount Everest. One of the conditions for this development assistance is keeping close tabs on the Tibetan community. (In October 2019, Chinese leader Xi Jinping pressed Nepal's government to sign an extradition treaty clearly designed to bring back Tibetan activists who escape over the borders.)

It was not until they reached a reception center in Kathmandu set up for the purpose of registering Tibetans and run by the U.N. High Commission for Refugees that the women felt safe.

They had been on the road for four months. Dechen's father never told either of them what he had paid, but the going price just for the smugglers who took them across the river was $10,000 a head.

All for lack of passports: Air China operates direct flights from Chengdu to Kathmandu that take just over three hours and cost roughly $250.

AFTER PHUNTSOG'S SELF-IMMOLATION, Dongtuk's mother sent her son into hiding. She didn't want him anywhere near the center of Ngaba, not even the center of Meruma or anywhere where he might do or say something stupid. So he would have to revert to the nomadic life, staying as far away from other people as possible. He spent a few months at his father's winter home, waiting until it was warm enough to head out to the grassland. Once the fresh growth of grass filled in the bald patches left by the melting snow, they set out for the hills with the animals.

Dongtuk traveled with Rinzen Dorjee. This reprieve would be his chance to get to know his half brother and to learn to ride a horse properly. They spent their days together riding on the hills above Meruma, often in silence. This was the Tibetan life, and he could see how much happier Rinzen Dorjee was to be out under the infinite sky instead of cramped and cross-legged in the monastery memorizing scripture and trying to find his voice in debate. They slept side by side in a black felt tent. Rinzen Dorjee told Dongtuk that he could only sleep properly in the open, listening to the grunting and rumblings of the yaks. Dongtuk, though, had terrible insomnia. He thought it was the most boring summer of his life.

The half brothers had been thrown together as children but never got to know each other well. The talkative, curious Dongtuk and the stoic Rinzen Dorjee were in different classes at Kirti and had their own sets of friends. But they endured many of the same experiences in those turbulent years: the school closure, the siege of the monastery, the protests and arrests, the self-immolations. Both worried about the threats to Tibetan culture, although Rinzen Dorjee cared less about the monastery than about his lifestyle as a nomadic herder. They both had been friends with Phuntsog from the village. Like Dongtuk, Rinzen Dorjee was horrified by the idea of flame consuming a human body, but he also admired the courage it took to perform such an act.

"He really figured out how to get the attention of the Chinese, didn't he?" he told Dongtuk.

"But for what purpose? What good has it done anyone?" Dongtuk retorted.

And so they debated as they rode through the grasslands by day and shared their tent by night. When an early September snow blanketed the slopes, they were children again. They lay on their backs, flapping their arms to make snow angels, then scampered to their feet to pack snowballs to hurl at each other. With a branch, they wrote in the snow, in as large letters as they could manage, the word *Bo,* meaning Tibet.

ॐ

Dongtuk's paperwork arrived a few weeks later. He dyed his hair again, put on his hipster clothing, and went straight to Lhasa and then to Dham. Unpredictably, after two failed attempts to escape Tibet, the third time was a charm. Unlike Dechen, he was thrilled by the zip line. (Later he learned that tourists paid good money for the adventure of riding zip lines across the gorges of Nepal.) He hid for a few days in a safe house on the Nepal side of the river, and then headed to Kathmandu, where he registered with the United Nations and shaved his head so that once again he could look like a monk. He traveled from Nepal to India, heading north to Dharamsala.

As soon as he arrived, he was taken in by the Kirti Monastery, settling into one of the dormitories that housed hundreds of refugee monks from Tibet. The Dharamsala branch of Kirti was opened in 1990 by Kirti Rinpoche, and is located up a steep pedestrian path from the Dalai Lama's headquarters. Dongtuk resumed his studies immediately.

Because Kirti had been at the center of the protests, the Dharamsala branch became something of a clearinghouse for information about the latest incidents. Despite the information blockade on Ngaba, residents passed on photos, texts, and videos. In February 2012, word spread through the monastery that a former Kirti monk from Meruma had self-immolated. Even before he was told the name, Dongtuk had a good idea who it was.

RINZEN DORJEE LIT HIMSELF on fire in front of one of Ngaba's schools. He didn't die immediately; he was taken to the prefecture hospital in Barkham. The family told Dongtuk that his half brother was not beaten or tortured, but that the police continued to interrogate him as he lay dying.

Their father was allowed to visit. In a small voice barely audible, Rinzen Dorjee apologized for making him travel so far. He sent wishes to his mother. And then he said—at least this is what Dongtuk was told—"Don't worry. I know I am going to die because I drank the gasoline. I don't regret what I did. I did it for the sake of all Tibetans and sentient beings."

Unlike other self-immolators, he didn't leave a farewell note or a video—which was no surprise because he was never much for words.

There was little press coverage of the event because Rinzen Dorjee was the twenty-first person to self-immolate, and by then it hardly seemed like big news.

PART FOUR

· · · · · · · · ·

2014 TO THE PRESENT

INDIA

Gonpo at home in Dharamsala, 2014.

WHEN GONPO ARRIVED IN DHARAMSALA IN 1989, SHE expected to stay for a few months. The purpose of the trip was to secure an audience with the Dalai Lama and to brush up on her Tibetan. It was supposed to be a sabbatical of sorts from her teaching job and a way to connect with her Tibetan roots. She'd brought her eleven-year-old daughter, Wangzin, with her. Gonpo left behind her husband and a young daughter, promising it wouldn't be a long separation.

She found the atmosphere in India intoxicating. More than 100,000 Tibetans were living there in exile, proudly displaying portraits of the Dalai Lama and waving the snow lion flag, openly debating the Tibet issue. The exile community was headquartered three hundred miles north of New Delhi in the former British resort town of McLeod Ganj, a village in upper Dharamsala developed by the British military in the mid-nineteenth century as a cantonment for troops administering the region. The British had been drawing up plans to turn it into a summer capital, when, in 1905, an earthquake devastated the town and forced their retreat to lower, firmer ground. After India's independence, the town was left with an inventory of empty real estate—quaint colonial buildings crumbling into the hillsides. When the Dalai Lama fled to India, a shrewd merchant who ran McLeod's general store prodded the Indian government to offer him the village as his base. It suited the needs of the Indian government to accommodate the Dalai Lama in a place that befitted his status but was comfortably out of the way so as not to irritate the Chinese government too much.

Dharamsala appealed as well to the Tibetans, who appreciated its relatively cool temperatures, mountain air, and auspicious name—"dwelling place of the dharma" in Hindi. All slopes and switchbacks with barely a horizontal surface in sight, Dharamsala didn't much resemble Tibet, but a snow-capped spur of the Himalayas was visible in the distance. Around the Dalai Lama sprung up an entire parallel universe of Tibet, hinting of home. The Central Tibetan Administration had its own ministers and parliament, schools, museum, library, and civil service employees—even a civil service exam. ("We don't have a country but we have bureaucracy," a spokesman told me, apologizing for the requirement that a press pass was needed to visit a school.) Empty storefronts filled up with hotels, cafés with multilingual menus and cuisine, English-language bookstores, yoga studios, and boutiques selling copper singing bowls and prayer beads.

The Dalai Lama gave Gonpo a warm reception. They'd met before in 1956, when he was a young monk and she was a girl accompanying her father on a trip to Lhasa. Even more than when she was a child,

Gonpo was giddy with excitement to see him. And to her astonishment, he too was happy to see her. Tibet's spiritual leader told her that he badly needed her help in Dharamsala. The exile government was dominated by refugees from central Tibet—the first generation to arrive in India after the Communist takeover. Tibetans from Amdo and Kham, the eastern regions, had not started arriving in large numbers until the 1980s and they often felt excluded. Their dialect was different, as were their tastes and customs. They needed better representation to fit into the Tibetan exile community. The Tibetan exile government had its own elected parliament, but the Dalai Lama had the right to appoint three representatives. He wanted Gonpo to be one of them.

Gonpo was in a unique position to help. She was respected by the people of Ngaba by dint of her father's reputation, but she had skills in her own right. She spoke and wrote impeccable Chinese and understood the workings and lingo of the Chinese Communist Party, having served on various committees in Nanjing. Her assistance would be invaluable in translating and analyzing documents in the on-and-off negotiations with Beijing.

It would have been hard enough to say no to His Holiness the Dalai Lama, but there were the people she met from Ngaba too. They begged her to stay; they evoked the name of her father. They even addressed her as *seymo,* or princess, a title she hadn't heard since she was a child. And the political situation back home in China was unstable. The 1980s had come crashing to an end with the crackdown at Tiananmen Square. Zhao Ziyang, the reform-minded Communist Party head, had been forced out during the student protests. Lhasa was under martial law. It wasn't clear if Gonpo would be penalized upon her return for having met with the Dalai Lama. Her patron, the Panchen Lama, had died suddenly in January 1989 at the age of fifty of an apparent heart attack, so she no longer had his protection.

After many tearful conversations with her husband over crackling telephone lines, Gonpo decided to stay a little longer. Then a little longer. She settled in a small walk-up apartment that had been built for Tibetan refugees by Norwegian donors. It would be sixteen years before she saw the family she'd left behind in China.

I MET GONPO ON my first trip to Dharamsala in 2014. I had heard about her from another Ngaba exile, who told me that she was a modest person who didn't like to talk to journalists. But one day, when I was visiting the exile parliament, I mentioned to the speaker that I was writing about Ngaba, and he insisted that I had to speak with Gonpo. He basically commanded her to come to his office to meet me. Gonpo, by then in her mid-sixties, was broad in the hips and wore her graying hair tied back in a bun, but struck me as girlishly endearing with her gapped teeth and bashful smile. She wore a long skirt with a colorful striped apron, a traditional garment in Lhasa for married women, now adopted by the exile government as the uniform for female civil servants. We sat around a low table in the speaker's office, sipping tea from small tulip glasses, making awkward small talk as we watched a monkey clamber outside on the windowsill. Gonpo told me she was not only a member of parliament, but also worked full-time translating documents. She told me she was very proud that she had translated the Tibetan constitution and election law into Chinese, showing by example how serious the Tibetans were about democracy. Then, she hastily excused herself, saying she had work to finish. Reluctantly, when the speaker prodded her, she scribbled her phone number in my notebook.

After a few days of trying and failing to pin her down for an appointment, a Tibetan translator I was working with suggested we drop in at her apartment on her day off. He knew where she lived—everybody knew everybody in Dharamsala. Her apartment building was tucked down an overgrown footpath in a clearing in danger of being swallowed up by the jungle. We made our way up an outside staircase onto a landing thick with potted plants, and warily knocked on the door.

To my relief, Gonpo wasn't upset that we'd dropped in unannounced. She ushered us into the cozy apartment, its bedroom separated from the sitting room by a lace curtain. She darted into the narrow galley kitchen to bring out tea and peanuts, sat down, and apologized for her earlier reticence.

"I usually try not to talk about the past. It makes me sad," she explained.

We talked for several hours that day. Although Gonpo did not cry, her eyes remained moist throughout as though she were living in perpetual grief. She pointed out on her walls, above the television, the black-and-white photographs, each of which conjured up a reminder of loss. The oldest, taken in 1954, showed her father, then in his forties, with the young Dalai Lama and the Panchen Lama, during a trip to Beijing where they were being courted to throw their support behind the Chinese Communist Party. From a few years later, a photo of her family standing in front of an elaborately carved wooden lintel of their house in Ngaba. Gonpo is the smallest, about five years old, and wears a tightly belted robe and boots. Her hair is shaved short like a boy's. It was taken in about 1957 and might have been the last photograph of their family before their expulsion from Ngaba. Then there was the family portrait that had been taken in the studio in Chengdu in the summer of 1966, everybody smiling, as though unaware that Mao was about to unleash the Cultural Revolution. Gonpo's parents and sister would be dead within the year.

Scattered around the side tables were fading color photographs from the 1980s, the most comfortable decade of her life, when she lived with Xiao Tu and their young daughters in Nanjing. The dissolution of that family was as painful as the loss of her parents. In the years after her departure for India, her husband was unable to get a passport to leave China, and it was too risky for her to return to China. She didn't see him again until 2005. Now they saw each other about once or twice a year, mostly during the holidays. Her relationship with Xiao Tu was good, she said. "He is a wonderful man. He understands my responsibilities." She is close to her older daughter, Wang-zin, who still lives in India. Her relationship with the daughter she left behind as a nine-year-old, now married to a Chinese man, was more complicated. They didn't see each other again until 2013.

"When the family gets together now, mostly what we do is cry," she said.

The fracturing of Gonpo's family parallels the estrangement of the Tibetan exile government from Beijing. If the Dalai Lama was able to return to Tibet, most likely Gonpo could as well. When she left for India, it was during that exhilarating period at the end of the Cold War when everything felt possible, including reconciliation between the Chinese Communist Party and the Tibetans. By 1988, the Dalai Lama had put the finishing touches on his "Middle Way" approach, in which he agreed to respect the territorial integrity of China in return for a measure of self-governance and the protection of the Tibetan re-ligion, culture, and language. The Chinese responded that they would negotiate with the Dalai Lama as long as he dropped the call for an independent Tibet. Tibetans tried to schedule talks in Geneva in Janu-ary 1989—while Gonpo was en route to India—but the Chinese com-plained that the Tibetans were trying to "internationalize" the issue, objecting in particular to a Dutch lawyer who was going to attend the talks. Every time Tibetans got their hopes up for a diplomatic break-through, the Chinese upped the ante with a new condition. The Chi-nese did finally agree to talks with the Dalai Lama's special envoy, Lodi Gyari, and there were nine rounds between 2002 and 2010, but they went nowhere. Another flurry of wishful thinking came out of the el-evation in 2012 of Xi Jinping to be the head of the Chinese Communist Party. His late father, Xi Zhongxun, a liberal vice premier, was thought to be sympathetic to the Tibetan cause and for decades wore a watch given to him by the young Dalai Lama. Xi's mother practiced Tibetan Buddhism. But Xi instead went on to usher in a hard-line assimilation-ist policy, roll back tolerance for free speech, and remove term limits for the presidency so he can stay in power as long as he likes.

The Dalai Lama officially retired as head of the exile government in 2011, giving up the leadership to an elected prime minister and ending centuries of theocratic rule. While the Dalai Lama is very proud of this experiment in democratic governance, it effectively scuttled further talks because the Chinese will not negotiate with an exile government, only with him. The rhetoric against him has continued unabated.

Gonpo was practically in tears when she spoke of the deadlocked negotiations. "His Holiness has openly stated that he is not seeking independence. We have given them all the political concessions we can. We have come to the bottom of the well," she said. "When I hear the words they use about His Holiness, the way they insult him, it gives pain to my heart and it only gives them more problems with Tibetans. I can't understand what they are thinking."

For Gonpo, it is all highly personal. Not only does the rift between China and the Tibetans run straight through her family, it runs through her psyche. Gonpo loves China as well as Tibet. She still speaks better Chinese than Tibetan. More than most Han Chinese people I know, she absorbed the lessons of socialism. She eschewed conspicuous display of wealth and was proud that she had shed her aristocratic roots and was, to use a Chinese Communist slogan, serving the people.

She told me she was proud that she worked full-time, even though it meant a long walk up and down a steep hill on the feet that still ached from the frostbite she'd suffered decades before in Xinjiang. She had resisted urgings over the years that she move to a nicer, more convenient apartment, preferring to live as simply as possible. "People think because I am the daughter of a king I would be spoiled, but it is not the case," she told me.

For Gonpo, the self-immolations are another tragedy she takes personally. Of the cases to date, about one-third have been from Ngaba and a disproportionate number of those from Meruma, the village named for the Mei dynasty. If the Mei rulers were still in power, these would be her subjects; many are literally the children and grandchildren of her father's generals and cabinet members. "I can't believe we are losing these precious young lives, one after another. I can barely bring myself to talk about it," she said. It was about all I could get her to say on the subject.

DURING THAT SAME OPTIMISTIC interlude at the end of the 1980s that brought Gonpo to India, many other Tibetans from Ngaba arrived. One of them was Delek, the boy with the perpetually runny nose who'd hidden in a laundry basket when his grandparents were beaten, the same boy who'd tended horses during the fighting of the Cultural Revolution.

After the dismantling of the communes in the early 1980s, Delek took over his family's yak herds and through his hard work, he managed to save enough money to travel. He left for a pilgrimage in 1989, intending to visit a few temples nearby, but decided to go onward to Lhasa. There he ran into some friends, who were hitching a ride on a truck to Mount Kailash. On his way back, he heard that the Dalai Lama was giving a teaching in Varanasi, India. Since he was already on the road, he decided to attend. And like Gonpo, he was awed by the vibrancy of the Tibetan exile community. He had tasted freedom and couldn't bring himself to go back.

Delek had little formal education, save for a few years at a Chinese government school with portraits of Lenin, Marx, and Mao on the walls. But he was intelligent and exceptionally disciplined and he was able to develop his reading and writing skills in the exile schools. He had acquired impeccable handwriting, which was an essential skill since Tibetan typewriters were rare. And he began interviewing fellow refugees from Ngaba trying to reconstruct what had happened since the coming of the Communists.

As a self-styled historian, Delek has become a well-known figure in Dharamsala. He goes by the name Amdo Delek—like many Tibetans without a family name he has affixed his birthplace onto his name. He has hollow cheeks that make his prominent nose look larger and wavy hair that he combs down over his forehead. He is so fit and tanned, his posture so ramrod straight, that he gives the impression of a retired executive who's just stepped off his yacht.

Delek lives on the grounds of the Tibetan Children's Village, one of the schools operated by the exile government for refugee children. His day job for many years has been as a caretaker of the school, and the position comes with an apartment. His sitting room is crammed full of every possible Tibetan motif. Besides the obligatory portraits of the Dalai Lama, there are prayer flags, snow lion flags, and prayer wheels. One of those wheels, shaped like a lazy Susan, sits on his coffee table. He spins it regularly as he speaks.

Because I was writing about Ngaba, Delek was one of the first people I sought out in Dharamsala. He proved to be a goldmine of information about Ngaba, dating back to its establishment by the first Mei kings. Delek's original research was focused on the events of the twentieth century. He wanted to record for posterity exactly who was killed by the Communists, who died in prison, who died fighting. He had compiled the names of the fighters who resisted when the Communists came to Aba in 1958. The names were all recorded in his exquisite handwriting in notebooks that filled the bookcases. He sought out people newly arrived from Ngaba, especially those of the older generation who, at last in a safe place, could describe what had happened. Some events Delek had witnessed himself—for example, the annihilation of the Tibetan men from Meruma who joined the Red Guard faction known as Hongcheng in 1968, thinking that their involvement had been condoned by Mao. He pulled out a blue child's notebook with pictures of seagulls on the cover and read out a list of names that were written in blue and red ink in his elegant handwriting.

Alak Jigme, Tashi Gorten, Garcho, Gupta, Thanku Alak, Dhonguk . . .

"They were slaughtered. In one day, fifty-nine men and one hundred horses were killed," Delek told me. I'd noticed that many older Tibetans similarly enumerated the number of horses killed along with the human fatalities.

Delek also kept track of family lineages. He was the one who first noticed that many of the self-immolators were descendants of resistance fighters. Phuntsog, for example, whose self-immolation began the trend, was the grandson of Dhondor, the rebellion leader from 1958. Rinzen Dorjee, Dongtuk's half brother, was the grandson of another resistance fighter. A beautiful teenage girl from Meruma who burned herself in December 2014 had a grandfather and an uncle who were leaders of the 1968 Red City rebellion.

To Delek, the family connections made sense of the madness. It also explained why so many resisters came from not only Ngaba, but Meruma. "Many of the king's ministers lived there. It was a very spirited place," he said. "They were influenced by family tradition to stand up to the Chinese." The older generation produced the fighters. The younger people, educated during the time of the 14th Dalai Lama, took his teachings about nonviolence to heart. They couldn't bring themselves to kill anyone but themselves.

BEING FROM NGABA CONFERRED a certain cachet in Dharamsala. The self-immolations were the most newsworthy thing that had happened out of Tibet in years. People collected the faces of self-immolators on their iPhones like so many baseball cards in the deck of martyrs. There was a wall in the official museum of the exile government devoted to their portraits. At the alley leading into the Dalai Lama's temple hung a large banner that read "Sacrifice of Life for Tibet" above grainy photos of the self-immolators. These were people once too obscure to merit their own photographs—they were perhaps the fourth sons and third daughters, easily passed over in the crowd, with almost no public profile. Now they were heroes celebrated at the home of the Dalai Lama himself.

Almost everybody I met from Ngaba knew somebody who had self-immolated or witnessed a self-immolation—if not a relative, then a classmate or a neighbor. Nobody knew more people who had self-immolated than Dongtuk. No matter that he was at the bottom of the

pecking order of exiles, a kid born out of wedlock with no money or family connections, this made him a minor celebrity in Dharamsala.

"Richard Gere is a friend of mine," Dongtuk told me when we first met in 2014. He'd met the actor, a longtime activist for Tibetan human rights, while giving him a briefing on self-immolations. After that comment, I was afraid that he was spoiled by the attention and would just give me a well-rehearsed spiel. But we ended up meeting frequently over cups of ginger lemon tea, the beverage of choice in Dharamsala, and a thoughtful young man emerged from beneath the bravado.

Dongtuk had spent a good deal of time trying to make sense of the self-immolations before he left Ngaba. At times, he seemed almost jealous of Rinzen Dorjee. Although Dongtuk was the one who excelled at the monastery school, who was the champion debater, witty and intelligent, it was Rinzen Dorjee who had made his mark on the world. It was Rinzen Dorjee's photo that was outside the Dalai Lama's temple. Dongtuk couldn't criticize what his brother had done. It would be unseemly given the revered place he holds in the pantheon of Tibetan martyrs, but he didn't exactly approve either. "I feel like there has to be a better way to express oneself," he told me. Dongtuk subscribed to the same theory I'd heard from other Tibetans—that those who burned themselves were motivated by their sense of powerlessness and frustration and their inability to speak up. Dongtuk had just started keeping a journal and hoped he could vent his passion for the Tibetan cause through his writing.

He showed me on his phone a 2009 photograph of the novice monks in his class at Kirti, about forty boys. Of them, two had self-immolated and three or four he thought were in prison. "Now that I think back on it, I'm sure I would not have been one of those who self-immolated, but maybe in prison, that I could imagine."

TSEGYAM, THE BRILLIANT YOUNG man who had taught at the Middle School in Ngaba when he was barely older than his high school students, now lives in India. He fled there in 1992 after serving eighteen months in prison for making pro-Tibetan posters. He eventually was hired as the Dalai Lama's private secretary, handling dealings with the Chinese government since his Chinese was fluent. Tsegyam travels with the Dalai Lama on most of his international appearances, and I can usually spot him in the backdrop of news agency photos. It was hard to pin him down for an interview, but when I finally found him, he spoke with animation about the intellectual awakening of the 1980s, a period for which he has considerable nostalgia. His office inside the Dalai Lama's complex in Dharamsala is lined with bookcases, some of them containing literary journals to which he'd contributed. With a touch of hometown chauvinism, he insists that Ngaba and other parts of eastern Tibet have been the most vibrant communities in terms of Tibetan scholarship and culture, producing in recent years the best-known Tibetan musicians and filmmakers. "Historically, Lhasa was the center of Tibet, but there are such restrictions there on intellectual life that the center has moved east to Amdo and Kham," Tsegyam told me. That of course depends on Chinese authorities keeping open a small crack in the window for free expression. Tsegyam has little contact with his family members in Ngaba. Since 2008, he's avoided direct communication with his family for fear they will be punished for his association with the Dalai Lama.

TSEPEY IS ANOTHER TIBETAN who had little choice but to leave China. He spent four years on the run after being identified as a participant in the 2008 protest in Ngaba. He remembered how the policeman who'd tracked him through his instant messaging account had boasted that "the Communist Party has control of the sky and earth." After slipping his captors, he hid out in the cornfields in Shenzhen. Eventually he managed to buy an unregistered SIM card (it was shortly before the Chinese government started requiring identification to buy a card). He used it to contact a Chinese friend with whom he had studied Buddhism. The friend drove all the way from Beijing to pick

Tsepey up. He brought him to Wutaishan, a Buddhist pilgrimage site. Tsepey hid out there for over a year pretending to be on a silent retreat.

Still, his crime wouldn't blow over. His name was in the police database and a reward was offered for his arrest. A forty-five-year-old man from Tsepey's hometown who was arrested for participating in a relatively small protest in 2008 died in custody, and his body was returned to the family covered with bruises, clotted blood, and burn blisters. Tsepey felt he could meet the same fate if he remained. "Once you are blacklisted as a political person, it is all over. You are never forgiven," he told me when we met in Dharamsala in 2015.

Tsepey did well in exile. His hair had turned silver, and he combed it into an updo. He wore a gold stud earring and thick wooden beads, a Western-style plaid button-down shirt open to midchest. He was full of plans for the future. He had married a fellow Tibetan exile; they were planning to have a baby and move to Australia, which offered asylum to former political prisoners. Tsepey figured that only when he was able to obtain an Australian passport would it be safe for him to return to China. He had a nephew who had self-immolated during the New Year's holidays in 2014 at the usual location outside Kirti Monastery. The young man, Dorjee, was the twenty-five-year-old son of Tsepey's half brother. He was from the same village, Cha. Although Tsepey was already in India, authorities blamed him because he was a known troublemaker and had shared his criticisms of the Chinese government with his nephew on WeChat. "They said I put these ideas into his head," Tsepey recalled. "That was crazy. My nephew never talked about anything of the kind."

NGABA HAD AN INFORMAL association of exiles with branches in Kathmandu and Dharamsala. I happened to be in Dharamsala during Losar, the Tibetan New Year, in 2014, and was invited to a holiday party at a rooftop café near the Dalai Lama temple. The older women had prepared the food at home and carried in trays of *momos* and *khapse*, a fried dough pastry shaped into bowties and sprinkled with powdered sugar. It was a mostly non-alcoholic affair. Bottles of Coca-Cola were lined up like bowling pins on a counter.

I noticed Dechen right away because she was the only woman in the room (besides me) who wasn't wearing traditional Tibetan clothing. She was wearing jeans and a denim jacket and carried a matching denim backpack. With chipped pink polished fingernails, she was tapping away on an iPad. When she looked up to greet me, she explained that she was sending New Year's greetings to her family back home.

Dechen had at that point been in India for two years. She told me she was "about eighteen." Tibetans are often unclear about their date of birth (they usually could tell you only what year of the Chinese/ Tibetan zodiac they were born in), but I was a little surprised to hear it from Dechen since she was so young and seemed to be well educated. She was attending a boarding school run by the exile government and was bursting with enthusiasm for her studies.

"In Ngaba, it was hard for me to be a good girl. Here, the teachers make me work and make me think about things," she told me. She was reading essays by Woeser, a Tibetan poet and activist who writes in Chinese. "I'm learning about the Cultural Revolution and everything that happened in the past, the things my parents and grandma wouldn't tell me about."

Dechen said that she wanted to be a journalist, perhaps one reason she was receptive to being interviewed. We stayed in touch, and on my next visit she invited me to meet Pema, whom she referred to as her mother. Tibetans are loose in describing family relations—they will often describe a cousin as a brother, an aunt as a mother. She and Pema were living in a neighborhood that was informally called Amdo Hill because it was home to so many Tibetans from that area. It was behind a commercial strip of backpacker cafés and souvenir shops. To get there, you had to make your way down a steep path strewn with loose stones and dangling electric wires. You then climbed a set of concrete stairs onto a long, narrow ledge off of which were identical rooms side by side like pigeon coops.

Pema and Dechen's room was no more than a hundred square feet and was painted a garish lime green. It had two hard beds pushed up against the wall with quilts rolled up, doubling as sofas during the day. Above a small brown mini-fridge were a wall hanging of the blue medicine Buddha and a portrait of the Dalai Lama. Pema had tried to beautify the place by putting a rug over the linoleum floor and arranging silk flowers in a vase on the table, but there was no way to disguise the dinginess. She missed home. Over the years the humble house she'd moved into as a young bride in Ngaba had acquired the trappings of upward mobility—the television set, the washing machine, the big wooden cupboard. "The electricity is better back home than here," she complained. "We never have a steady supply in India."

Pema went back and forth about whether she had done the right thing in coming to India. She loved that she could openly display the portrait of the Dalai Lama. She attended many of his public teachings in India and was always thrilled when she saw his car coming out of his compound. But she didn't feel at home in India. She told me she preferred Chinese people to Indians and that she quarreled frequently with her landlord. "The Indians hate the Tibetans. They are always raising our rent." (The next time I saw her she had moved to a room a few doors away that was nearly identical, but painted a Pepto-Bismol pink.) Pema didn't have to work in India since her son, the reincarnated monk, was sending her money, but she was bored and lonely. She thought at times about returning to Ngaba. "The rule was so repressive. There was never a single day that I felt at peace. I was always agitated, fearing something would happen," she told me. "But at home, the development was much higher. The food was better. Even when I was poor, I could eat tsampa."

It is not out of the question for her to go back. The Chinese embassy in New Delhi issues a blue passport-like booklet for what it calls the Overseas Chinese National. On weekday mornings, you can see hundreds of Tibetans lined up as early as three A.M., in effect with their tail between their legs, soliciting the Chinese government for the paperwork that will allow them to live again under Chinese rule in Tibet.

India is not a signatory to the 1951 Convention Relating to the Status of Refugees, so the treatment of Tibetans is subject to the Indian government's moods, which have veered in recent years toward reconciliation with the economic powerhouse of China. These days India doesn't give Tibetans registration certificates, and without them it is difficult to rent an apartment, get a driver's license, or be hired for a proper job. Only those who were born in India between 1950 and 1987 are eligible to apply for Indian citizenship.

To stay in India or to try to go home: I met many Tibetans spinning with indecision. Their families send them photos on WeChat of new cars and motorcycles, remodeled houses and appliances—the creature comforts that have made life more comfortable inside China over the past decade. The unemployment rate among young Tibetans in India is about 50 percent. Even the souvenir shops selling Tibetan mandala and singing bowls are mostly run by Kashmiri Muslims. "Everybody knows that the economic situation is better over there than here. People feel it is better to go back home than to live here in a shack," said a young engineer from Ngaba who was trying to return.

On the other hand, it feels like an admission of failure to go back to China after making the effort to escape, the money paid to smugglers, the treks through the snow, and the harrowing crossing into Nepal by zip line. Tibetans are rightfully afraid that they will be prosecuted upon their return for whatever it is they may have done in India, attending anti-Chinese demonstrations or talking to journalists. As Tibetans who lived in India, they will be constantly under suspicion, having to guard their words and watch their step at every turn.

The Chinese government says that 80,000 Tibetan exiles have returned to live or to visit since the 1980s. "Back to the motherland," boasted the headline of a 2014 article on a Chinese-government website. It quoted an elderly returnee exclaiming, "My hometown has gone through enormous changes. Living conditions are a lot better than before. There is also freedom of religion. Returning home was the right choice!"

Although the Chinese claims of a stampede to the homeland are exaggerated, it is undoubtedly true that more Tibetans are leaving India than arriving. The Tibetan population in India peaked at 118,000 in the mid-1990s. By 2009—the date of the last census—it had slipped to 94,000. Many have left for Western countries, but Chinese authorities also have succeeded in plugging leaks in the borders to the west, reducing the number of new arrivals to a trickle. A reception center in Dharamsala, a modern yellow-and-green brick compound, inaugurated in 2011 by the U.S. ambassador to India with U.S. funding, was practically empty the last few times I visited. Delek told me that the Tibetan Children's Village used to receive 1,000 new students annually until 2009, when China sealed the borders. Now enrollment is dropping so steeply that he fears he might lose his job.

THE DALAI LAMA TURNED eighty in 2015, a milestone marked with much foreboding. There is a sense in the international community that both he and the Tibetan exile movement are past their prime. It is perhaps no surprise that impoverished Nepal is easily bullied into controlling Tibetan refugees, but larger, richer countries are also cowed by the world's second-largest economy. Beijing administers diplomatic loyalty tests, punishing countries that host His Holiness, rewarding those who do not. In 2014, South Africa denied the Dalai Lama a visa to attend a gathering of Nobel Peace Prize laureates. The meeting was moved to Rome, where Pope Francis declined to grant the Dalai Lama an audience. The Indians too are afraid of the Chinese. A celebration entitled "Thank you India" in 2018 to mark the upcoming sixtieth year of the Tibetan exile community in India had to be scaled back after the Indian government barred its officials from attending.

The Dalai Lama's mortality hangs heavily over the Tibetans. Picking a successor by reincarnation is admittedly a dysfunctional system. Beijing has indicated that it alone will control the selection of the next Dalai Lama. The idea of these Communist technocrats weighing in on matters of reincarnation prompts much hilarity. ("Reincarnation is not the business of the Communist," the Dalai Lama told me, joking that the Party should first identify a reincarnation of Mao Zedong if they sincerely accept Buddhist teachings about rebirth.) But the consequences of Chinese meddling could be deadly. If the Tibetans select one Dalai Lama and the Chinese another, it will create a schism likely to be more fraught than what occurred after the Panchen Lama's death in 1989, when there were also competing reincarnates. And the next Dalai Lama, whether chosen by the Chinese or the Tibetans, might not be as persuasive in conveying the message of nonviolence.

To ensure the continuity of his teachings, the Dalai Lama has said he might choose a successor in his lifetime. Most recently there have been indications that he will name a panel of lamas shortly before his ninetieth birthday to come up with a plan. However, the Dalai Lama's delay in planning for the inevitable worries Tibetan intellectuals.

"He is acting very irresponsibly," said Jamyang Norbu, a Tibetan novelist and essayist who now lives in Tennessee. "The Chinese have already set up a commission to pick the next Dalai Lama. If we don't get in on the game, they will do it before us. They will find some cute little Tibetan boy they can control."

The Dalai Lama's compound is conspicuously devoid of grandeur, its architecture more evocative of a 1970s junior high school than the magnificent Potala Palace. Shoehorned into the hillside, the compound has a temple and office buildings, and is surrounded by terraces of poured concrete large enough to accommodate most of the Tibetan population of Dharamsala for public ceremonies. Through a small waiting area and metal detector is a walkway with trellises of roses where His Holiness receives visitors. Whether or not the Dalai Lama is the repository of infinite wisdom one can debate, but his patience indeed seems infinite when it comes to the devotees who come to prostrate themselves before him, kiss his robe, hold their children up to have their cheeks stroked. From Tibetan nomads to movie stars, European parliamentarians, artists, and of course journalists, the reception line appears endless. In recent years, many Chinese Buddhists have made the pilgrimage, traveling discreetly for fear they will get in trouble with their government. The Dalai Lama makes a special effort to see the Chinese visitors, hoping they might soften their government's attitude toward Tibet.

The Dalai Lama is relentlessly optimistic, almost exhaustingly so—about his own health and longevity and about China and the future of Tibetans within China. When I met with him, he pointed to a speech Xi Jinping gave in Paris speaking of Buddhism's role in Chinese culture. He recalls his friendship with Xi Jinping's father, Xi Zhongxun, a liberal vice premier. He bristles at the suggestion that China has won and that Tibetans have lost: "I don't consider China powerful at all. They may be powerful in their economics and weapons, but in terms of moral principles, they are very weak. The whole society is full of suspicion and full of distrust."

We talked a good deal about Ngaba and more generally about the Amdo region where he was born. The Dalai Lama left his home at the age of four for Lhasa, and Lhasa for India at the age of twenty-four, so he relies on visitors to brief him on conditions inside. "One Chinese man who just came back from Tibet told me that outwardly there was lots of development, new roads, new buildings. The economic conditions were quite good. However, he told me that the Tibetans are not at all happy internally. When he told me that, and he was sitting where you are sitting now, he had tears in his eyes."

Among the many religious figures who come to India to seek the Dalai Lama's wisdom are a contingent of Jewish leaders, and he invariably turns the question on them of how to preserve a civilization in exile. "You wrote about the Jewish people losing a homeland two thousand years ago, and how you're still here. Mine has just lost its homeland, and I know it's going to be a very long road into exile," the late Elie Wiesel told *The New Yorker,* recalling a conversation with the Dalai Lama in the 1970s. "How did you survive?"

Having largely conceded in the fight for independence, the Tibetan exile government has lowered the bar for success. Survival is now the goal. Although you can still hear the rallying cry of *Rangzen*—Freedom—Tibetans talk more nowadays about the freedom to preserve their culture, memories, and language both inside and outside China. They try to keep alive the story of a people on the losing side of history. In Dharamsala, the Library of Tibetan Works and Archives holds more than 100,000 Tibetan-language titles ranging from the Buddhist canons to treatises on medicine and astronomy to modern poetry. The exile government runs the schools that keep the language alive among the younger generation of Tibetans and encourages the teaching of Tibetan inside.

The Dalai Lama takes pride in the fact that so many Tibetans insist on studying their own language. "Actually, during the Cultural Revolution, some local Chinese official vowed that within fifteen years, the Tibetan language must be eliminated. But we're still here," he said. Since he has retired as head of the exile government, remaining only the Tibetan spiritual leader, he sees himself mostly as the inspiration for the continuation of the civilization. "That's my responsibility, the preservation of Tibetan culture, the culture of peace and compassion."

These sound like modest and achievable goals. Certainly the survival of the culture should not be threatening to a superpower that is poised to become the world's largest economy. Unfortunately, my travels inside Tibet suggest otherwise.

EVERYTHING BUT
MY FREEDOM

Tibetans in Meruma attending a propaganda lecture, December 2019.

I FIRST TRAVELED TO NGABA IN MID-2013. ALTHOUGH nothing in Chinese law prevented my visit—indeed, when I called the prefecture's press office I was told it was permitted—I knew from others that Chinese police were stopping foreigners at checkpoints. Already the number of self-immolations had surpassed one hundred and the town was under lockdown. I went in at dusk, my favorite time of day for discreet travels through the Tibetan plateau. After picking up a taxi in a nearby town, I shrank inconspicuously into the shadows of the back seat. As the taxi weaved through the darkened landscape, empty except for clusters of tents, the stillness of the night was interrupted only by a brief blinding camera flash. The authorities had photographed our vehicle, but failed, it seemed, to detect my presence in the back. The taxi continued on its way along the empty road. When we reached the checkpoint just behind Kirti Monastery, the soldiers were in the middle of a shift change, and we slipped right through.

I breathed a sigh of relief, but perhaps too quickly. As we approached the market area in front of Kirti, it felt to me as much like a war zone as any I'd visited in a career that had brought me to Baghdad, Sarajevo, and the Gaza Strip. It was that strange mix of the mundane and the military—people shopping for the evening's provisions amid the clutter of stalls, pretending everything was normal when obviously it was not. All around us were canvas-topped army trucks, jeeps in camouflage, police cars mounted with cameras. An armored personnel carrier was stationed in front of the department store on the main intersection. I raised my cellphone briefly to take a photo out the window, but then thought better of it and slipped the phone back into my bag.

As I became more familiar with Ngaba, I appreciated the ways that the town—and the Tibetan situation—had been transformed by the self-immolations. The Chinese government alternated between the use of the stick and the carrot in trying to quench the fires. The prefecture government had begun a blitz of development designed to turn the town into a showpiece of modernity. The main road was made one-way so that traffic moved in an orderly loop from the market to the Middle School. The Tibetan-themed murals and signage had been added the same year.

As everywhere in China, large red billboards touted the latest Communist Party propaganda.

TOGETHER WE WILL BUILD A BEAUTIFUL HOME.
BEND LOW. LISTEN TO WHAT PEOPLE SAY.

Some of the Tibetans I met said they believed the Communist Party had in fact listened to the message conveyed by the self-immolations, which was an unequivocal register of discontent. The government had cancelled the unpopular water diversion project that could have dried up the Ngaqu River. The plans to house 60,000 Chinese workers and their families on the southern banks of the river were shelved, although the designated land was being used for military barracks and a new government complex, accessed by an ostentatious bridge with four lanes for traffic and enormous lacquered gates topped with the Tibetan symbol of the endless knot.

Shi Jun, the Party secretary for Ngaba prefecture, whose doctrinaire policies many blamed for the unrest, left Ngaba in 2012, and although he was promoted to a provincial position, his departure made for a less provocative atmosphere. Photos of the Dalai Lama that had been removed from Kirti Monastery were replaced—how long they'd be allowed to remain nobody could predict. A group of Ngaba businessmen had raised money to set up a refuge for ducks and cows that had been saved from the slaughterhouse, part of the Buddhist custom of animal release as a way to gain merit. It is located on the north bank of the river behind Se Monastery.

During a trip to Ngaba in 2014, I saw many nomads pitching white waterproof canvas tents that had been distributed by the local government for free, replacing the bulkier traditional tents made of black felt. The government also distributed free lumber to build pens for yaks and freed up grant money for Tibetans to make additions to their homes.

"I don't approve of people setting themselves on fire. It is a terrible loss of life, but I have to admit we are getting more from the government," a housewife from Ngaba, whose family had gotten money for home improvement, told me. "The self-immolators made sacrifices that improved our lives."

Now there were plans afoot to turn Gonpo's former palace into a tourist attraction. They even put a signpost near the turnoff of the road to direct people to the palace, but as of my last visit nothing had been started, and I was told the local Party secretary who proposed the project had switched jobs.

Peeking between the doors, I could see grass growing from the roof. The enclosing wall was patched with yak dung, but the building itself wasn't in bad shape. The wooden balconies that had held the toilets still protruded from the sides. The palace had been used for decades as a government warehouse. Neighbors meanwhile had erected a shrine to the late Mei king in front of the palace. It was a small square house straddling a stream, painted crimson red with a painting of a dharma wheel on the front door.

More showcase projects were under construction in Meruma village. Facing Route 302 were new houses painted daffodil yellow with the same Tibetan murals as those in downtown Ngaba. "This is a face project. They built twenty or thirty really nice model homes to show officials," a fifty-four-year-old former nomad told me. He gave me a tour of his less impressive house off the main road. It was a drab rectangular box of concrete blocks. It cost only $10,000, but was really just a shell. The man said he'd poured concrete himself to make a floor and stapled tiles to make a ceiling, but he had run out of money for windows and could use the house only to store barley.

Everywhere you looked in Ngaba, something new was popping up. Local authorities were developing new tourist sites for Chinese following the route of the Long March through the Ngaba region. On the road west of Ngaba, they were developing fishing ponds, which were clearly for Chinese tourists only, since Tibetans generally do not eat fish.

How many Chinese are living in Ngaba is something of a mystery, since many of the new migrants have kept their legal residency in their former hometowns. Virtually all the fruit and vegetable vendors and most of the restaurant owners were Chinese or Hui Muslim. The 2008 earthquake in Sichuan, with its epicenter in Wenchuan, also in Ngaba prefecture, had brought a fresh influx of Chinese migrants whose homes and workplaces had been destroyed, but plenty of middle-class Chinese were moving in too. Walking around downtown Ngaba one evening, I saw crowds of young men and women in business attire spilling out of offices, animatedly speaking Chinese as they headed to the popular hot pot restaurants. They chattered outside the karaoke club with its lurid rainbow lighting. A shiny Range Rover without license plates whizzed down the main street, a sight that I recognized from Beijing, suggesting newly rich Chinese or their offspring with Party connections.

For all the development, it appeared that few new jobs were going to Tibetans. I toured the airport in Hongyuan when it was under construction in 2014 and saw that all the workers were Chinese. The construction crews for new housing were all Chinese. A friendly young man working for the Ngaba prefecture office who gave his name as Zou Shuangquan told me that Tibetans didn't like to do construction work. "The Tibetans don't really look for jobs. The nomads have yaks. They can dig for caterpillar fungus. They can make more money that way than in regular salaried jobs," said Zou, who, as it happened, was one of the Chinese officials I spoke to who was most well disposed to Tibetan culture and one of the few seriously studying the language.

The only place I encountered Tibetan construction workers in Ngaba was at a Tibetan-owned hotel where two women were maneuvering a wheelbarrow of building material up an unfinished staircase. One of the women, slim and delicate-featured, was wearing a padded jacket in the oversaturated orange favored by Buddhists, but it wasn't until she yanked off her woolen cap exposing her clean-shaven head that I realized she was a Buddhist nun. Her name was Yangchen. Her Chinese was good; she told me she'd taught herself by watching television and reading books. Her family was poor, so she was doing construction work for 100 yuan a day, half of the going rate for Chinese workers. "I was lucky that a Tibetan gave me this job. Most of the businesses and shops are owned by Han Chinese, so naturally they prefer to hire Han Chinese," Yangchen said in a matter-of-fact tone, no bitterness in her voice.

For the most part, the young Tibetans I met were as obsessed with getting secure jobs as people of their generation anywhere. It should go without saying: The Tibetans are not some exotic isolated tribe trying to preserve an ancient civilization against the advance of modernity. They want infrastructure, they want technology, they want higher education. But they also want to keep their language and culture and their freedom of religion.

Since there is so much workplace discrimination against Tibetans in the private sector, many young Tibetans aspire to civil service jobs. That entails many sacrifices, though, including accepting a limitation on the practice of Buddhism. "What opportunities do we have in Ngaba? We have to become collaborators with the Communist Party or we herd yaks and pick caterpillar fungus," an educated twenty-four-year-old man named Tashi told me.

"If I stayed in Tibet, maybe I would become a teacher and make 2,000 yuan [$300] a month," a young man named Dorjee who now lived in India told me. "Then if I wanted to advance my career, I'd have to join the Communist Party. We can't compete with the Chinese in the private sector. There is such a gap in the level of education we receive in Tibet compared to what the Chinese students are getting."

I saw this for myself when a photographer and I visited one government-run elementary school in a town not far from Ngaba. We walked into a classroom, where there were approximately thirty children about six years old milling around the room and playing. We looked around for a teacher, but there were none to be found. No adults at all, other than myself and the photographer. When the children spotted us—two adult females—they rushed back to their seats, three to a desk designed for two, and looked up expectantly, ready for us to begin the lesson. One of the children gestured to a classmate, pointing out that she had a nosebleed. I had to explain apologetically that we weren't teachers and couldn't offer them anything more than a Kleenex to wipe off the blood. (A teacher later told me that when we'd visited the teachers were on their lunch break, but the photographer had been there early in the morning and there was no teacher in the classroom then either.)

Time and again I heard the same story. Almost everybody was better off financially than they'd been a decade ago, like everybody in China. But Tibetans were still poor—even by the standards of rural China. And they could see that the Chinese newcomers in town had a higher standard of living.

TRAVELING THROUGH THE TIBETAN plateau was rough. Once on my way to Ngaba, I stopped for the night in a small town, Darlag. Trying to find my way on a dark, rainy night when the electricity was out, I tumbled into an open sewage ditch. It wouldn't have been so bad except that when I reached the hotel, the water wasn't working either and so I couldn't bathe.

I stayed with a Tibetan family in a village a few hours outside of Ngaba. (I am not naming the village in order to protect my hosts.) Other than the main road, nothing was paved. In order to enter the house, you had to climb over stones slick with mud and rainwater. The house was in a relatively new neighborhood, laid out by the government, where the houses were squeezed together. Although each home had a walled courtyard, it was just large enough for storage of the yak dung used for fuel, not for keeping animals. Most people in the neighborhood were former nomads who had been encouraged to sell their herds and settle down. The houses were made of mud and brick with horizontal wooden beams that supported the roof. The beams extended slightly beyond the structure to form a decorative pattern, a row of circles. In the home of my hosts, a lightbulb and a cassette player were powered by a solar panel since the town's electrical supply was minimal. The interior was essentially one long room, with a sleeping area separated by a polythene tarp. The walls were papered with garishly colored photos from magazines—birds, flowers, plump babies, pop stars—a style that you see frequently in Tibetan homes.

The centerpiece of the home was a stove for both heat and cooking. A kettle of water was kept hot at all times, all the quicker to make a porridge out of tsampa, which they ate at every meal, quickly and quietly licking the porcelain bowls clean.

My hostess was a widow in her late fifties, who lived with some of her adult children. Like many Tibetans of her generation, she was orphaned at an early age; her father died in prison and her mother of starvation during the Communist reforms of the 1950s. Despite a lifetime of adversity and hard work and the toll of multiple childbirths, the widow was a trim, energetic woman who exuded competence and calm. She started her day with full prostrations before a tiny altar, a routine that would challenge the fittest of my gym-rat colleagues, cleaned the stove, drew water from the well to refill the kettles. The family was a little wealthier than most in the village because they had relatives outside sending money, but still they were poor. The house was always cold and the family members wore woolen ski caps inside. Everybody appeared to be underweight, especially a daughter in her twenties. The family told me she had tuberculosis, but they couldn't find the proper medicine. A relative I met, a sixty-five-year-old woman, showed me tablets somebody had sold her for high blood pressure, telling her they came from the United States. She asked me to read the label, which identified the product as containing snakeskin and ginseng. I wasn't happy to inform her I didn't think it actually came from the United States.

Sanitation was poor. People relieved themselves by the river, always going out with a rock in hand to scare away the stray dogs. One morning, I made the mistake of exiting the gate before I had a chance to pick up a stone. I had barely stepped out of the courtyard when a large yellow dog zipped around the corner and sunk his teeth into my thigh before dashing off again.

The village did have a public toilet, sort of, by the main road, but it was nothing more than a roofless concrete box over a pit in the ground and a long walk from most houses.

As best I could tell, the only government service provided was policing. Aside from the monastery, the largest structure in the village was the Public Security Bureau, which dominated a small commercial strip. I couldn't imagine why there was so much security in this village where the population of two thousand was mostly made up of retirees, and where there hadn't been a protest or self-immolation. Police cars were continually circling the monastery and a small parking lot where buses stopped. It seemed almost all the vehicles in the village were security vehicles. I learned this the hard way when I was trying to get back to the village. There were no taxis, so a Tibetan friend and I put out our thumbs to hitch a ride. It was dusk and the road was empty, until over the ridge we were heartened to see the headlights of a car. But when it approached we could tell from the license plates that it was the armed police. This was open plateau, bare of trees or anything else to hide behind, no place to run without raising suspicion. We had no choice but to slink into the back seat.

"*Ni hui shuo putong hua?*" the plainclothes officer asked. Can you speak Chinese? I kept my mouth shut and my head down, pretending I didn't understand. Fortunately we were protected by the dim lighting. When the car reached the village, my friend muttered her thanks and we hopped out without incident.

CHINA ANALYSTS OFTEN SPEAK of an implicit bargain that the Communist Party made with the Chinese people: economic growth in return for their acquiescence to a one-party state. The Party is trying the same formula with Tibetans, and it might have even worked, since many Tibetans I've met are genuinely appreciative of the economic gains achieved under seventy years of Communist Party rule. It's not all propaganda. Tibetans don't want to go backward. If only the Chinese government offered Tibetans the same terms of the deal they do Han Chinese. Not the rights offered in democratic countries, elections or even freedom of speech, but the fundamental rights that have been offered to most Chinese citizens. The right to travel freely in their own country. The right to get passports. The right to send their kids to be educated abroad. The right to travel abroad themselves. The right to study their own language. The right to display the portrait of their spiritual leader.

A Tibetan businessman, one of the entrepreneurs who rebuilt Ngaba in the 1980s and is now an affluent man, expressed it most memorably and succinctly. This is a man with two homes, two cars, including a late-model Japanese SUV, the latest iPhone and iPad. But despite decades of trying, despite the lack of any arrest record, he has been unable to obtain a passport.

"I have everything I might possibly want in life, but my freedom," he told me.

By 2014 and 2015, the self-immolations had tapered off, replaced by a new form of protest. Solo protesters were going out into the streets waving portraits of the Dalai Lama and shouting pro-Tibetan slogans. The International Campaign for Tibet counted fourteen reported incidents in the last half of 2015 and a smaller number in each subsequent year. Similar to the profile of the self-immolators, many solo protesters have been Kirti monks from Meruma. They have received sentences ranging from two to three years.

The level of fear among Tibetans is comparable to what I've seen in North Korea. On a trip to Jiuzhaigou, the tourist resort where Tsepey worked, I asked a young Tibetan woman a bland question about the musical performance we were watching. She blanched and told me she didn't have permission to speak to me. A Tibetan academic I had met at a government-sponsored lecture hung up the phone when I called, not out of rudeness but out of fear.

China is becoming what political scientist Stein Ringen has termed the "perfect dictatorship." The government's control already is so complete, their surveillance of online communications so thorough, the closed-circuit cameras so ubiquitous, the biometric tracking of the population so advanced, that they maintain order almost seamlessly. China's new approach is less barbaric than the methods used by other regimes to control dissent—for example, the gassing of civilian populations by Syria's Bashar Assad—but it is no less stifling. By

2020, China was supposed to have 626 million closed-circuit cameras installed—one for every two people, according to a British tech consultancy. Advances in facial recognition technology already allow security services to identify people who participate in protests, as well as those who jaywalk or jump turnstiles. New social security cards have been rolled out in Ngaba and other Tibetan areas since 2015 that use advanced biometric data, such as iris scans, for identification. A "social credit" system that is under development will enable the government to punish offenders instantly by revoking privileges such as the ability to buy train tickets. China may not yet be the technological dystopia that critics fear, but that is the direction in which it is headed. The intimidation reaches far beyond China's borders. Tibetans living outside China (and other overseas Chinese, for that matter) assume that their emails and texts—especially those on WeChat—are monitored and that what they say can have negative repercussions. Several Tibetans I know in New York say that their communications with their families back in Tibet are constrained by fears that anything negative could be misconstrued as criticism of the government and that they are often unsure what is really going on at home.

Uighurs have it even worse than Tibetans; as of this writing, up to one million Uighurs are being held against their will in "patriotic education" camps where they do menial work for little to no pay and undergo Communist Party indoctrination. Their children are often placed in boarding schools to learn Chinese. The Chinese government says the camps provide vocational training and were designed to prevent Islamic militancy. The internment camps were developed by Chen Quanguo, a hard-line assimilationist, who spent five years as Communist Party secretary in the Tibet Autonomous Region before assuming the same role in Xinjiang in 2016.

Even if they are not corralled in internment camps, Tibetans live under a relentless assault of China propaganda. They are encouraged, sometimes ordered, to display portraits of Xi Jinping and Chinese flags in their home. ("My mother has a picture of Xi Jinping in her bedroom," a Tibetan from another part of Amdo told me.) For the

October 1, 2019, celebrations of the anniversary of the founding of the People's Republic of China, Ngaba students had to participate in a "motherland" singing competition: "Express your infinite love for the Party and give a gift to the 70th anniversary of the founding of New China." Among the recent posts by the Ngaba county local government was one from December 2019 showing Tibetans in Meruma attending a conference to "strengthen grassroots social governance." A photo showed Tibetans sitting on the ground, their cloaks pulled up around their heads. It was 31 degrees that day. There is only so much you can intuit from a photograph, but I'd guess they didn't want to be there.

Early indications for 2020 are not promising. In March, parents in Ngaba were informed that the #3 primary school would switch its language of instruction to Chinese. The school was the last in the country that taught primarily in Tibetan, and the switch of languages—to take effect in the fall—is already triggering protests and petitions from educators and parents. Chinese authorities have also seized upon the coronavirus emergency to impose new controls on the population. A mandatory smartphone application assigns people a color code—green, yellow, or red—indicating their likeliness to be sick or contagious and can be used to bar their entry into public spaces. The technology could remain in place long after the epidemic has passed.

I DIDN'T WORRY ABOUT what might happen to me personally while traveling in the Tibetan plateau. I was traveling legally with a valid visa and press card; the worst that was likely to happen to me was that I'd be detained for a day and escorted out of town. The source of my anxiety was what might happen to the Tibetans who helped me, or even talked with me. They could get in serious trouble—possibly being arrested or fired from their jobs.

The Chinese too have limits on their freedom of speech, but they have much, much more latitude than minorities. Even with the erosion of civil liberties under Xi Jinping, Han Chinese usually can get away with speaking to journalists and voicing minor criticisms of their government.

When I talked to Tibetans inside China, I did so inside private homes or other secluded settings, even if we were having innocuous conversations that didn't touch on politics. I was careful when hiring Tibetan translators and drivers for fear that I would get them in trouble. That created some difficulties in reporting this book since many Tibetans do not speak much Chinese. At times, I used my broken Chinese to interview Tibetans who also spoke poor Chinese, and we managed to communicate despite our limited vocabularies. At times I recorded more complicated expressions in Tibetan in order to have them translated later. Other times, younger family members interpreted what elders said into Chinese.

Over the course of my reporting, I interviewed dozens of people in Ngaba. But when writing this book, I decided to concentrate on those living abroad and elsewhere in China so that they could convey the nuance of their life stories. I realize from many years of interviewing defectors, refugees, and exiles that people on the outside often speak more candidly about the place they left than those who chose to remain. I tried to guard against that by choosing subjects whose accounts could be corroborated by relatives and friends still living inside Tibet. With a few exceptions (Tsegyam, the school official, and Tsepey, the former model/performer), the people in this book left Tibet not for political reasons but to further their education or personal growth.

For the most part, they were regular people who hoped to live normal, happy lives in China's Tibet without having to make impossible choices between their faith, family, and their country.

At the heart of the predicament is the Dalai Lama. Many Tibetans have told me they could more easily resign themselves to life within China if only the government would stop maligning the Dalai Lama.

No matter what the Dalai Lama says, the Chinese government never tires of denouncing him. Their hatred of him appears boundless. We journalists used to joke that he was like Lord Voldemort—the antagonist of the Harry Potter series, he whose name cannot be mentioned and (in many parts of Tibet) whose image cannot be seen. I had a hint of this myself in 2014 when I was transiting through the Lhasa airport on my way back from Nepal. Although I was only changing planes I knew my bags might be searched, so I took care not to carry anything sensitive. I even gave away my Kindle. All I had was a guidebook, which I figured would be suitably innocuous—the Lonely Planet guide to Nepal. It turned out that was precisely the book they were looking for. As soon as my bag went through the luggage scanner, the uniformed border guard reached inside and pulled out the guidebook. He expertly flipped to page 315, where he found the offending item. In a sidebar running along the bottom of the page, there were several historic photos, including one so small I had to squint to recognize that it was the Dalai Lama.

"*Nie kai wanxiou*," I told him. You've got to be kidding.

We argued. I suggested that he rip out the offending page and give me the rest of the book. I pointed to the manufacturer's suggested price of $27.99. He shook his head and stashed the book behind his desk, no doubt with a stack of others confiscated from unwitting travelers. The guard was a Tibetan, a tall man with erect posture in a Chinese paramilitary uniform, and he was smiling slightly, as though to indicate he knew it was stupid but he had a job to maintain and a family to support and that he had no choice but to go along with an absurd and counterproductive Chinese policy.

To purge the memory of the Dalai Lama, however, is impossible. Tibetans content themselves in places where the photograph is banned by worshipping instead Avalokitesvara, the thousand-armed bodhisattva of compassion whose likeness graces Tibetan monasteries. The Dalai Lama is considered the reincarnation of Avalokitesvara, who stands in for the missing spiritual leader. "It doesn't matter if we don't have the photo. We know where he is," a Tibetan in Lhasa told me.

The avowed atheists of the Communist Party no doubt fear the Dalai Lama for the devotion he inspires in Tibetans, but they seem to underestimate its tenacity. In the seven years I lived in China, traveling through Tibetan regions, I never ceased to be surprised by how emotional Tibetans get when speaking about the Dalai Lama. I saw a well-educated, avowedly secular Tibetan I worked with overcome when we met the Dalai Lama for an interview. This was a man in his thirties, a hard-bitten cynic and a man of reason, who was critical of the Dalai Lama's leadership of the exile community. It didn't matter; he practically melted in the presence of His Holiness.

I happened to be in China in 2015 shortly before the Dalai Lama's eightieth birthday and I passed through Ngaba. Although the self-immolations had tapered off by then, the town was under tight control as the authorities geared up to prevent celebrations. I had conducted my interview not long before and still had photographs on my phone, having ignored advice to delete them. I just couldn't resist the bragging rights. I showed the photos to a few Tibetans, and suddenly it was as if I were an official emissary. Previously closed doors opened to me. A few days later, when I was loading up the car to leave Ngaba, I was approached by a group of young Tibetans. They were in their teens and twenties, outwardly secular, denim-wearing, smartphone-carrying, Chinese-speaking young Tibetans. They had a special request. They knew that the Dalai Lama was planning to spend his birthday in Los Angeles and wanted me to bring him gifts. My driver had already popped open the trunk of the car for our suitcases, and before I could intervene, the young Tibetans started loading in gifts. There were five-pound sacks of barley flour to make tsampa, more sacks of dried vegetables, and a smaller bag of meat-stuffed momos. I tried to protest. I lived in New York, not Los Angeles. I explained that New York and Los Angeles were far apart, and in any case I had no plans to visit Los Angeles anytime soon. Furthermore, I was catching various connecting flights on my way home and surely wouldn't be able to get the food past U.S. Customs.

"It doesn't matter. It's about our heart and our intentions," one of the men responded.

It was useless to argue any further. As we drove out of town in the

Volkswagen stuffed with Tibetan food, I consulted with my inner Dalai Lama. What would the bodhisattva of compassion advise in this situation? We were headed east toward Chengdu, when I remembered I had met a very poor, disabled woman in a nearby village. We detoured off the main road, found her house, and unloaded the trunk with the offerings for the Dalai Lama inside her gate before driving back to modern China.

NOTES

THIS IS PRIMARILY A BOOK OF ORAL HISTORY STITCHED together from the recollections of Tibetans from Ngaba. As a journalist who had to familiarize myself with Tibet quickly, I relied on the work of many scholars who know more than I ever would in multiple lifetimes. These endnotes serve to credit their work and to guide readers who want to explore in more depth the topics raised in this book. In most references, I do not include page numbers since so many of us are reading electronically. Web links to specific articles change frequently so I've cited them only when they look likely to remain intact in the near future. Most of the many human rights reports and academic journals I've cited are easily accessible—at least to people living in an environment with uncensored Internet.

The physical descriptions of the places in this book are my own. I visited most of the locations in the book: Ngaba, Chengdu, Lhasa, and Lixian, where the king and queen killed themselves; Jiuzhaigou, where Tsepey worked; the Nepal side of the border; Dharamsala; Nanjing; and of course Beijing, where I lived for seven years.

Tibetan names are a slippery proposition. Places have different names just as they have different and conflicting histories. There are Chinese names and Tibetan names, which have changed over time. The academic standard to romanize Tibetan, the Wylie system, accurately reflects the Tibetan script, but not the pronunciation. I've tried to use the spellings that are most common and recognizable, easiest to find on search engines, so that curious readers can pinpoint them. Ngaba unfortunately is among the most elusive quarries; I've seen it spelled a half-dozen different ways, and even the pronunciation varies between *Ngaba* and *Ngawa* depending on the dialect of Tibetan. Perhaps it only adds to the mystery of the place.

As for personal names, Tibetans often have multiple names, but not always family names. They will change names during a lifetime—if, for example, a name is deemed unlucky or to reflect a change in status, such as the way boys entering Kirti Monastery take the new first name Lobsang. Many Tibetans have nicknames, and I've often used them both for the sake of simplicity and for the protection of the people I'm writing about.

AUTHOR'S NOTE

Under the Chinese administrative system, Ngaba is actually a county with a downtown area (which I refer to as Ngaba town) and small townships surrounding it that are in turn divided into villages. The entire population of the county is about 73,000. There is also the much larger Ngaba prefecture, which has a population of nearly 1 million and is about the size of a smallish U.S. state. This can be confusing because the capital of the prefecture is incorrectly labeled as Ngaba on some maps; in American terms, this would be roughly the equivalent of labeling Albany as New York City. The official name of the prefecture is the Aba Tibetan and Qiang Autonomous Prefecture. (The Qiang are another ethnic minority, although related to the Tibetans.)

The 50,000 figure for the number of security personnel stationed in Ngaba comes from Kirti Monastery's information officer, Kanyag Tsering, who says they were told this by government officials.

PART ONE: 1958–1976

CHAPTER I: THE LAST PRINCESS

Gonpo's full name is Gonpo Tso Mevotsang. *Tso* means "lake" and is often appended to female names in Amdo.

The descriptions of life inside the Mei king's court come primarily from my interviews with Gonpo in India. In Ngaba, I interviewed an elderly neighbor who witnessed the expulsion of Gonpo's family from the palace. I also read testimonies that were compiled for a 2015 commemoration to mark the centennial of the king's birth. These included accounts by his sister, Dhondup, and her husband, as well as by former ministers of the king's court. I visited her palace several times, but was unable to go inside. A Chinese website provided many of the statistics about the method of construction used for the palace and the interior décor.

For the history of the kingdom, I was lucky to find a book privately published in 1993 by the king's former personal secretary, Choephal, *A Brief Recollection of the Union of the Mei King and the People for Posterity*. It is the most detailed history I've found about the kingdom, although written as something of a hagiography of the late king.

More objective might be recollections of an American missionary, Robert Ekvall, who visited Ngaba in the 1920s and was similarly impressed by the Mei's governance and the literacy of the royal family. Transcripts of an interview conducted in 1979 are contained in the Billy Graham Center Archives at Wheaton College, Illinois. https://www2.wheaton.edu /bgc/archives/transcripts/cn092t01.pdf.

Ekvall also wrote a novel, *The Lama Knows* (Chandler & Sharp, 1981), which takes place near Ngaba and, although fictional, offers rich descriptions of the time and place.

Another missionary, Robert Dean Carlson, traveled through Ngaba in the 1940s. His recollections are available in the same archives. https:// archon.wheaton.edu.

After his death, the Mei king won praise in an official Chinese government history. I thank Jianglin Li for referring me to the Aba Tibetan and Qiang Autonomous Prefecture *Anthology of Literature and History,* Book 6, published in 1987.

Daniel Berounský of Charles University, Prague, contributed a fascinating essay, "Kirti Monastery of Ngawa: Its History and Recent Situation," to an issue of *Revue d'Études Tibétaines* in 2012 that was devoted to the self-immolations. http://himalaya.socanth.cam.ac.uk/collections /journals/ret/pdf/ret_25.pdf.

CHAPTER 2: EAT THE BUDDHA

This chapter draws heavily on the groundbreaking work of scholars Jianglin Li and Matthew Akester, who discovered and translated firsthand accounts of both Tibetans and Chinese of their encounters during the Long March of 1935 and 1936. Akester coined the title "Eat the Buddha!" for a paper he and Li posted on their blog; it was through that paper that I discovered Ngaba was one of the first places where Communists and Tibetans collided, and it was one of the inspirations for me to choose Ngaba as the place to write about. Their complete paper, "Eat the Buddha! Chinese and

Tibetan Accounts of the Red Army in Gyalrong and Ngaba 1935–6 and Related Documents," can be found on their blog, http://historicaldocs .blogspot.com/2012/05/red-army-in-ngaba-1935-1936.html.

The memoirs of Wu Faxian, the Red Army soldier who wrote of eating votive offerings in monasteries, were published in Chinese under the name *Months of Hardship* (Star North Books, 2006). In English, Sun Shuyun's *The Long March: The True Story of China's Founding Myth* (Doubleday, 2007) is based largely on interviews with Red Army survivors; they make clear that they felt the Tibetan plateau was a foreign country.

In conversations with Edgar Snow, Mao described the Red Army's confiscation of food as "our only foreign debt," saying that someday they would have to repay the "Tibetans for the provisions we were obliged to take from them." Edgar Snow, *Red Star Over China* (Grove Press, 1973), pages 203–204.

On the origins of the Tibetan people, the legend about their descent from an ape and an ogress was first written in post-tenth-century Buddhist works that describe the Tibetans' progenitors as emanations of the bodhisattva of compassion, according to Matthew Kapstein's *The Tibetans* (Wiley-Blackwell, 2006). I found his book to be very helpful, along with R. A. Stein's *Tibetan Civilization* (Stanford University Press, 1972). On the history of the Tibetan empire, I turned to Sam van Schaik's *Tibet: A History* (Yale University Press, 2011).

Tsering Shakya, a leading Tibetan historian, summed up the nuances of the question of who is a Tibetan in a 1993 essay, "Whither the Tsampa Eaters?" The entire essay is published online. https://www.academia.edu /691679/Whither_the_Tsampa_Eaters?auto=download.

On the question of how the Mei and other mini-kingdoms survived within the Chinese empire, I refer to Jack Patrick Hayes's *A Change in Worlds on the Sino-Tibetan Borderlands: Politics, Economies, and Environments in Northern Sichuan* (Lexington Books, 2014). He writes that in order to rule cheaply and easily, both the Ming and Qing dynasties "co-opted existing structures by assigning local leaders official and imperial titles." Max Oidtmann of Georgetown University also shared with me some of his research on the legal overlay provided by the Qing dynasty over existing Tibetan chieftains in Amdo.

On the confusing terminology about Tibet's legal status, see Amanda

Cheney's "Tibet: Lost in Translation: Sovereignty, Suzerainty and International Order Transformation, 1904–1906," *Journal of Contemporary China* 26 (2017), and a paper by Ryosuke Kobayashi, "The Political Status of Tibet and the Simla Conference (1913–14)."

CHAPTER 3: RETURN OF THE DRAGON

An invaluable source was the memoir *My Tibetan Childhood: When Ice Shattered Stone,* by Naktsang Nulo, translated by Angus Cargill and Sonam Lhamo (Duke University Press, 2014). The book is one of the few accounts available in English translation of the harrowing and underreported experiences of ordinary Tibetans in the eastern reaches of the plateau during the 1950s. The author lived in Gansu province, not far from Ngaba, and belonged to the Chukama clan, which was constantly fighting with the Mei kingdom, a war that is described in some detail in the book. As Tibet scholar Robbie Barnett notes in an excellent introduction, most other accounts were written by elite Tibetans and aristocrats from Lhasa, which was not nearly as hard hit in the early years under Communism. Barnett's introduction also provides a very cogent explanation of the importance of the eastern reaches of the Tibetan plateau in Tibetan culture, history, literature, and economy, despite the fact that these areas were sometimes not considered to be Tibet proper.

For authoritative accounts of how Tibet fell under Chinese rule, I turned to Tsering Shakya's *The Dragon in the Land of Snows: A History of Modern Tibet Since 1947* (Penguin Compass, 2000) and Melvyn Goldstein's three-volume *A History of Modern Tibet,* especially the first volume, *The Demise of the Lamaist State, 1913–1951* (University of California Press, 1989).

The Dalai Lama described his early encounters with Mao and the Chinese Communist Party in his memoir, *My Land and My People.* The passage I quote is from a republished edition with a new foreword (Hachette Book Group, 1997), pages 87–88. The description of his education is on pages 34–35. I also relied on John Avedon's biography of the Dalai Lama, *In Exile from the Land of Snows,* first published in 1979 (Vintage Books, 2015) and on Pico Iyer's *The Open Road* (Vintage Books, 2008).

For the section on the Mei king's reaction to the Communist Party, I relied on Delek, an amateur historian of Ngaba, who was both a source for and a major figure in this book. An older exile from Ngaba, Jamyang Sonam, born in the 1920s, was interviewed in 2014 by a translator working with me.

The king's former ally, Ma Bufang, would later become Taiwan's ambassador to Saudi Arabia.

CHAPTER 4: THE YEAR THAT TIME COLLAPSED

While Mao's Great Leap Forward is now widely recognized as one of the world's greatest man-made disasters, the Tibetan experience is often dismissed as something of a sideshow. An exception is *Hungry Ghosts: Mao's Secret Famine* (Free Press, 1997) by Jasper Becker, who has included a chapter about Tibetans. Dutch historian Frank Dikötter also deals with Tibetans in his books about the impact of the Communist revolution: *Mao's Great Famine: The History of China's Most Devastating Catastrophe, 1958–1962* (Walker Books, 2010); *The Tragedy of Liberation: A History of the Chinese Revolution, 1945–1957* (Bloomsbury Press, 2013); and *The Cultural Revolution: A People's History, 1962–1976* (Bloomsbury Press, 2016).

An important new book about the Great Leap Forward is Yang Jisheng's *Tombstone: The Great Chinese Famine, 1958–1962* (Farrar, Straus & Giroux, 2012). The book was first published in Hong Kong—the famine still being a taboo subject on the mainland. Yang concludes that 36 million people died in the famine and that another 40 million were not born.

The expression *dhulok,* translated as "collapse of time," was used by many of the older people I met from Ngaba. I have only found one written reference to the term. It is in Tsering Wangmo Dhompa's *A Home in Tibet* (Penguin Books, 2013), a gorgeously written memoir by a Tibetan-American poet who returned to her mother's home village in Kyegu, about two hundred miles west of Ngaba.

The quote about the Han being the "bulwark" of the revolution comes from a chapter by Warren W. Smith, "The Nationalities Policy of the Chinese Communist Party and the Socialist Transformation of Tibet," in *Resistance and Reform in Tibet,* ed. Robert Barnett and Shirin Akiner (C. Hurst, 1994), page 57.

The massacre in Marang village, Ngaba, is described in a compilation of testimonies published by the Tibetan Centre for Human Rights and

Democracy in 2018 under the name *Ancestor's Tomb*. The author, identified only by a pseudonym, Mar Jang-Nyug, is a writer and university student from Ngaba.

There were some reports about fighting as well in *Neibu Cankao,* a limited-circulation publication of the official Xinhua News Service, intended only for government officials.

The most extensive research on the death toll among Tibetans during this period was conducted by Jianglin Li. Li is the author of *When the Iron Bird Flies: The 1956–1962 Secret War on the Tibetan Plateau* (Linking Publishing Company, 2012). She uses official Chinese government and military sources, some of them classified, to document the suppression of the Tibetan resistance in eastern Tibet. Its key findings are also summarized on the *War on Tibet* blog: http://historicaldocs.blogspot.com/2013/05/when -iron-bird-flies-summary-of-findings.html.

In *Tibet, Tibet: A Personal History of a Lost Land,* Patrick French extrapolates the Tibetan death toll from data published by the Chinese government, and analyzed earlier by the demographer Judith Banister. He points out that death rates in provinces with large Tibetan populations were almost double those elsewhere in China.

On the 1937–1938 massacre in Nanjing, Japanese historians have suggested a death toll of anywhere from 20,000 to 200,000, while the Chinese say more than 300,000 were killed and most of them were civilians.

Once a supporter of the Communist Party, the Panchen Lama was able to travel with relative freedom in the Tibetan regions. Horrified by what he observed, he presented a scathing critique to the government in 1962. Known simply as the 70,000-Character Petition, the document was kept secret from all but the upper echelons of the Chinese government until 1996, when a copy was obtained by the Tibet Information Network. An English translation was published by the Tibet Information Network in 1998, entitled *A Poisoned Arrow: The Secret Report of the 10th Panchen Lama.* Some of the figures about the percentage of the population imprisoned and killed come from the Panchen Lama's report and his subsequent research.

The CIA's involvement in Tibet is the subject of several books, which are succinctly synopsized by Jonathan Mirsky in *The New York Review of Books:* "The CIA's Cancelled War," April 19, 2013. The United States pulled the plug in 1972 on the eve of Richard Nixon's historic visit to China, after which U.S. policy returned to what Mirsky aptly describes as "kowtowing to the Chinese and hollow good wishes for the Dalai Lama."

CHAPTER 5: A THOROUGHLY CHINESE GIRL

China modeled its ethnic minorities policy after the Soviet Union, according to Warren Smith's illuminating essay in *Resistance and Reform in Tibet,* referred to earlier. In the 1954 census, China recognized thirty-nine minorities; a decade later, they expanded that to fifty-six minorities.

The poster hailing the integration of ethnic minorities into the new China was released in 1955. It can be seen on chineseposters.net.

The full text of the sixteen-point statement of the Central Committee of the Chinese Communist Party, "Concerning the Great Proletarian Cultural Revolution," is widely available online.

For the atmosphere in Beijing in 1966, the exact language of the slogans, and other background on the Cultural Revolution, I turned to *Mao's Last Revolution* by Roderick MacFarquhar and Michael Schoenhals (Harvard University Press, 2009).

The editorial about sweeping away the "monsters and demons" (*nuigui sheshen,* literally "cow monsters and snake demons") was published June 1, 1966, by Chen Boda, Mao's political secretary, and is also available on Marxists.org.

CHAPTER 6: RED CITY

The Chinese scholar Li Jianglin provided me with her translations of Chinese-language accounts of the Cultural Revolution. These include an internally published memoir by Dajie, a Tibetan official of the Communist Party from neighboring Golok, where the rebellion spread, *Knowledge and Memory in Golok* (Xining, 2008). Another reference is Cai Wenbin's *Zhao Ziyang in Sichuan* (Hong Kong, 2011). Zhao Ziyang, the Chinese leader who was purged for his sympathy to Tiananmen Square protesters, had served earlier as Party secretary in Sichuan, where he also had a reputation as a reformer. According to this biography, Zhao was personally responsible for rehabilitating "Hongcheng" Tashi, the leader of the Red City movement.

From Tibetan sources, Matthew Akester provided a translation of the relevant section from *Wounds of Three Generations,* a work of oral history published by Kirti Monastery in exile (Dharamsala, 2010).

When I was reporting in Ngaba, I was unable to meet with Hongcheng Tashi, who is in his eighties, but I did interview at some length his younger brother, Louri, who was a contemporary of Delek's and participated in the fighting.

A better-known Tibetan rebellion during the Cultural Revolution took place in 1969 in Nyemo county and was led by a Buddhist nun who was later executed. It is described in Melvyn Goldstein's monograph *On the Cultural Revolution in Tibet: The Nyemo Incident of 1969* (University of California Press, 2009).

CHAPTER 7: EXILE

Gonpo had very little contact with people outside her farm and didn't interact much with the Kazakhs, Uighurs, and Mongols who lived in the area. The farm was run by the Xinjiang Production and Construction Corps, a military organization set up in 1954 on Mao's orders to develop the frontier region. Sadly, Qinghe (Qinggal in Uighur) is now the site of one of hundreds of reeducation camps in which over one million Uighurs are being imprisoned for reeducation.

Xiao Tu, or Little Rabbit, is a common nickname for Chinese born during the year of the rabbit. In order to protect his privacy, I'm not using his full name.

The lyrics of the song come from Geremie Barmé's *Shades of Mao: The Posthumous Cult of the Great Leader* (Routledge, 2016). They are possibly from a later version of the song that Gonpo remembers, although all versions are more or less the same.

On the ban on intermarriage between Han and Uighurs, see James Palmer's "Blood and Fear in Xinjiang," *Foreign Policy,* March 2, 2014. Nowadays, some local governments are encouraging intermarriage as a way to promote assimilation.

Chinese universities reopened in 1968, but only admitted students who were recommended by their Party work units. Limited entrance exams resumed in 1973, but it was not until 1977 that China reinstated the *gaokao,* the nationwide entrance exam that is used to this day.

PART TWO: INTERREGNUM, 1976–1989

CHAPTER 8: THE BLACK CAT AND THE GOLDEN WORM

Eloquent descriptions of the giddy atmosphere in 1980s China can be found in Orville Schell's *To Get Rich Is Glorious* (Pantheon Books, 1984).

The description of the rebuilding of Kirti Monastery and the role of the businessman Karchen comes largely from a market trader named Pema who is introduced in chapter 13.

On the herbs sold by Tibetans, the Latin name of *beimu* is *Fritillaria cirrhosa*. I haven't found an English name. The bulb is used to make cough syrup.

On the caterpillar fungus or *yartsa gunbu,* known as *chongcao* in Chinese, statistics about the contribution to the Tibetan economy come from Daniel Winkler, an environmental consultant and mycologist. The anthropologist Emilia Roza Sulek published a book on the subject, *Trading Caterpillar Fungus in Tibet* (Amsterdam University Press, 2019). In 2008, I followed a Tibetan family hunting for caterpillar fungus to report a story for the *Los Angeles Times,* and I can attest personally to the strain on the eyes and lungs. Although the worm still provides a large part of Tibetans' disposable income, the supply is dwindling due to overharvesting and warming temperatures.

Far too little research has been conducted on the incentives for Han Chinese to move to Tibetan areas. The most detailed that I found was *The Long March: Chinese Settlers and Chinese Policies in Eastern Tibet* (International Campaign for Tibet, 1991).

Tibet advocacy groups argue that the policy of moving Chinese into Tibet violates a provision of the Fourth Geneva Convention stating that an "occupying Power shall not deport or transfer parts of its own civilian population into the territory it occupies" (Article 49, paragraph 6). The same provision is most often cited in discussions of Israeli settlement activity. See www.tibetjustice.org/reports/wbank/index.html.

CHAPTER 9: A TIBETAN EDUCATION

In addition to my own interviews with Tsegyam, I spoke with one of his brothers and consulted the profile that was published in 1999 by Human

Rights Watch. It is available on their website, https://www.hrw.org /legacy/reports/1999/tibet/Tibetweb-01.htm.

The execution that Tsegyam witnessed as a boy took place in March 1971. Alak Jigme Samten was the man whom young Delek remembered blowing smoke into the mouth of his dying companion in Meruma in chapter 6. The other man executed was Gabe Yonten Gyatso, a rebel leader from Golok, where the Red City uprising had spread.

Barkham, the capital of Ngaba (Aba) prefecture, had a surprisingly robust literary scene in the 1980s and 1990s. It was also home of Alai, a well-known half-Tibetan writer who won China's prestigious Mao Dun Literature Award. In the mid-1980s, he was editor of the *New Grasslands Journal* and Tsegyam was one of the contributors.

The Tibetan who described the Dalai Lama to me as "like Santa Claus" is Dechen, who is introduced in chapter 13.

CHAPTER 10: A PEACOCK FROM THE WEST

On the process of rehabilitation or *pingfan,* I turned to Hsi-cheng Chi's *Politics of Disillusionment: The Chinese Communist Party Under Deng Xiaoping* (Routledge, 1991).

The passage about the exhumation of the Mei king's body comes from an interview with Jamphel Sampo that was included in a book privately published in 2012 for the centennial of the king's birth.

Gonpo doesn't remember meeting with Delek in 1984, as she was one of dozens of the king's former subjects who came to greet her, but he has a clear recollection of the meeting.

PART THREE: 1990–2013

CHAPTER 11: WILD BABY YAK

Under China's complicated family planning regulations, some minorities have exemptions from the one-child-per-family limit. The regulations are applied unevenly and vary greatly by region. Anecdotally, I've heard of Tibetan women being forced to abort; I've also met nomadic families with more than ten children.

On Tibetan family arrangements and the prevalence of single mothers, I refer to Melvyn Goldstein's "When Brothers Share a Wife," *Natural History* (March 1987). The village Goldstein studied was in Nepal, but was ethnically Tibetan. Although the practice of polyandry was more common in western Tibet, I heard of several cases in Ngaba, and many of the Ngaba residents I met said they were raised by a single mother.

The television series about the Long March was aired on CCTV in 2001, and featured a propagandistic spin on the Chinese Communist Party. In the episode shot in Meruma, Mao talks with a "living Buddha" (Chinese terminology for a reincarnate lama) about Buddhism and Communism.

MAO: I believe in Marxism.

LIVING BUDDHA: If Marx has the surname Ma, he must be Chinese.

MAO: No. He's German.

LIVING BUDDHA: Why did you change to believe in the Marxism started by a German?

MAO: That's because Marxism can solve the problems China is facing today. . . .

MAO: Please do not worry, living Buddha. The future in China will for sure have freedom of religion.

LIVING BUDDHA: With your wisdom, you can at least win the people's support and make peace of the world.

CHAPTER 12: A MONK'S LIFE

As a journalist without a background in Tibetan Buddhism, I found it difficult to understand the education system of the monasteries. One very helpful source was Georges B. J. Dreyfus's *The Sound of Two Hands Clapping* (University of California Press, 2003).

The Third National Forum on Work in Tibet took place July 20–24, 1994, and was considered pivotal in changing the direction of Tibet policy. See *Cutting Off the Serpent's Head: Tightening Control in Tibet, 1994–1995,* by Robert Barnett and the staff of Tibet Information Network (Human Rights Watch, 1996). The quote I've used is on page 212.

Copies of lectures and tests used for "patriotic education" were provided by the information office of Kirti Monastery's branch in Dharamsala.

CHAPTER 13: COMPASSION

The Dalai Lama's seemingly innocuous call for Tibetans not to wear the skins of protected animals ended up causing much turmoil. According to a report from Dharamsala, at least $75 million worth of skins were destroyed in eastern Tibet. The Wildlife Trust of India reported that in Ngaba prefecture 10,000 people attended a public bonfire where three truckloads of furs were burned. "Police were unable to prevent the burning, due to the large crowd. Eight people including two Chinese and six Tibetans were arrested here. This is considered to be the largest collection of animal skins burnt in the last fortnight," the Wildlife Trust reported. Environmental News Service, February 24, 2006.

The description of Lhundup Tso's childhood and upbringing came from an interview with her sister in India in 2014.

The water diversion project did not go forward, Ngaba residents believe, because officials feared the town could erupt in large-scale protests. But a similar project was proposed in late 2018 to divert water from the Yellow River (Machu in Tibetan) to the Qinghai provincial capital of Xining. See https://freetibet.org/news-media/na/china-launches-mass -yellow-river-diversion-project.

China is famous for its engineering projects to divert water from the south to the arid north, and the projects often trigger protests, not just in Tibetan areas.

For a deep dive into how Chinese development is impacting the Tibetan plateau, I recommend Michael Buckley's *Meltdown in Tibet: China's Reckless Destruction of Ecosystems from the Highlands of Tibet to the Deltas of Asia* (St. Martin's Press, 2014). A quicker but nonetheless excellent read on the subject is Sulmaan Khan's "Suicide by Drought: How China Is Destroying Its Own Water Supply," *Foreign Affairs* (July 18, 2014).

CHAPTER 14: THE PARTY ANIMAL

On the railroad, see Pankaj Mishra, "The Train to Tibet," *The New Yorker*, April 16, 2007. He quotes the poet Tsering Woeser referring to the train as a "colonial imposition."

Chinese ambitions have led to the construction around the country of oversized airports with impressive architecture and facilities, but few flights or passengers. I toured the Hongyuan airport in 2014 when it was under construction. My colleague David Pierson did a humorous story about this phenomenon: "Plenty of New Airports but Few Passengers in China," *Los Angeles Times,* March 13, 2010.

The Associated Press, quoting Chinese state media, reported on large-scale military exercises: "Chinese Military Exercise on Tibetan Lands," June 29, 1999.

On Jiuzhaigou, I spent two days at the resort in 2013 and saw for myself the gala that Tsepey described—a multi-ethnic homage to the Chinese Communist Party. The performance I saw opened with a Tibetan woman singing "Wo ai ni Zhongguo" (I Love You, China).

The Shugden worshippers are adept at getting publicity for themselves, holding raucous protests outside venues where the Dalai Lama is speaking, accusing him of being a "false Dalai Lama" and a "dictator" who opposes their freedom of religion. Reuters reported in 2015 that the Shugden movement is funded and coordinated by the Chinese Communist Party in order to discredit the Dalai Lama. See David Lague, Paul Mooney, and Benjamin Kang Lim, "China Co-opts a Buddhist Sect in Global Effort to Smear Dalai Lama," Reuters, December 21, 2015.

Tibetans say that pro-Shugden monasteries are suspiciously well funded and protected by the Chinese government. I personally observed Chinese paramilitaries stationed in specially built guardhouses to protect a shrine to Shugden at Ganden Monastery near Lhasa.

State Religious Affairs Bureau Order #5 ("Measures on the Management of the Reincarnation of Living Buddhas") decreed: "It is an important move to institutionalize management on reincarnation of living Buddhas. The selection of reincarnates must preserve national unity and solidarity of all ethnic groups and the selection process cannot be influenced by any group or individual from outside the country."

The story of how this child became a pawn in the battle between the Chinese government and the Dalai Lama is covered in Isabel Hilton's *The Search for the Panchen Lama* (Norton, 2000).

The forestry data is quoted by Daniel Winkler in "Forests, Forest Economy and Deforestation in the Tibetan Prefectures of West Sichuan," *Commonwealth Forestry Review* 75, no. 4 (1996). A researcher for the Sichuan Communist Party Policy Research Department is quoted saying that state-owned forestry companies have to meet a quota that is up to three times higher than the sustainable yield. Another Chinese researcher is quoted complaining that Ngaba prefecture's forest cover was reduced from the 1950s to the 1980s from 19.4 percent to 10 percent.

On the resettlement villages seen by Tsepey: The relocation of nomads into sedentary housing is a major concern for Tibetans, who say that herders are pressed into selling off their animals and losing their livelihood and lifestyle. The Chinese government says the relocations are necessary to prevent overgrazing and to protect the fragile ecosystem of the plateau. I don't explore it in this book because it was not happening on a large scale around Ngaba county, although it was in nearby Jiuzhi and in Hongyuan. In Golok, just to the northwest of Ngaba, I drove past sprawling resettlement colonies, cheerless chockablock rows of concrete boxes. Human Rights Watch addressed the subject in "They Say We Should Be Grateful: Mass Housing and Relocation Programs in Tibetan Areas of China" (June 2013). For an academic analysis, also see Jarmila Ptackova's "Sedentarisation of Tibetan Nomads in China: Implementation of the Nomadic Settlement Project in the Tibetan Amdo Area; Qinghai and Sichuan Provinces," *Pastoralism: Research, Policy and Practice* (2011).

CHAPTER 15: THE UPRISING

I am unsure of the anti-riot device that was used to spew gravel into Dongtuk's eyes. He was certain that it was not tear gas. I suspect that it was similar to the gravel-dispersal vehicles developed for the use of the Israeli military.

For an excellent analysis of the 2008 uprising, see "The Tibet Protests of Spring 2008: Conflict Between the Nation and State" by Robbie Barnett, *China Perspectives* (March 2009). The full article is online. Barnett points out that the protests shocked Beijing because they had often pointed to Tibetan communities in Sichuan, Qinghai, and Gansu as exemplars for the successful governance of ethnic minorities. While incidents of unrest are common in China—often protests against pollution, corruption, or layoffs—the Tibetan protests in 2008 were a direct challenge to Chinese rule over Tibetans.

The initial Xinhua report (which is referenced in Barnett's essay), dated March 20, read, "URGENT: Four Rioters Shot Dead Sunday in Aba of SW China, Police Sources."

On casualty figures from 2008 protests in Lhasa, see "Leaked Internal Document Shows China Used Machine Guns to Kill Tibetans in March 2008 Protest" (August 20, 2014). Available on the website of the Tibetan Centre for Human Rights and Democracy: https://tchrd.org/?s=leaked+internal+document.

Overall casualty figures are so wildly far apart as to make an accurate count elusive. According to a comparison in Barnett's article, the Tibetan exile government claimed 219 Tibetan protesters were killed throughout the region, the International Campaign for Tibet (ICT) 140 protesters, and the Chinese government just 8 protesters. The Chinese government and ICT more or less agreed that either one or two security personnel were killed, along with 18 bystanders.

James Miles of *The Economist* happened to be in Lhasa at the time of the protests and was the only Western journalist there. Along with foreign tourists, he witnessed Tibetans stabbing and bludgeoning random passersby who they thought were Chinese or Hui Muslim. "It was an extraordinary outpouring of ethnic violence of a most unpleasant nature to watch, which surprised some Tibetans watching it." James Miles interview on Tibet, CNN.com, March 20, 2008.

I also wrote about the attacks on civilians, as did many of my colleagues: "Tales of Horror from Tibet," *Los Angeles Times,* March 22, 2008. In a subsequent piece from Golok, I addressed long-festering Tibetan-Hui tensions that lay behind some of the violence: "Tibetan-Muslim Tensions Roil China," *Los Angeles Times,* June 23, 2008.

Again, Ngaba residents didn't share these sentiments and Muslim businesses in Ngaba were not targeted.

CHAPTER 16: THE EYE OF THE GHOST

Photographs of Tibetans being taken away in trucks and wearing signboards around their necks were provided to me by the information office at Kirti Monastery in Dharamsala. They also showed me copies of the examinations used during the patriotic education training.

On Zhang Qingli's attack on the Dalai Lama and on the Dalai Lama's response: Ching-ching Ni, "China Steps Up Criticism of Dalai Lama," *Los Angeles Times,* March 10, 2008; Somini Sengupta, "Dalai Lama Threatens to Resign," *New York Times,* March 19, 2008.

On the music that inspired Dongtuk and his friends, I refer to Lama Jabb's essay "Singing the Nation: Modern Tibetan Music and National Identity." This essay was first published online in *Revue d'Études Tibétaines,* No. 21 (October 2011). I wrote in 2008 about the arrest of a popular folk musician in Golok: "China Silences a Tibetan Folk Singer," *Los Angeles Times,* June 8, 2008.

The lyrics to Tashi Dhondup's "1958–2008" and other songs were translated into English by *High Peaks Pure Earth* (highpeakspureearth .com), a website that provides news, commentary, and poetry about Tibet as well as translations from the Tibetan and Chinese.

CHAPTER 17: CELEBRATE OR ELSE

On the Lhakar or "White Wednesday movement," *High Peaks Pure Earth* did a useful explainer that is posted on its website.

Tibetans around China were forced to celebrate Losar. "In Tibet, 'Happy New Year' Is Not a Wish; It's an Order," *Los Angeles Times,* February 23, 2009.

On fake Twitter accounts that propagate upbeat news about Tibet, see Andrew Jacobs, "It's Another Perfect Day in Tibet," *New York Times,* July 21, 2014.

On China's attempt to portray Tibetans as happy, one of the most striking examples was an exhibit in 2008, *Tibet of China: Past and Present,* installed in the sprawling Cultural Palace of Nationalities in Beijing. There were large Technicolor photographs of apple-cheeked Tibetans with cornucopias of food, contrasted with displays of gruesome torture implements purportedly used on serfs in old Tibet. Most of the visitors were Chinese families; the children looked terrified. I attended with the Tibetan poet Tsering Woeser.

CHAPTER 18: NO WAY OUT

The popularity of basketball among Tibetans inspired a recent documentary, *Ritoma,* directed by Ruby Yang and released in 2018.

"One Passport, Two Systems; China's Restrictions on Foreign Travel by Tibetans and Others," Human Rights Watch, July 13, 2015. The quote from the Tibetan blogger is in the report.

CHAPTER 19: BOY ON FIRE

Videos of the scene in Ngaba in the aftermath of Phuntsog's self-immolation are available on the website https://freetibet.org/about/human-rights/case-studies/phuntsog.

Radio Free Asia reported in detail on the court cases that arose from Phuntsog's self-immolation: "Kirti Monk Sentenced for Murder," August 29, 2011.

Much of the information about the self-immolations came from the Tibetan writer and poet Tsering Woeser. She analyzed the final statements of the self-immolators in some detail for Radio Free Asia. Her book *Tibet on Fire* (Verso, 2016) is the most detailed account I've read of the self-immolations.

Tapey and other self-immolators are featured in a CCTV documentary produced in 2012: "Facts about the Self-Immolations in the Tibetan Area of Ngapa." As of this writing, a thirty-minute version of the video was available on YouTube: https://www.youtube.com/watch?time_continue=83&v=IDIhI528-hA. According to Woeser, the documentary was intended primarily for foreign audiences and was not available on Chinese sites.

CHAPTER 20: SORROWS

At the height of the self-immolations, Chinese authorities allowed U.S. ambassador Gary Locke to visit Ngaba prefecture, but permitted him to go only as far as Songpan, a quiet town free of protests and a hundred miles away from Ngaba county. Ed Wong, "U.S. Ambassador Confirms Meeting with Tibetans in Western China," *New York Times,* October 17, 2012. A few years later, the government brought a group of journalists to the region, again avoiding the downtown area of Ngaba county.

Among the journalists who managed to sneak into Ngaba were Tom Lasseter, then of McClatchy Newspapers, who hid under two backpacks and a sleeping bag, and Jonathan Watts of *The Guardian,* who folded his six-foot-three frame into the back of a car. Holly Williams of Sky News was detained along with her crew on her way out from a visit to Ngaba. Videos of their visit give a good sense of the level of security.

On China's domestic security spending, see Chris Buckley, "China Internal Security Spending Jumps Past Army Budget," Reuters, March 4, 2011; Human Rights Watch, "Heavy-Handed Security Exacerbates Grievances, Desperation," October 12, 2011.

Christopher Beam wrote a fascinating piece about the hardship of life in Ngaba without connectivity: "Beyond China's Cyber Curtain," *The New Republic,* December 5, 2013.

The quote from Lama Sobha is found in "Harrowing Images and Last Message from Tibet of First Lama to Self-Immolate," International Campaign for Tibet, February 1, 2012.

The papers delivered at the conference in Paris were published by *Revue d'Études Tibétaines* under the collective heading "Self-Immolation: Ritual or Political Protest?" December 6, 2012. The entire issue is available online: http://himalaya.socanth.cam.ac.uk/collections/journals/ret/pdf/ret_25 .pdf. Daniel Berounský's paper on the history of Ngaba and Kirti Monastery is included in this issue.

On self-immolation among Chinese Buddhists, the most detailed study is James Benn's *Burning for the Buddha: Self-Immolation in Chinese Buddhism* (University of Hawaii Press, 2007). Benn also has an essay in the above-cited *Revue d'Études Tibétaines.*

The quote about the self-immolators asserting their moral superiority is from James Verini's "A Terrible Act of Reason: When Did Self-Immolation Become the Paramount Form of Protest?" *The New Yorker,* May 16, 2012.

A wealth of history and analysis about the phenomenon of copycat suicides was gleaned from Loren Coleman's *Suicide Clusters* (Faber & Faber, 1987).

One of the inspirations for my book was Orhan Pamuk's novel *Snow* (Vintage, 2006), based on a cluster of suicides in the Turkish city of Batman.

The quote comparing the Tibetan self-immolators to the Tunisian fruit vendor comes from Jamyang Norbu's blog, *Shadow Tibet,* at https:// www.jamyangnorbu.com/blog/: "Igniting the Embers of Independence," October 14, 2011.

Kirti Rinpoche testified before the Tom Lantos Human Rights Commission, November 3, 2011. Full testimony available at https://human rightscommission.house.gov/sites/humanrightscommission.house.gov /files/documents/Kirti%20Rinpoche%20Testimony.pdf.

The letter complaining about Shi Jun was discovered by Tsering Woeser, who reprinted it on her blog, *Invisible Tibet,* February 18, 2012. *High Peaks Pure Earth* republished it in English translation. The dislike of Shi Jun was not unanimous among Tibetans in Ngaba. Several of the businessmen I met praised his contributions to the business community. His career has advanced considerably since his tenure in Ngaba. He was appointed vice minister of the Ministry of Public Security in May 2017 and vice minister of the United Front Work Department in August 2018, according to *Global Times*: http://www.globaltimes.cn/content/1143562 .shtml.

CHAPTER 21: THE ZIP LINE

On the situation of Tibetans in Nepal, Human Rights Watch issued a report, "Under China's Shadow: Mistreatment of Tibetans in Nepal," April 1, 2014. I reported on the issue the following year from the border town of Kodari: "Tibetans Lose a Haven in Nepal Under Chinese Pressure," *Los Angeles Times,* August 6, 2015.

The border crossing between Tibet and Nepal has shifted since 2015 due to damage from the 2015 earthquake.

PART FOUR: 2014 TO THE PRESENT

CHAPTER 22: INDIA

John Avedon's *In Exile from the Land of Snows* (referenced earlier) was very informative on the origins of the Tibetan exile community in Dharamsala.

On the disenchantment of the permanent refugees stuck in India, *Dharamsala Days, Dharamsala Nights* was published in 2013 by an aid worker writing under the pseudonym Pauline MacDonald and provides intelligent criticism of the exile government.

Tim Johnson offered a dispiriting assessment of the future of the Tibet movement in *Tragedy in Crimson: How the Dalai Lama Conquered the World but Lost the Battle with China* (Bold Type Books, 2011).

I turned to Tsering Shakya's above-referenced *The Dragon in the Land of Snows* on the frustrations of the dialogue between the exile government and Beijing.

Xi Jinping's Paris speech took place March 28, 2014, at UNESCO headquarters. Ian Johnson writes of the fascination of both father and son, Xi Zhongxun and Xi Jinping, with Buddhism in "What a Buddhist Monk Taught Xi Jinping," *New York Times,* March 24, 2017; the article is adapted from Johnson's book *The Souls of China: The Return of Religion After Mao* (Pantheon, 2017).

Elie Wiesel's conversation with the Dalai Lama was recounted in Evan Osnos's "The Next Incarnation," *The New Yorker,* September 27, 2010.

On the differing interpretations of *Rangzen,* Tsering Wangmo Dhompa has a revealing passage on page 189 of *Home in Tibet* that I quote here: "Freedom, as I have been taught to understand as a political being in exile—(is) to be protected by law, to be able to live my life as I choose, absent from tyranny and persecution. . . . The elders tell me they equate freedom with the right to live as Buddhists, which entails being able to perform their rituals, have access to lamas and to monasteries, and be able to participate in retreats and studies. They might even refer to an aspired state of mind: to be free of attachment, anger, stupidity, jealousy, and arrogance."

After I finished reporting this book, I learned from a mutual friend that Tsepey had died in Sydney, Australia, of a virulent flu. He was forty years old and left behind a wife and child.

CHAPTER 23: EVERYTHING BUT MY FREEDOM

Stein Ringen, *The Perfect Dictatorship: China in the 21st Century* (Hong Kong University Press, 2016).

The language situation appears to be better in Ngaba than in Lhasa. When I visited in 2017 I was shocked to find that public street maps were only in Chinese and English. A Burger King at the airport similarly offered menus in Chinese and English, not Tibetan, and the magazine for Tibet Airlines contained no Tibetan aside from some decorative calligraphy on the cover. A Tibetan complained that many official documents, including the passport application, were only in Chinese.

On Chen Quanguo, the former Party secretary for Tibet: There may be one precedent for the mass incarceration of Uighurs for political reeducation. In 2012, hundreds of Tibetans who had attended a prayer festival in Bodh Gaya, India, presided over by the Dalai Lama were detained upon their return and held for months in military camps. Most of the pilgrims were senior citizens and sufficiently well connected that they had obtained Chinese passports and had traveled legally to India. It is unclear why they were allowed to travel in the first place, only to be arrested upon their return, but the timing suggests that the detentions were ordered by Chen Quanguo, who had recently arrived in Tibet. See Edward Wong, "China Said to Detain Returning Tibetan Pilgrims," *New York Times,* April 7, 2012. Also see "Has the World Lost Sight of Tibet?" A ChinaFile conversation, November 20, 2018, http://www.chinafile.com/conversation/has -world-lost-sight-of-tibet.

GLOSSARY

Aba—The Chinese name for Ngaba.

Aba (Ngaba) Tibetan and Qiang Autonomous Prefecture—A division of modern Sichuan province covering 32,000 square miles that contains Aba county (Ngaba).

Amdo—The Tibetan name for the northeastern region of the Tibetan plateau, which now falls in parts of Qinghai, Gansu, and Sichuan provinces.

beimu—An alpine lily often collected by Tibetans for use in traditional medicine.

bodhisattva—A person who has obtained Buddhahood but has decided to be reborn instead for the benefit of others.

caterpillar fungus (*Cordyceps sinensis*)—A fungus collected by Tibetans and prized in traditional medicine.

chorten—The Tibetan term for the Sanskrit stupa, a Buddhist votive structure.

chuba—The traditional Tibetan robe, sometimes called *lawa* in the Amdo dialect.

Chushi Gangdruk—The Tibetan guerrilla movement set up in 1957 to fight the Chinese Communist forces, supported for a time by the CIA.

Cultural Revolution—Mao's decade-long campaign from 1966 to 1976 to purge China of capitalist and reactionary elements. Tibetans sometimes use the term more broadly to include the forced collectivization that began in the 1950s.

danwei—(Chinese) A work unit to which each Chinese citizen was assigned.

Democratic Reforms—The name given to the phase of expropriation and class struggle that was imposed on Tibetan areas from 1956 onward.

dunglen—Literally, "strumming and singing." A style of Tibetan folk music.

dzi—A striped agate bead highly prized by Tibetans.

dzomo—A hybrid bred from a cow and a yak, used to produce dairy. (The male is called *dzo.*)

gaokao—(Chinese) The Chinese university entrance exam.

Golok—A region northwest of Ngaba and the name of its people, which means "rebellious" or "unsubdued" in Tibetan.

Hui—Ethnically Chinese Muslims.

hukou—(Chinese) The household registration document required of all Chinese citizens.

jiji fenzi—(Chinese) Activists who supported the Chinese Communist Party. The Tibetan term is *hurtsonchen,* although many use the Chinese term instead.

Kham—The southeastern portion of the Tibetan plateau, which now lies partly in Sichuan, Qinghai, and Yunnan provinces.

Khampa—The people of Kham.

khapse—A fried dough pastry usually eaten during the New Year.

khata—A ceremonial scarf.

kora—Circumambulation around a monastery, temple, stupa, etc.

Lhakar—Literally "White Wednesday." A movement to promote Tibetan identity by speaking only Tibetan language and wearing Tibetan clothing on Wednesdays.

liang piao—(Chinese) The rationing coupons issued in China from the mid-1950s until the early 1990s.

Lobsang—A Tibetan name meaning "noble minded." All Kirti monks have this as the prefix of their ordination name.

Losar—Tibetan New Year.

lungta—Literally "wind horse," a symbol of good luck or vitality in Tibetan culture, commonly printed on prayer flags, especially the small paper ones that are thrown into the air like confetti.

mani—The most familiar Tibetan mantra, *om mani padme hum,* associated with the Bodhisattva Avalokitesvara.

momo—A Tibetan dumpling.

Monlam—Tibetan prayer festival.

pingfan—(Chinese) Political rehabilitation.

Qiang—An ethnic minority living primarily in Sichuan province.

Rangzen—Tibetan word meaning "freedom" or "independence."

rinpoche—An honorific term usually denoting a high lama.

sangha—The Buddhist community of monks, nuns, and lay disciples.

stupa—A ceremonial structure, usually with a dome shape, that contains relics and sacred texts. Also known as a chorten in Tibetan.

tawa—An Amdo Tibetan term for the lay community living next to a monastery.

tejing—(Chinese) Special police.

thamzing—The struggle sessions used during the Mao era to persecute alleged class enemies.

thangka—A Buddhist scroll painting.

three jewels—The Buddha, the dharma, and the *sangha* (the Buddhist monks and nuns).

Tibet Autonomous Region—The designation given in 1965 by the People's Republic of China to the territory of the former Lhasa government.

torma—Offering cake usually made of barley flour and butter, much used in Tibetan ritual.

tsampa—The Tibetan staple food made of roasted ground barley.

tulku—A reincarnate lama or, specifically, a child recognized as the reincarnate successor to a lineage of spiritual masters, such as the Dalai Lama.

tusi—(Chinese) The Chinese imperial term for traditional local rulers invested with central authority.

Uighur—A Turkic-speaking, mostly Muslim ethnic minority living in Xinjiang.

wujing—(Chinese) Armed police.

Xinjiang—(Chinese) Literally "New Frontier." The northwestern region of China, bordering Russia, Kazakhstan, Kyrgyzstan, Tajikistan, Afghanistan, Pakistan, and India.

ACKNOWLEDGMENTS

THIS BOOK IS DEDICATED TO LOBSANG CHOKTA TROTSIK. We met in 2014 thanks to an introduction from the poet Tsering Woeser. Trotsik, as I knew him (he took his nickname from his village in Ngaba) was the vice president of Tibetan Writers Abroad PEN, a writer, and a voracious reader. He immediately understood my fascination with Ngaba and my approach to telling its story through the lives of ordinary Tibetans. He introduced me and vouched for me to many other people from Ngaba whose stories form the backbone of this book. On February 12, 2015, Trotsik was stabbed to death at a bus station in New Delhi, a senseless murder I am still struggling to understand. His death at the age of thirty-three was an incalculable loss to his family, his community, and really anybody who cares about the future of the Tibetan culture and language. He had been working to improve digital access to Tibetan literature and was passionate about the need to spread awareness beyond the subject of Buddhism. I can only imagine how much was lost with his premature death.

Matthew Akester provided invaluable guidance on this project at every step of the way. When I was still trying to decide which Tibetan community to profile, I stumbled on the blog he wrote with Jianglin Li. I consulted with him frequently during the writing, editing, and fact-checking process. Akester is also responsible for the evocative phrase "Eat the Buddha!," a title he gave to the study he and Li co-authored about the Red Army's sweep through Ngaba during the 1930s. Jianglin Li has plowed so much new ground in her research about the Red Army's misadventures in Tibet from the 1930s through the 1950s, and she was generous in sharing with me some of the Chinese documents and sources she uncovered.

I met Tsering Woeser during that eventful year of 2008 and we attended the exhibit *Tibet: Past and Present* at the Cultural Palace of Nationalities in Beijing. It was hard to see her subsequently because she was often under surveillance, but her guidance was invaluable, as was her blog, probably the best day-to-day source of what's happening in Tibet. I also want to thank Dechen Pemba and the staff of *High Peaks Pure Earth,* a website that translates and curates writing in Tibetan and about Tibet, including the work of Woeser.

In India, the Tibetans featured in this book sat patiently through extended interviews over repeated cups of ginger lemon tea. Amdo Delek shared with me decades of research; Gonpo Tso Mevotsang relived painful memories to allow me to tell her story, and her daughter, Wangzin Lhamo, and other members of the family helped me gather mementos and photos. I interviewed dozens of people from Ngaba who, while not all subjects of this book, filled in many details. Kunchok Gyatso, also known as Kungam, who ran an association of former political prisoners in exile, was especially helpful. Tashi Phuntsok and Tsering Wangchuk of the exile government's Department of Information and International Relations helped me navigate the exile bureaucracy. Penpa Tsering, who had been speaker of the Tibetan parliament in exile, helped convince the initially reluctant Gonpo to speak with me. Kirti Rinpoche, abbot of the monastery, was generous with his time and facilitated other interviews at Kirti. Kanyag Tsering and Lobsang Yeshi run a small but well-equipped information office at Kirti Monastery in Dharamsala that provided photographs and documents, including the test papers given during the patriotic education sessions. Among the many human rights activists who were helpful were Kate Saunders, formerly of the International Campaign for Tibet, Bobbi Nassar, and Kerry Wright. I frequently consulted reports from the ICT, as well as Human Rights Watch, Amnesty International, and the Tibetan Centre for Human Rights and Democracy. Radio Free Asia often reported first on breaking news out of Ngaba.

Nobody has done more to inform a generation of journalists about Tibet than Robbie Barnett. Somehow he manages to simplify without being simplistic, to be simultaneously eloquent and plainspoken. His insights can be found throughout this book, as should be evident from the many references and endnotes.

Early readers of the manuscript were my uncle, David Schmerler, who also served as cameraman during an interview with the Dalai Lama; and my friend Julie Talen, a screenwriter and filmmaker with an unfailing sense of story. I talked through my ideas regularly with Margaret Scott.

My original reporting on Tibet was done for the *Los Angeles Times*. Photographer Carolyn Cole accompanied me on trips to Ngaba, Dharamsala, and Nepal; besides taking stunning photos, she proved an equal partner at reporting. My colleagues at the Beijing bureau Jia Han, Jon Kaiman, Nicole Liu, Mark Magnier, Julie Makinen, Ching-Ching Ni, David Pierson, and Megan Stack all played a part. Tommy Yang uncovered much of the original research that went into this book and helped with fact-checking all the way to the end. I thank former foreign editor Marjorie Miller for sending me to Beijing, and her successors Mark Porubcansky, Kim Murphy, and Mitchell Landsberg for shaping my reporting into coherent stories and giving me a long enough leash to satisfy my obsession with this place. Editors Norman Pearlstine and Scott Kraft gave the most valuable gift of all—freedom—in allowing me an extended leave of absence.

Over seven years living in Beijing, I was educated by the never-ending conversation about China's past and future that took place in our homes, restaurants, and coffee shops. Many of my colleagues in Beijing also covered Tibet issues and gave their advice and insight freely. Evan Osnos wrote a profile of the Dalai Lama for *The New Yorker*, which is quoted in this book; and Ed Wong of *The New York Times* irritatingly scooped me often on stories about Tibet, but remains a good friend. Andrew Jacobs wrote one of the funniest pieces I've ever read about Tibet. Hannah Beech, Ed Gargan, and Jane McCartney were all obsessed with Tibet long before me, as was Tim Johnson, who also authored a book on the subject. Barely a few days went by when I didn't consult with Gady Epstein about my work. Jonathan Watts, Holly Williams, and Tom Lasseter all traveled before me to Ngaba. Other fellow travelers in Beijing who shared ideas, meals, reading recommendations, and companionship were Jonathan Ansfield, Tina Beeck, Angus Cargill, Lillian Chou, Sheila Fay, Claudio Garon, Jen Lin-Liu, Melinda Liu, Jane Perlez, Keith Richburg, Didi Tatlow, Greg Thurman, and Lijia Zhang. Madeleine Grant traveled with me in Amdo. Back in the United States, colleagues and fellow writers offered guidance: Anna Boorstin, Molly Fowler, Robin Golden, Lee Hockstader, Terri Jentz, Ruth Marcus, Nomi Morris, Lena Sun, Margaret Scott, Burton Wides, and Laura Wides-Muñoz. Eden Mullon, Nicholas Demick, and as always my mother, Gladys Demick, were a source of support throughout.

I am in awe of the wealth of research done by the academic community about Tibet, especially in light of the obstacles placed by the Chinese government. I repeatedly consulted the work of many scholars: the late Elliot Sperling; historian Tsering Shakya, whose work is cited repeatedly in this book; Andrew Fisher on the Tibetan economy; Gray Tuttle's writings about Amdo; and Max Oidtmann, who explained to me the subtleties of the Qing dynasty's relationship with the Tibetans. Among the China scholars: Orville Schell, whose books about both China and Tibet educated throughout.

Flip Brophy, my agent and friend, has been with me every step of the way, ably assisted in recent years by Nell Pierce. Nobody helped to shape this book as much as Julie Grau, who transformed me from a daily newspaper writer into an author. Thanks as well to Cindy Spiegel and Mengfei Chen of Spiegel & Grau. I didn't think anybody could compensate for their loss, but Andy Ward earned my respect and gratitude, as did Marie Pantojan. Bella Lacey of Granta Books offered invaluable advice throughout.

In New York, I enjoyed the hospitality of the Council of Foreign Relations while writing this book, as an Edward R. Murrow Press Fellow. The fellowship provided me with travel stipends and a relatively quiet space to work in New York. Thanks to Janine Hill and Victoria Harlan, our fellowship coordinators, and to Elizabeth Economy, the council's director for Asia studies.

New York was an excellent place to learn about Tibet. I benefited from many lectures and films hosted by the Modern Tibetan Studies Program at Columbia University's Weatherhead East Asian Institute and from the excellent collection at Columbia's C.V. Starr East Asian Library. Events at the Asia Society, China Institute, Rubin Museum, and Trace Foundation, as well as the yearly gathering of Tibetans in New York organized by Machik, filled in my education.

There are some conspicuous absences in these acknowledgments. As this book is going to press, the atmosphere in China is very unforgiving and I am not naming many people—Tibetans, Chinese, and others—for fear that their help would be misconstrued as somehow anti-China. Friends, interpreters, interview subjects, experts, and consultants who would prefer not to have their names in print: PD, W, DD, LD, J, T, T, K and D and family, among other people from Ngaba, D, S, R and T, LC, and LD. I hope you know who you are and accept my gratitude anonymously.

ILLUSTRATION CREDITS

Photos from the *Los Angeles Times* are copyright © 2008–2015 *Los Angeles Times*. Used with permission.

Cover: A monk walks through the grounds of Kirti Monastery past a stove where juniper branches are burned as incense. The papers littering the ground are *lungta,* prayer flags printed with the symbol of a wind horse, which are customarily thrown into plumes of smoke during incense-burning ceremonies. Carolyn Cole, *Los Angeles Times,* 2014.

Page iv: The palace of the Mei king in Ngaba. Courtesy of the Mevotsang family.

Page xi: Downtown Ngaba. Courtesy of the author.

Page 1: Rolling landscape. Carolyn Cole, *Los Angeles Times,* 2014.

Page 3: The royal family of Ngaba. Gonpo is center front with her father, the king, behind her, 1957. Courtesy of the Mevotsang family.

Page 13: The Chinese Red Army on their way to the Tibetan plateau, crossing Jiajinshan Mountain, June 1935. Sovphoto/Getty Images.

Page 26: From left to right, the young Panchen Lama, the Mei king, the Dalai Lama, and other officials on a 1954 tour of China. Courtesy of the Mevotsang family.

Page 37: Amdo Delek as an adult. Carolyn Cole, *Los Angeles Times,* 2014.

Page 54: The last photo of Gonpo's family, taken in Chengdu in 1966, months before the start of the Cultural Revolution. Only she (top left) and her aunt (top center) would survive. Courtesy of the Mevotsang family.

Page 65: A bonfire of Buddhist scriptures, Lhasa, 1966. Tsering Dorje, from the book *Forbidden Memory: Tibet During the Cultural Revolution* by Tsering Woeser (Lincoln, Neb.: Potomac Books, 2020). Used with permission.

Page 75: Gonpo and Xiao Tu. Courtesy of the Mevotsang family.

Page 87: Man walking yaks down the road. Jia Han, *Los Angeles Times,* 2008.

Page 89: A Tibetan woman with caterpillar fungus. Jia Han, *Los Angeles Times,* 2008.

Page 106: Tsegyam, 2016. Courtesy of the author.

Page 118: Gonpo, her husband, and their daughters, in a taped-together photo. The four were rarely together. Courtesy of the Mevotsang family.

Page 129: Boy lying in the grass at a prayer festival. Carolyn Cole, *Los Angeles Times,* 2014.

Page 131: Boy in Meruma, 2014. Carolyn Cole, *Los Angeles Times.*

Page 140: Kirti Monastery, 2014. Carolyn Cole, *Los Angeles Times.*

Page 149: Worshippers sitting outside Kirti Monastery, 2014. Carolyn Cole, *Los Angeles Times.*

Page 159: Dancers and models in Tibetan costume, Jiuzhaigou, 2007. Ian Cruickshank/Alamy stock photo.

Page 169: Lhundup Tso, Pema's niece. Courtesy of Kirti Monastery.

Page 183: Monks under arrest in Ngaba, 2008. Courtesy of Kirti Monastery.

Page 192: Chinese police marching in Ngaba, 2011. Courtesy of Kirti Monastery.

Page 201: Checkpoint in Ngaba. Courtesy of Kirti Monastery.

Page 209: The monk Phuntsog. Courtesy of Kirti Monastery.

Page 218: Photos of self-immolators, Dharamsala. David Schmerler, 2015.

Page 228: A monk in Kodari, Nepal, looking at the border with Tibet, 2014. Carolyn Cole, *Los Angeles Times.*

Page 239: A Tibetan woman peering into her donated Chinese tent, Ngaba, 2014. Carolyn Cole, *Los Angeles Times.*

Page 241: Gonpo at home in Dharamsala, 2014. Carolyn Cole, *Los Angeles Times.*

Page 261: Tibetans in Meruma attending a propaganda lecture, December 2019. Ngaba County Government on Weibo.

INDEX

Page numbers in italics indicate illustrations.

BARBARA DEMICK is the author of *Nothing to Envy: Ordinary Lives in North Korea,* a finalist for the National Book Award and the National Book Critics Circle Award, and *Logavina Street: Life and Death in a Sarajevo Neighborhood.* She was a reporter with the *Los Angeles Times* and headed the paper's bureaus in Beijing and Seoul. She was also a correspondent for *The Philadelphia Inquirer* out of the Balkans and Middle East.

Demick grew up in New Jersey and graduated from Yale College. Her work has won many awards, including the Samuel Johnson Prize (now the Baillie Gifford Prize) for nonfiction in the United Kingdom, the Overseas Press Club's human rights reporting award, the George Polk Award, the Robert F. Kennedy Journalism Award, and Stanford University's Shorenstein Journalism Award for Asia coverage. She was a press fellow at the Council on Foreign Relations, a Bagehot fellow in business journalism at Columbia University, and a visiting professor of journalism at Princeton University. She lives in New York City.

ABOUT
THE TYPE

This book was set in Bembo, a typeface based on an old-style Roman face that was used for Cardinal Pietro Bembo's tract *De Aetna* in 1495. Bembo was cut by Francesco Griffo (1450–1518) in the early sixteenth century for Italian Renaissance printer and publisher Aldus Manutius (1449–1515). The Lanston Monotype Company of Philadelphia brought the well-proportioned letterforms of Bembo to the United States in the 1930s.